Summary of Contents

M000086619

FULL STACK JAVASCRIPT DEVELOPMENT WITH MEAN

BY **ADAM BRETZ**
& **COLIN J. IHRIG**

Full Stack JavaScript Development with MEAN

by Adam Bretz and Colin J. Ihrig

Product Manager: Simon Mackie   **English Editor:** Kelly Steele

Technical Editor: Don Nguyen   **Cover Designer:** Alex Walker

Published by SitePoint Pty. Ltd.

48 Cambridge Street Collingwood
VIC Australia 3066
Web: www.sitepoint.com
Email: business@sitepoint.com

ISBN 978-0-9924612-5-6 (print)

ISBN 978-0-9924612-4-9 (ebook)
Printed and bound in the United States of America

About Adam Bretz

Adam Bretz is a software engineer focusing on client and server side JavaScript. Adam earned his Bachelor of Science in Computer Science in 2007 from Millersville University of Pennsylvania. At a previous job, Adam was part of the team of engineers that helped migrate the company from PHP to a pure JavaScript solution. Adam currently resides in the Pittsburgh area with his wife, Jenna.

About Colin J. Ihrig

Colin J. Ihrig is a software engineer, working primarily with Node.js. Colin is the author of Pro Node.js for Developers, and is currently the managing editor of SitePoint's JavaScript channel. Colin received his Bachelor of Science in Engineering, and Master of Science in Computer Engineering from the University of Pittsburgh in 2005 and 2008, respectively.

About SitePoint

SitePoint specializes in publishing fun, practical, and easy-to-understand content for web professionals. Visit http://www.sitepoint.com/ to access our blogs, books, newsletters, articles, and community forums. You'll find a stack of information on JavaScript, PHP, Ruby, mobile development, design, and more.

To Mom and Dad — thanks for getting me a Nintendo when I was seven and a computer when I was ten. — Adam

This book is dedicated to my wife, Alaina, my sons, CJ and Carter, and my mom. I love you all so much! — Colin

Table of Contents

Preface

With modern tools, it is possible to create production-grade applications using only JavaScript, HTML, and CSS. The combination of MongoDB, Express, AngularJS, and Node.js, all JavaScript technologies, has become so popular that it's been dubbed the MEAN stack. This book will explore the MEAN stack in detail.

We'll begin by covering Node.js, as it lays the groundwork for all our server-side work. You will learn how to get Node running on your local machine, as well as download modules using npm, Node's package manager. The key aspects of the Node.js programming model will also be covered.

From there, we'll move on to MongoDB, a NoSQL database. You'll learn how to interact with Mongo from a Node application, and how to create, retrieve, update, and delete data from a Mongo store.

After you have a solid grasp on Node and Mongo, the book will move on to the Express web server. We'll address the basics of Express applications via topics such as routes and middleware. Building on previous chapters, we will cover the integration of Node, Mongo, and Express.

Our coverage of the MEAN stack will wrap up with several chapters on AngularJS. These chapters will detail Angular fundamentals such as data binding, directives, controllers, routing, and services. Wrapping up the book will be chapters on debugging and testing MEAN applications.

Full-stack JavaScript is not fully encompassed by the MEAN stack. There is an entire ecosystem of JavaScript tools to learn about, and this book will introduce a few of them. We will present task runners Gulp and Grunt, which are extremely useful for automating mundane, repetitive tasks. We'll also investigate JSHint, a linting tool used to improve code quality. Along the way, we'll also be developing an example human resources application from scratch using the MEAN stack.

Who Should Read This Book

This book is suitable for intermediate-level web designers and developers. Experience of HTML, CSS, and JavaScript is assumed.

Conventions Used

You'll notice that we've used certain typographic and layout styles throughout this book to signify different types of information. Look out for the following items.

Code Samples

Code in this book will be displayed using a fixed-width font, like so:

```
<h1>A Perfect Summer's Day</h1>
<p>It was a lovely day for a walk in the park. The birds
were singing and the kids were all back at school.</p>
```

If the code is to be found in the book's code archive, the name of the file will appear at the top of the program listing in this way:

```
                                                    example.css
.footer {
  background-color: #CCC;
  border-top: 1px solid #333;
}
```

If only part of the file is displayed, this is indicated by the word *excerpt*:

```
                                              example.css (excerpt)
  border-top: 1px solid #333;
```

If additional code is to be inserted into an existing example, the new code will be displayed in bold:

```
function animate() {
  new_variable = "Hello";
}
```

Where existing code is required for context, rather than repeat it, a ⋮ will be displayed:

```
function animate() {
  ⋮
  return new_variable;
}
```

Sometimes it's intended that certain lines of code be entered on one line, but we've had to wrap them because of page constraints. An ➥ indicates a line break that exists for formatting purposes only, and should be ignored.

```
URL.open("http://www.sitepoint.com/responsive-web-design-real-user-
➥testing/?responsive1");
```

Tips, Notes, and Warnings

Hey, You!

Tips will give you helpful little pointers.

Ahem, Excuse Me ...

Notes are useful asides that are related, but not critical, to the topic at hand. Think of them as extra tidbits of information.

Make Sure You Always ...

... pay attention to these important points.

Watch Out!

Warnings will highlight any gotchas that are likely to trip you up along the way.

Supplementary Materials

http://www.learnable.com/books/mean1/
The book's website, containing links, updates, resources, and more.

https://github.com/spbooks/mean1/
The downloadable code archive for this book.

http://community.sitepoint.com/category/javascript

SitePoint's forums, for help on any tricky web problems.

books@sitepoint.com

Our email address, should you need to contact us for support, to report a problem, or for any other reason.

Want to Take Your Learning Further?

Thanks for buying this book. Would you like to continue learning? You can now receive unlimited access to courses and ALL SitePoint books at Learnable for one low price. Enroll now and start learning today! Join Learnable and you'll stay ahead of the newest technology trends: http://www.learnable.com.

Introduction

Web programming is a task that takes years to truly understand. Part of the complexity comes from the sheer number of moving parts. Effective programmers need at least a basic understanding of many topics, including networking, protocols, security, databases, server-side development, and client-side development, amongst others. For many years, this also included working with a medley of programming languages.

Client-side programming alone requires an understanding of three languages: HTML for markup, CSS for styling, and JavaScript for functionality. While front-end development has its own complexities, the good news is that development is more or less locked into the "big three" languages. The server side has been a different story altogether. The server has been the domain of languages like Java, PHP, Perl, and just about any other language you can think of. The majority of web applications also utilize a database for data persistence. Historically, communicating with a database has required developers to also understand SQL.

Creating a simple web application requires developers to understand HTML, CSS, JavaScript, SQL, and a server-side language of choice. In addition, there's no guarantee that the server side will be written in a single language. Optimistically, developers need to understand at least five separate languages to create a simple app, and that's without considering the data interchange format used for client-server communication. Remember, the x in Ajax stands for XML. Many web applications have recently moved away from XML in favor of the simpler JSON, but this is still another layer that developers must understand.

Although HTML, CSS, and SQL aren't strictly considered programming languages, they each have their own syntax and quirks that developers must know. Completely understanding five "languages" and constantly context switching between them is a daunting task. If you've ever attempted this, you have likely mixed up syntax on more than one occasion.

This has lead to specialization among developers with different teams working on front-end and back-end development. Unfortunately, this doesn't always ensure that projects are completed faster or with higher quality. In fact, it often results in more back and forth, debates, and programmers who are less knowledgeable about a project's big picture. There was a very clear-cut need for a language to be used across the entire development stack. The remainder of this chapter explains how JavaScript grew into the role of a full-stack language in a way that no other language could.

The Rise of Full-stack JavaScript

JavaScript has long been the de facto standard for client-side scripting. JavaScript burst onto the scene in 1995 after Brendan Eich developed what was known as Mocha at the time over the course of just ten days. In September 1995, Netscape Navigator 2.0 was released with Mocha, which by then had been renamed LiveScript. JavaScript finally settled into its current name by December 1995. The name was chosen because Netscape was attempting to ride the coattails of Sun's Java programming language, which was trendy at the time.

During the initial browser wars, Microsoft's Internet Explorer and Netscape's Navigator were constantly trying to one-up each other. As a retort to Navigator's JavaScript, Microsoft released its own implementation, named JScript, with Internet Explorer 3.0 in August 1996. JavaScript was submitted to Ecma International, an international standards organization, in November of 1996 and JavaScript was standardized as ECMA-262[1] in June 1997.

---

[1] http://www.ecma-international.org/publications/standards/Ecma-262.htm

Earlier on, JavaScript earned a reputation as being a language lacking in performance and only used by amateur developers. Yet browser vendors invested a lot of time, energy, and money into improving JavaScript over the years. The result is that modern JavaScript engines are highly optimized pieces of software whose performance is far beyond anything of the original JavaScript interpreters. On the client-side, it is unlikely that any competing languages (such as Dart) will dethrone JavaScript in the near future, as it's the only language supported by every major browser. Couple that with overall improvements in computing, and the result is a language that is suitable for just about any general-purpose computing task.

Node.js

In 2009, Ryan Dahl created Node.js, a framework used primarily to create scalable network applications. Node.js is built on top of Google's V8 JavaScript engine[2] (the same one used in Chrome) and Joyent's libuv,[3] an asynchronous I/O library that abstracts away the underlying platform. Node made JavaScript a viable alternative for server-side programming. Additionally, Node provided a full system JavaScript API that was never really achieved before due to the sandboxed environment that browsers provide. With the advent of Node, JavaScript developers could access the file system, open network sockets, and spawn child processes.

One of Node's top features is the ability to pack a lot of functionality into a small amount of code. Node flaunts this right on the project's home page.[4] The code that follows is taken directly from the Node home page, and implements a trivial web server in just six lines:

```
var http = require('http');
http.createServer(function (req, res) {
  res.writeHead(200, {'Content-Type': 'text/plain'});
  res.end('Hello World\n');
}).listen(1337, '127.0.0.1');
console.log('Server running at http://127.0.0.1:1337/');
```

Listing 1-1. A trivial web server written in Node

---

[2] https://code.google.com/p/v8/

[3] https://github.com/joyent/libuv

[4] http://www.nodejs.org

There's no need to fully understand the code now, but we'll provide a quick run-down. The first line requires the `http` modules, which provide functionality for creating HTTP clients and servers. Next, a server is started that listens on port 1337. When a connection is received, the server responds with the message `Hello World`. The last line of code simply prints a message to the console in order to let the developer know what's happening.

The Node.js Ecosystem

Node was not the first attempt at a server-side JavaScript implementation,[5] but it has certainly proven to be the most successful by far. One way of gauging a technology's popularity is by the size of the ecosystem around it. Node has been adopted by huge companies like Walmart, PayPal, LinkedIn, and Microsoft. It has even given rise to completely new companies such as StrongLoop, NodeSource, and npm, Inc.

Perhaps even more impressive than the list of companies using Node is the collection of third-party modules being developed for Node. In the few short years since Node's creation, over 77,000 third-party modules have been published to npm, Node's package manager. According to Module Counts,[6] a website that tracks the number of modules in various repositories, the npm registry is growing at a rate of approximately 170 modules per day at the time of writing. The next closest package manager in terms of growth rate is PHP's Packagist at 73 modules per day. Figure 1.1, taken from Module Counts, illustrates the growth of the Node module system compared to various languages' package managers. npm has been annotated for your viewing pleasure.

---

[5] http://en.wikipedia.org/wiki/Comparison_of_server-side_JavaScript_solutions
[6] http://modulecounts.com/

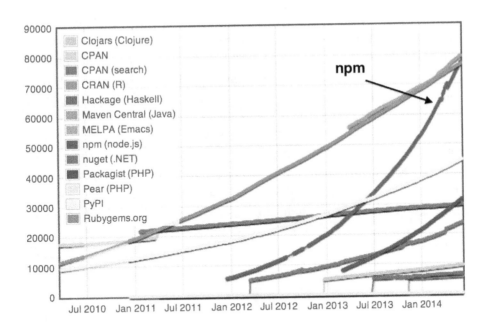

Figure 1.1. Growth of various package managers

With the sheer number of modules available, developers can typically find at least one to solve just about any problem they encounter. (Of course, these modules are in various stages of development, and not all are production ready.) As previously stated, one of Node's biggest use cases is the development of web servers. So, as you might expect, there are a number of modules that implement web servers. The most popular of these modules is Express, which currently powers more than 26,000 web applications around the world.[7] Based on the Ruby language's Sinatra framework, Express is self-described as a "fast, unopinionated, minimalist web framework for Node.js."[8] Express will be explored in detail over the course of several chapters later in this book.

MongoDB

While Node was invading the server space, another movement was gathering pace in the world of databases. For years, the primary method of working with data stores had been to issue SQL queries to relational databases. Yet there's another type of data store that doesn't rely on SQL. This class of database, known as NoSQL, doesn't

---

[7] http://expressjs.com/applications.html

[8] http://expressjs.com/

even use the familiar table structures of relational databases. NoSQL databases store data in a variety of formats, such as documents or key-value pairs, and are less rigid and structured than relational databases. This lack of structure often leads to simpler prototyping and ease of development. NoSQL databases tend to be slightly faster, as there's no need for them to enforce the rigid table structure of relational databases.

In 2007, a company named 10gen (now MongoDB, Inc.) began working on a NoSQL database that would become a component in a planned platform as a service (PaaS) offering. In 2009, the database known as MongoDB[9] (a play on the word hu**mongo**us) was open sourced. MongoDB is a document-oriented database that stores information as Binary JSON (BSON) documents. By using a flavor of JSON, Mongo is incredibly simple to read and write objects from JavaScript code. Just as Node replaces another server-side language with JavaScript, MongoDB replaces SQL with queries based on JavaScript objects.

AngularJS

While JavaScript has always been a client-side programming language, its use in the browser has changed drastically over time. Back in the Netscape Navigator days, JavaScript was used for very simple page interactions. Use cases consisted of tasks such as changing an image's `src` attribute on mouse over or powering collapsible menus. The effects were simple, but provided a level of interactivity unable to be achieved with HTML alone.

As technology continued to evolve, JavaScript evolved with it. A major breakthrough for web applications came with the widespread availability and adoption of high-speed Internet. This opened the door for Ajax applications that make background requests instead of full page loads. Network performance is key in Ajax applications, as a slow connection will make the page appear unresponsive. Applications gradually transitioned towards fewer and fewer page loads, and more Ajax requests. Eventually, the Single Page Application (SPA) was born. In the strictest sense SPAs have just a single page load, and request all other data via Ajax calls.

AngularJS[10] is one of most popular frameworks for creating SPAs. Angular was created in 2009 (a busy year for JavaScript) by Miško Hevery and Adam Abrons. Angular owes much of its popularity to being backed by Google, Hevery's employer.

---

[9] http://www.mongodb.org/
[10] https://angularjs.org/

It applies a model-view-controller (MVC) approach to web applications, and has several noteworthy features. First, Angular provides two-way data binding between views and models. This saves developer time, as Angular automatically keeps everything in sync. Another interesting feature of Angular is that many tasks, including templating, can be done in augmented HTML.

Angular will be covered in greater detail later in the book, but it's worth looking at a partial example now to illustrate how powerful it really is. Here's an Angular controller named PeopleCtrl that sets the people property in the data model:

```
app.controller('PeopleCtrl', ['$scope', function($scope) {
  $scope.people = [
    {
      firstName: 'Colin',
      lastName: 'Ihrig'
    },
    {
      firstName: 'Adam',
      lastName: 'Bretz'
    }
  ];
}]);
```

Listing 1-2. A simple Angular controller that manipulates a model

The people property of the model is an array containing two simple objects representing people. Now here's an Angular view template that can be used to display the model data:

```
<div ng-repeat="person in people">
  {{person.lastName}}, {{person.firstName}}
</div>
```

Listing 1-3. A simple Angular view template

The <div> is just a standard HTML <div> element, while ng-repeat is known as an Angular directive. This particular directive is employed to loop over the elements of an array, and the double curly braces are used to access data from JavaScript. For now, there's no need to completely understand what's going on here, just realize that Angular takes care of a lot of tasks for you out of the box.

Summary

This chapter has introduced the concept of full-stack JavaScript, as well as some of its most popular constituents. Using the technologies described here, it is possible to create a production grade application using HTML, CSS, and JavaScript alone. The combination of MongoDB, Express, AngularJS, and Node.js has become so popular that it has earned its own title: the **MEAN stack**, whose logo can be seen in Figure 1.2. This titling borrows from the LAMP stack, which consists of Linux, Apache (web server), MySQL, and PHP.

Figure 1.2. The MEAN stack logo

The rest of this book explores the MEAN stack in detail. We'll begin by covering Node.js, as it will lay the groundwork for all our server-side work. We'll learn how to make Node run on your local machine as well as download modules using npm. The key aspects of the Node.js programming model will also be covered.

From there, we'll move on to MongoDB. We'll learn how to interact with Mongo from a Node application, as well as how to create, retrieve, update, and delete data from a Mongo store. In covering Mongo, we'll also learn how to access a MySQL[11] database from Node.js. While not technically inline with the MEAN approach, relational databases are too popular to simply not acknowledge.

After gaining a solid grasp on Node and Mongo, we'll move on to the Express web server. We'll cover the basics of Express applications via topics such as routes and middleware. Building on previous chapters, we'll cover the integration of Node, Mongo, and Express. We'll also introduce hapi.js,[12] an alternative to Express. hapi is an up-and-coming framework developed and battle-tested at Walmart.

---

[11] http://www.mysql.com/
[12] http://hapijs.com/

Our coverage of the MEAN stack will wrap up with several chapters on AngularJS. These chapters will cover Angular fundamentals such as data binding, directives, controllers, routing, and services.

Full-stack JavaScript is not fully encompassed by the MEAN stack. There is an entire ecosystem of JavaScript tools to learn about, and this book will introduce a few of them. We'll cover task runners Gulp[13] and Grunt,[14] which are extremely useful for automating mundane, repetitive tasks. We'll also address JSHint,[15] a linting tool used to improve code quality. **Linting** tools analyze source code and report potentials issues, a feature that's especially useful in non-compiled languages such as JavaScript.

We'll conclude our exploration of the JavaScript tool ecosystem with discussions on Node Inspector[16] and Mocha.[17] Node.js comes with a built-in debugger that is anything but user-friendly. Node Inspector addresses this shortcoming by allowing Google Chrome's developer tools to act as a front end to Node's built-in debugger. Mocha, on the other hand, is a Node.js-based testing framework. We'll show you how to create and run individual tests and test suites.

If this sounds like a lot of material, you're right. And if you think it'd make a lot more sense with concrete examples, you'd be right again. Throughout the various chapters, we'll provide many standalone code samples that you can try out. Yet we'll also be developing a comprehensive example application along the way. The example app is a human resources (HR) application that can be used for tracking employees and teams in a small- to medium-sized company. This app will be developed over certain chapters sprinkled throughout the book.

It's worth pointing out that there are several MEAN stack boilerplates in existence,[18] but this book doesn't use any of them. We feel that it's better to understand all the technologies independently rather than expect all applications to follow a single format. Once you understand the basics of technology, picking up one of the boilerplates should be a piece of cake.

---

[13] http://gulpjs.com/

[14] http://gruntjs.com/

[15] http://www.jshint.com/

[16] https://github.com/node-inspector/node-inspector

[17] http://visionmedia.github.io/mocha/

[18] http://mean.io/

Node.js Introduction

To date, there have been over ten different server-side implementations of JavaScript.[1] While Node.js is the most successful, it is far from being the first. Engineers have spent considerable time and effort trying to make JavaScript run on a web server—but why? What is it about JavaScript that makes it so well-suited to being a server-side language? Ultimately, it boils down to two factors: familiarity and non-blocking asynchronous I/O.

Familiarity with JavaScript

Looking at GitHub usage,[2] JavaScript is the prevailing language. As evidenced in Figure 2.1, the raw amount of JavaScript code continues to grow, outpacing all the other popular scripting languages available today. The graph represents the number of new GitHub repositories created that list JavaScript as the primary language.

---

[1] http://en.wikipedia.org/wiki/Comparison_of_server-side_JavaScript_solutions
[2] http://redmonk.com/dberkholz/2014/05/02/github-language-trends-and-the-fragmenting-landscape/

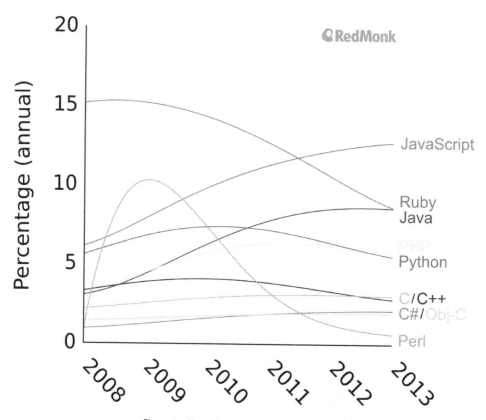

Figure 2.1. New GitHub repositories by language

JavaScript was created in 1995 by Brendan Eich during his time at Netscape Communications Corporation. By 1996, the official ECMA specification had been submitted with both Microsoft and Netscape implementing JavaScript in their flagship browsers. Over the subsequent twenty years or so, there have been new versions of the ECMAScript specification, JavaScript libraries such as jQuery, client-side JavaScript MVC frameworks, JavaScript controlling robots with Tessel,[3] and the rise of server-side JavaScript. If you have ever worked on a web page in the last twenty years, you've had some exposure to JavaScript.

The ubiquity of JavaScript is one of the reasons why it is so attractive as a server-side language. If the web server is written in JavaScript, developers that know

---

[3] https://tessel.io/

JavaScript can be active contributors, regardless of their specialization. JavaScript, the language, is the same both client-side and server-side using Node. Rather than having people specialize in one part of development versus another, there is now the opportunity to be a JavaScript developer and work on any aspect of a web application. One single language can be used to complete an entire website without requiring developers to learn multiple—sometimes wildly different—programming languages.

One of the expressions you'll often hear from people trying to learn Node is "It's just JavaScript." The existing JavaScript knowledge base that has been building over twenty years is still useful, and continues to be useful in Node.js programming. By leveraging an already popular language in a different environment, Node.js instantly turned any developer familiar with JavaScript into an entry-level full-stack developer, just by sticking with JavaScript.

The Problem with I/O

Any non-trivial web server will eventually have to execute some I/O. The nature of the I/O can be anything from reading from a disk, querying a database, or communicating with another web server. Even with modern computers, I/O is *still* the slowest part of any system. Figure 2.2 presents an excellent summation of the cost of I/O.

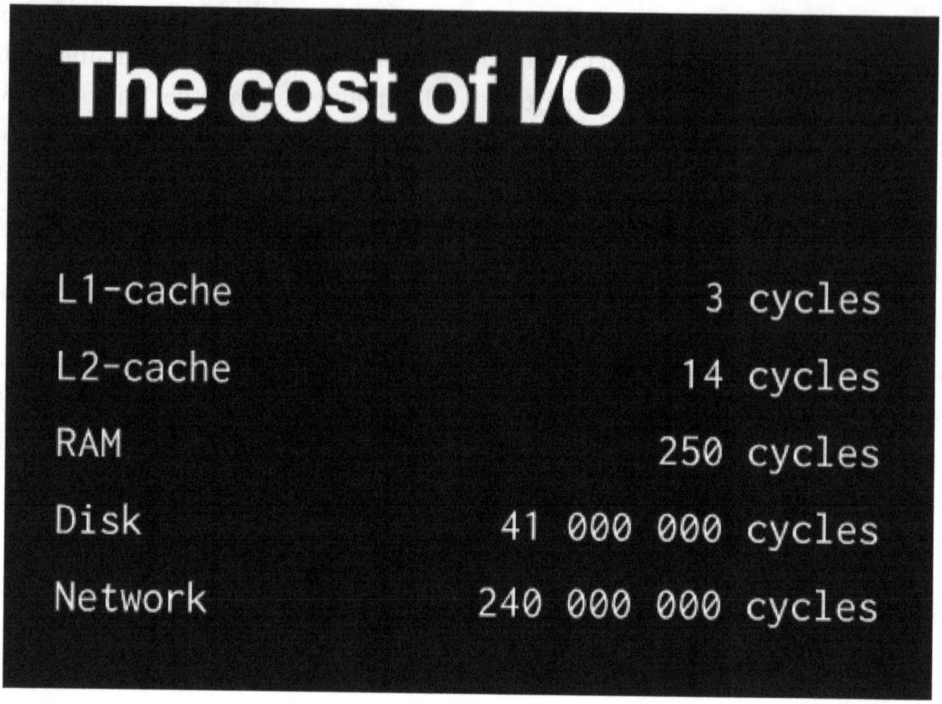

The cost of I/O

L1-cache	3 cycles
L2-cache	14 cycles
RAM	250 cycles
Disk	41 000 000 cycles
Network	240 000 000 cycles

Figure 2.2. The cost of I/O[4]

Figure 2.2 illustrates that disk and network I/O are orders of magnitude slower than RAM and CPU cache. For servers that have to respond to hundreds of thousands of requests per minute, this cost can quickly grow into a crippling performance problem. Let's take a look at an imaginary web server that does a very common web server task: communicate with a database.

An Example Web Server

Suppose we have a simple web server written in stock PHP and we know nothing about threads or asynchronous programming. All this server does is take input from the query string (after it's sanitized for SQL injection attacks, of course) and run a query on a database. When the database responds, the server will process the response and send a view of the data back to the client, as shown in Figure 2.3.

---

[4] Source: http://blog.mixu.net/2011/02/01/understanding-the-node-js-event-loop/

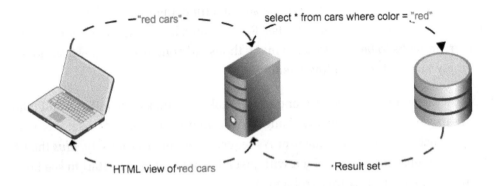

Figure 2.3. Example request life cycle

Here are the steps of the life cycle:

1. A request comes in to the web server. The client has requested every car in our database that is "red."

2. A second remote server houses our corporate database. Our web server creates a database query and sends it off to the remote server housing our database.

3. The database engine runs the query and assembles the results.

4. The database server responds to our web server with the results.

5. The web server receives the query results and turns them into JSON so that the results are easier to process.

6. The server reads from the local file system to find an appropriate HTML document to display the results.

7. The server responds to the request and returns HTML with all the red cars in our database.

This is a typical request life cycle for many web servers. Looking through the life cycle outlined and Figure 2.3, I/O latency is apparent during several of the steps. Steps two, three, and four all introduce I/O: network, disk, and disk, respectively. If we use the *very* rough numbers from the information given in Figure 2.2, we have approximately 322,000,000 cycles wasted waiting for blocking I/O operations. I/O activity that blocks other processing from happen in a running program is known as **blocking I/O.**

If web servers only had to serve one person at a time, there would be no problem with those 322,000,000 blocked cycles. Realistically, however, any public-facing web server needs to be able to serve many thousand concurrent requests and have extremely high uptime and low latency.

Suppose user A makes a request, and user B makes a request one millisecond later. In our sample server, without any changes to the architecture or code, user B is going to experience latency every time user A's request does any I/O activity, *plus* the I/O activity of their own request. Even with just a few users, you can start to see how this would create a cascading problem.

Stepping Around the I/O Problem

I/O is not a new problem. As long as there have been web servers, engineers have had to solve scalability issues. Many existing web servers built with more traditional programming languages, such as Java or PHP, solve scalability concerns with threads or parallel processes. While these approaches can help with the latency and I/O issues of concurrent users, they are often complicated and require more hardware as the load on the web server increases. Additionally, threads and parallel processes aren't free. Most companies have a finite amount of resources so increasing hardware becomes cost-prohibitive at a certain point.

JavaScript (and Node) by convention is a **non-blocking** language. Rather than having to solve the I/O issues after the language was created, it has a simple solution already built into the core of the language: callbacks. A **callback** is a function that is executed when I/O operations finish or produce an error. Instead of waiting and thus creating latency for other users, an operation starts and a callback function is supplied. When the I/O is complete, the supplied callback function executes. There is still a delay in waiting for the I/O to finish, but other logic can execute freely during this time.

Thinking back to how JavaScript was initially used and designed, this pattern makes sense. In JavaScript, functions are first-class citizens so they can be passed around and declared as easily as an integer. Combined with the client-side uses for JavaScript, such as event handling and Ajax requests, JavaScript was built to be non-blocking and has been used in that fashion for many years.

In Ajax requests, a request is made (network I/O, because of the wait on the server) and you supply a callback to it. At this point, the browser window is not blocked and the user is still free to click on any enabled element on the page. When the request completes, the callback supplied to the Ajax request is executed. Common Node.js conventions recommend that developers follow this same pattern. While many of Node's core I/O function offer synchronous versions, both the community and the Node documentation strongly encourage opting for the asynchronous versions.

Example Web Server Revisited

Let's examine how our simple web server example would work using Node.js. Functionally, it would be the same. As mentioned, the Node.js ecosystem is *extremely* vibrant thanks to the npm registry and GitHub, so any plugin or module our PHP server was using almost certainly has a Node counterpart.

Let's analyze how our new Node.js-powered web server will behave for user A and B now. When user A's request reaches step two, an asynchronous call will be made to the database server. A callback function will be passed along that's executed when the response from the database server comes back. User B's request will be right behind, and instead of having to *wait* for A to finish, B can start processing immediately and queue up another request to the database server. No threads or additional resources are required to service both requests. This will allow A and B to have a latency equal to roughly the total time for all the I/O for each of their requests, completely independent of how many other users may be making requests of the web server.

 This Doesn't Magically Speed Up Requests to the Database Server

Remember, this will not speed up requests to the database server. It just prevents the I/O activity from blocking additional service requests as they come in. This allows our web server to handle more concurrent requests without requiring additional hardware or configuration.

Real World Data

We've described the advantages that a server running JavaScript can bring, but let's look at some numbers. One of the big players in the Node.js arena is PayPal. They rewrote their account overview page using Node.js and a wrapper around the Express.js framework. PayPal migrated from a Java web server to a JavaScript web server and posted the performance benchmarks shown in Figure 2.4.

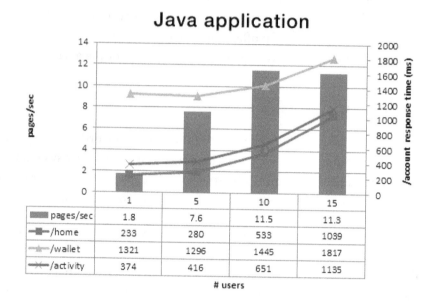

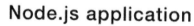

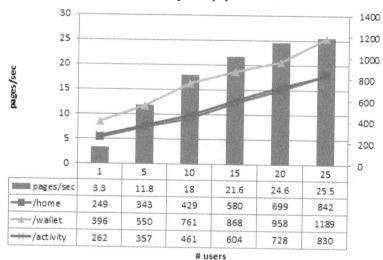

Figure 2.4. Node.js compared to Java web server[5]

The key points of this graph are:

---

[5] Source: https://www.paypal-engineering.com/2013/11/22/node-js-at-paypal/

1. The Node.js web server could handle double the number of requests per second compared to the Java server. This is especially impressive because the Java web server was using five cores and the Node.js server was using one.

2. There was a 35% decrease in the response times for the same page. This amounts to about 200ms time savings for the user, a noticeable amount.

These results were published in 2013 on the PayPal Engineering site.[6] Considering PayPal was using an older version of the Node.js framework on only one core, we can assume that these numbers would be even *more* impressive if they ran these tests today. According to this article, the replacement server was built almost twice as fast that the old version with fewer people and 33% fewer lines of code.

It's results like this that continue to propel Node.js out of research and development and into battle-tested, production-ready web servers that run faster, have lower latency, are built with less resources, and usually cost companies less money because of the reduced hardware needed when loads increase.

Your First Node.js Server

We've talked enough! Let's set up our environment so that we can expand on the server in Listing 1-1.

Installing Node.js

The preferred method of installing Node.js is to download it from the Node.js website.[7] Node.js is cross-platform and there are installation packages available for Windows, OS X, and Linux. When the download is complete, install Node.js on your computer. To verify that everything worked correctly, open a terminal and type node -v. You should see a printout of the version of Node that's currently installed.

REPL

One of the first things you'll probably discover by accident is what happens when you just enter node in the terminal without any arguments. The terminal input character will change to > and the usual terminal commands won't function. This

[6] https://www.paypal-engineering.com/2013/11/22/node-js-at-paypal/
[7] http://nodejs.org/download/

is normal. When you execute node without arguments, you launch the Node.js **REPL**, which stands for read-eval-print loop. REPL gives you a JavaScript sandbox to play in. It can be treated as a Node.js script file, and all the usual functions and modules are available in this environment. Go ahead and try out a few simple Node commands by entering the following lines:

```
3+1
console.log('hello world')
var x = 5;
var http = require('http')
```

There are a few REPL-specific commands available to you, which can be displayed by typing .help. We encourage you to play around with the REPL tool, especially if you're yet to feel comfortable with JavaScript for anything more than just client-side event handling. REPL includes all the features of Node proper. It can be a great place to try code presented in this book or from sources out on the Web.

Writing the Server

Launch your favorite text editor, because we're going to write our first Node.js web server. One of the nice aspects about using JavaScript is that all you need is a terminal and a text editor—no complicated or bloated IDE is required.

Create a file called **app.js** and copy the contents of Listing 1-1 into it. It should look like this:

```
var http = require('http');
http.createServer(function (req, res) {
  res.writeHead(200, {'Content-Type': 'text/plain'});
  res.end('Hello World\n');
}).listen(1337, '127.0.0.1');
console.log('Server running at http://127.0.0.1:1337/');
```

Listing 2-1. A trivial web server written in Node

Listing 2-1 is the default Node web server that's often shown in examples of Node. The aforementioned code snippet will respond with "Hello World" any time you make a request to http://127.0.0.1:1337. You can verify this using either a web browser or the curl command in a terminal window.

Let's refactor this example server to show what can happen when I/O is introduced into the web server. We'll make a simple web server that sends the contents of the currently running file back to the requesting client. Listing 2-2 uses both `http` and a new module: `fs` for "file system." In a future chapter, we'll delve deep into the details of both `fs` and `http`, so don't worry if you feel a little lost right now. We'll cover the high level of what is happening with the new `fs` calls that follow:

```javascript
var http = require('http');
var fs = require('fs');

http.createServer(function (req, res) {
  if (req.url === '/favicon.ico') {
    return res.end();
  }
  console.log('Incoming request to ' + req.url);

  var i = 2;
  res.writeHead(200, {'Content-Type': 'text/plain'});

  setTimeout(function() {
    fs.readFile(__filename, {
      encoding: 'utf8'
    }, function (error, contents) {
      if (error) {
        console.error(error);
        return res.end();
      }

      console.log('sending response for ' + req.url);
      res.end(contents);
    });
  }, 5000);

  while(i--) {
    console.log('Loop value: '  + i + '\r');
  }
}).listen(1337, '127.0.0.1');

console.log('Server running at http://127.0.0.1:1337/');
```

Listing 2-2. A Node server with file I/O

The core of the code is the same as Listing 2-1. We've created a server and are listening on local port 1337. We are writing the data to `res`, our response object, the same as before. We needed to add the check for `/favicon.ico` because some browsers request these files unexpectedly and that would change our results. The `while` loop is just to add some synchronous code to demonstrate what happens when you mix synchronous and asynchronous code. `fs.readFile` reads a file from the disk into a buffer. When the read is complete, the supplied callback is executed and passed in an error object and the file contents. `__filename` is one of several global objects; it just gives us the path to the currently executing file.

Our Server in Action

Start the server and open two (or more) tabs in your browser of choice. In one tab, make a request to `http://localhost:1337/one` and in another tab, quickly make a request to `http://localhost:1337/two`; then watch the terminal for the logged output. You should see a log entry about an incoming request, information about our `while` loop, an entry about another incoming request, and then the `while` loop again. Finally, a response will be sent back to the requesting client—the very file that is currently executing.

The terminal output from the server should be very similar to this:

```
Incoming request to /one
Loop value: 1
Loop value: 0
Incoming request to /two
Loop value: 1
Loop value: 0
sending response for /one
sending response for /two
```

Listing 2-2 demonstrates the non-blocking nature of JavaScript and Node. When the first request comes in, it executes `setTimeout` and we supply a callback function. The second request is still queued and has yet to begin processing. JavaScript recognizes that `setTimeout` is an asynchronous call, queues up the supplied callback function, and continues linear execution. The `while` loop will execute and then stop for this request because there is no more synchronous code to execute for `/one`. The request to `/two` can start processing. Again, once the code finishes the `while` loop, other requests can be serviced if there are any. Neither new requests nor the `while` loop have to wait the 5,000 milliseconds to start processing.

Once the 5,000 milliseconds have elapsed, the callback function supplied to `set-Timeout` will execute and we will try to load the currently executing file. Again, we pass another callback function into `fs.readFile` that will run after the file is completely loaded into a buffer. During that time, other requests could be queued up and start executing synchronous code, exactly like the window during the `set-Timeout`. After the file is read into a buffer, we call `res.end(contents)` and send the results back to the requesting client. This simple web server is meant to demonstrate that even though there is I/O happening, more requests can be made to the server and synchronous code can execute without waiting for the I/O to finish.

The next chapter will go into the nuts and bolts of Node to provide a better idea of *how* the callback system works, as well as how to leverage it in our own web servers to increase throughput.

Summary

This chapter introduced Node.js, the most successful server-side implementation of JavaScript. We discussed the reasons why Node has been successful as a server-side technology: because it uses a language that's familiar to many developers — JavaScript — and that it provides non-blocking asynchronous I/O. We finished the chapter by writing our first trivial Node server.

In the next chapter, we're going to discuss how Node's modules and the Node package manager (npm) work.

Chapter **3**

Modules and npm

As we discussed in Chapters 1 and 2, one of the keys to the success of Node is the wide array of modules that are available to developers. There are open-source modules on GitHub for the majority of problems developers face when building a web server. Then there are modules available for social authentication,[1] validation,[2] and even server frameworks such as ExpressJS[3] and Hapi.[4] Not every module is massive and complicated, though; there are simple modules for coloring console text,[5] formatting dates and times,[6] and cloning[7] JavaScript objects.

As developers, we try not to reinvent the wheel if we can help it. We preach "code reuse" constantly and Node does not disappoint in this area. To fully appreciate the Node ecosystem, it is important to understand how modules and the Node package manager (npm) function.

---

[1] https://github.com/jaredhanson/passport
[2] https://github.com/hapijs/joi
[3] https://github.com/visionmedia/expressjs.com
[4] https://github.com/hapijs/hapi
[5] https://github.com/marak/colors.js/
[6] https://github.com/moment/momentjs.com
[7] https://github.com/pvorb/node-clone

npm

npm is the package manager for Node. It is a Node module that is installed globally with the initial installation of Node. By default, it searches and loads packages from the npm registry.[8] In addition to being a package registry, it also acts as a user-friendly resource for developers to discover new modules. npm is the heart of the Node module ecosystem, so let's now discuss some of the commands you need to know to use it effectively.

npm install

`npm install`, like many of the npm commands, can perform many different tasks depending on the arguments supplied. Simply executing `npm install` will install all the modules listed in the **package.json** file in the current directory. We'll talk more about the **package.json** file in a moment, but for now, think of it as a list of module names. `npm install` will look at the **package.json** file and install all the listed modules into a local **node_modules** folder.

Generally, when starting a new project that you've pulled from a source control provider, this is the first step to getting the code to run properly. This will give you the correct environment and dependencies, allowing you to be up and running very quickly.

`npm install <name>` tries to install the most recent version of the module <name> into the local **node_modules** folder. When you find a module that you'd like to try, simply install it with `npm install name` and npm will handle the rest. As a simple exercise, open up a terminal and type the following:

```
npm install colors
```

If you are watching the terminal, you should see several GET requests and 200 status codes. Those requests and responses is npm calling out to the npm registry, looking for the module-named `colors`, and downloading it into the local **node_modules** folder.

---

[8] https://www.npmjs.org/

Global versus Local Installations

npm install without any modifying arguments will always install the Node modules locally in the **node_modules** folder of the current directory. This is generally the desired behavior; however, some modules can be run directly from the command line. Think of these global modules as new commands that are written using Node and JavaScript. These kinds of modules are ones that you might want to use outside of a particular project and have access to them globally. We've already encountered one global module already: npm. Another example of this is the express-generator module. express-generator adds a command to the terminal that lets the user create a generic ExpressJS application server (file structure and boilerplate code) with a single command and some arguments.

Since we will be using this module later, let's install it globally now. Type this into your terminal:

```
npm install express-generator --global
```

Unless you have made changes to the permissions of your file system, you will get an EACCES error during the installation. This is normal. The EACCES error means that npm lacks permission to write to the location that global modules are installed. A quick Google search will net you several ways to solve this problem, but we're going to present the one that is without added security issues and does not require running npm as a more privileged user.

Global Installation Setup

In a terminal, navigate to your home directory and run npm config set prefix ~/npm. This will configure the prefix option globally for npm. You can verify that this worked correctly by running npm prefix, and the results should point to a directory under the current user ending with **/npm/bin**. This command tells npm to read and write from this directory during global operations instead of the default location, to which the current user probably lacks the permission to write.

Your last task will be to ensure that "~/npm" is included in your $PATH variable. If you skip this step, you won't be able to run any of the global modules easily from the command line and will instead have to provide a complete path to the module in the ~/**npm** folder.

Setting the $PATH

$PATH is an environment variable found in Unix-like operating systems. It is a list of directories where executable programs are located. Applications rely on this value to help look up external applications when running. For example, if you're employing an IDE (integrated development environment), it will use the $PATH value to find items such as external compilers, debuggers, or installed source-control applications. It is referred to as %PATH% in Windows operating systems.

Trying to reinstall the `express-generator` module should work fine now with no EACCES errors. This is a one-time setup and going forward, global module installations will be seamless. To make sure `express-generator` was properly installed, create a temporary directory and navigate your command line to it. Run `express` and you should see notifications that several files and directories are being created. If you list the folder contents, you should see **app.js**, **package.json**, and several sub-folders.

npm search

`npm search` is a quick way to query the npm registry without leaving the terminal. Suppose you wanted to display a file that was written in Markdown. Remember, you are entering into the Node module ecosystem—there are well over 20 existing modules for working with Markdown. In most cases, it would make no sense trying to write your own. Existing modules already have tests and have been vetted by the community over time. So rather than rolling your own, let's try to find one on the npm registry.

In a terminal, enter `npm search markdown`. The first time you run the search command, it will take a while; this is normal. When the results come back, you'll see a long list of all the available Node modules that contain "markdown" either in the title, description, or tags.

At this point you could pick and install one using `npm install <name>`. If you want to learn more about the package and read up on the documentation, try `npm docs <name>`. If the package is properly configured, it should launch a web browser and take you to the module's home page.

If you prefer an alternative to the command line for searching, you can go directly to the npm home page and use the search feature provided there.[9] The search results show module popularity, number of stars, dependency lists, and other useful data points.

npm, both the command and the website, is a vital piece of the Node ecosystem. We have only touched on a few important commands to be up and working quickly. We encourage you to check out the npm documentation to learn more of the commands.[10] Further in this chapter, we'll discuss one more npm command in depth: `npm link`.

package.json

We now know that running `npm install` will look for a **package.json** file and install the packages listed there. Let's examine a simple **package.json** file:

```
{
  "name": "hr",
  "version": "1.0.0",
  "scripts": {
    "start": "echo \"Run the correct js file to start your
➡application\" && exit 0",
    "populate": "node ./bin/populate_db"
  },
  "dependencies": {
    "async": "0.9.0",
    "debug": "0.7.4",
    "express": "4.2.0",
    "mongoose": "3.8.11"
  }
}
```

Listing 3-1. A sample **package.json** file.

Let's discuss each of the top-level keys of this file:

- name: is the name of the module. Generally, this is the <name> argument given to `npm install <name>`. This is required, but only needs to be unique if you

---

[9] https://www.npmjs.org/
[10] https://www.npmjs.org/doc/

plan on publishing the module to the npm registry. The name shouldn't have "node" or "js" in it. You should also avoid using any non-URL-safe characters, because name is used to create a URL when it's on the npm registry.

▨ version: is the version of the package expressed as **major.minor.patch**. This is known as semantic versioning, and it is recommended to start with version 1.0.0.

▨ scripts: This key serves a unique purpose, providing additional npm commands when running from this directory. For example, if you entered npm run start inside a folder with this package.json file, you'll see "Run the correct js file to start your application" logged in the terminal. If you run npm run populate, npm will try to execute node ./bin/populate_db. This file is yet to exist, so the command will fail. The key can be any valid JSON key and the value can be a node command or a shell script.

▨ dependencies: This is generally where the majority of information in any **package.json** file is stored. dependencies lists all the modules that the current module or application needs to function. The key is the module name and the value is the version of the module that's required. There are many ways to express a version inside the package.json file. You can state specific versions or a range of versions by combining >=, ~, and ^ (for example, >= 0.9.x,~3.x, and ^0.5.x). It is also possible to set a version to point directly to GitHub: "git://github.com/flatiron/winston#master", for example. The specifics and details of npm versioning can become extremely complicated, especially when working with ^, ~, and modules with versions less than 1.0.0. For a complete write-up about the semantic versioning npm uses, read the documentation on Github.[11]

Trying to write a **package.json** line by line in a text editor is not recommended. npm has a built-in command that will walk you through creating a valid file. Run npm init in the terminal and it will guide you through a series of prompts. This will generate a simple **package.json** file that's in line with the community standard and the latest specification from npm.

npm init is pretty self-explanatory about what each of the fields means. The one exception is the main value. main should be the filename or path to the JavaScript that should be used when a user requires your module. In general, the default value of **index.js** is fine.

---

[11] https://github.com/npm/node-semver

Now that we have a **package.json** file in the current directory, let's try `npm install` again with with some new arguments:

```
npm install colors --save
```

This command will install `colors` into the **node_modules** directory, and also update `dependencies` inside **package.json** to include an entry for the `colors` module. Now the next developer can simply type `npm install` and be ready to code, avoiding time wasted looking for modules referenced in the code.

The node_modules Folder

As we have demonstrated, the **node_modules** folder is where npm installs local modules. This is also the first place Node looks when you `require` a module. Let's install the ExpressJS framework and examine its **node_modules** folder.

In a new folder, install Express via `npm install express`. If you open this location with a file browser or terminal, you should see a **node_modules** folder. If you keep drilling into this directory, you'll soon realize that many of the submodules have their own **node_modules** folder. This is how Node handles modules that depend on other modules.

Module Dependencies

Looking closer at the file structure, several of the subfolders inside `express` have their own **node_modules** folder. Let's look inside the **send** directory. Its structure looks like this:

```
|send
|-lib
|-node_modules
|---finished
|-----node_modules
|-------ee-first
|---mime
|-----types
```

Listing 3-2. Node module directory structure

Express uses the send module, which in turn uses the finished and mime modules. finished also uses the ee-first module. By looking at the tree structure, it becomes easy to visualize a module's dependencies and subdependencies.

Because every module has its own node_modules folder, you'll probably see duplication. For example, if another module that Express uses requires ee-first as well, the ee-first folder would appear a second time in a different location.

By forcing every module to have its own node_module folder, rather than having a single directory of every module, it allows developers to be very specific with the particular module's version that they want to use. For example, if module A used version 1 of the "cookie" module, but module B was using version 2.x, there could be no guarantee that module A would continue to function properly if every module was saved into the same folder. How would npm decide which version to install in a global module directory?

require()

The require function is specific to Node and is unavailable to web browsers. At its core, all require does is execute JavaScript based on the supplied argument. When you require a module, you execute the JavaScript code that makes up the specified module. Node then returns an object that has function and values attached to it, just like any other JavaScript object.

Looking back through the code examples, you may have noticed require('http') in a few different places. Let's re-examine the simple server from Listing 1-1:

```
var http = require('http');
http.createServer(function (req, res) {...}).listen(1337,
➥'127.0.0.1');
console.log('Server running at http://127.0.0.1:1337/');
```

Listing 3-3. Simple Node server with logic removed

The code in Listing 3-3 should look familiar; this is the example Node server we've talked about several times already in the first two chapters of the book. It's a very basic web server that listens for requests on host 127.0.0.1 on port 1337. We've removed most of the internals of the code so that we just focus on the require logic. On the first line, we are setting the http variable to the result of require('http').

`require('http')` will cause Node to try to locate a module named `http` in a series of predefined locations. If the named module cannot be found in the current location, Node will try the next one. The lookup procedure roughly works in this way:

1. Check to see if the module named is a core module.

2. Check in the current directory's **node_modules** folder.

3. Move up one directory and look inside the **node_modules** folder if present.

4. Repeat until the root directory is reached.

5. Check in the global directory.

6. Throw an error because the module could not be found.

This list sums up the primary points of the Node module lookup algorithm. There are more details in the official documentation,[12] but these steps should be enough for the most common use cases.

Node will make several attempts to find the required module before throwing an error. In the case of the `http` module, because it's a core module it will only have to go to step 1. The module has been resolved, the code for the `http` will execute, and a JavaScript object will be returned that has functions and values attached to it. `createServer()` and `STATUS_CODES` are examples of data attached to the resultant `http` object. If you want to see the full `http` module, check the Node source code.[13]

Looking at how `require` works when passed a module name should solidify the discussion about the **package.json** file and how important the `name` key is. The `name` key is not only what's used to install a module with npm, but also how it's included in your code for use.

Let's look at another example. Write this into a script file:

---

[12] http://nodejs.org/api/modules.html
[13] https://github.com/joyent/node/blob/master/lib/http.js

```
javascript
var colors = require('colors');
console.log('Hello world'.green);
```

Listing 3-4. Requiring non-core module

We want our console logs to really pop, so let's colorize them! `colors` is *not* a core module, so Node will start a recursive lookup to try finding a module with the name `colors` as specified in its **package.json** file.

Go ahead and execute `node require_test`. If you've previously installed the `colors` module from earlier in this chapter, you should see "Hello world" logged to the console in green. If not, you will see an error such as `Error: Cannot find module 'colors'`. Install the `colors` module and rerun **require_test.js**.

Other Uses for `require`

The `colors` module is a good example of a node module that's easy to install and use. It also demonstrates another facet of `require()`. Looking back to Listing 3-4, you'll notice that the code is `"Hello world".green`. The code is invoking a `green` method on a string object. Unaltered `String` objects are without a `green` method, so the `colors` module added various color methods to the `String` prototype.

Remember, at its core `require` merely executes some JavaScript code. In the example of the `colors` module, it returns an object, but it *also* attaches items to the `String` prototype chain. `require` can be used to execute "run once" code as well, such as database initialization, constructing log singletons, changing built-in types and objects, and any other single-run code.

`require` can also accept a path to a file. This is useful for modules that you don't plan to publish the the npm registry. Shortly, we're going to write a simple module that we can reuse across multiple files. You can load the module with the following command: `var ourModule = require('./path-to/our-module')`.

The ability to point `require` at any arbitrary files allows developers to break their applications down into smaller parts and keep logic housed in single modules. In any web server, there is going to be boilerplate initialization logic. Instead of being forced to have this logic in the main application code, it can be housed in a separate file and executed with `require` once in the main application startup. If you create several applications that all share some boilerplate code, this small JavaScript file could even be shared across multiple projects.

Writing a Module

The final section of this chapter is going to cover writing our own module that we can use in an example Node script. We're going to create a very simple module that exposes several math functions. Let's name it "mmm" for MEAN Math Module.

Before we start writing the module, one quick note about a Node convention. While writing or viewing Node code, you'll often see `exports`, `require`, and `module` that seem to lack a definition. All JavaScript files that Node executes are automatically wrapped in a function with several parameters passed into it:

```
(function (exports, require, module, __filename, __dirname) {
   // The code we write will be here
});
```

Listing 3-6. Node automatic wrapping function

Node wrapping developer code in this way has several advantages. First, it helps prevent accidental global variables. This wrapping code creates an additional scope level that prevents improperly declared variables from being globally accessible. A second advantage is that every Node file automatically adheres to this predefined pattern.

It should now be clear why we have access to `exports` and `require` in our own code. They are automatically passed in to every file that is executed. Don't write that wrapping function; let Node put it there for you, in case it ever changes in subsequent versions. If you'd like to see how this works, check out the Node source code for this feature.[14]

---

[14] https://github.com/joyent/node/blob/master/src/node.js

Module Functionality

Before we dive right into the Node and module aspects, let's write some JavaScript code that executes basic math functions— addition, multiplication, and factorial—on integers:

```
                                                              mmm.js
function add (number1, number2) {
  return parseInt(number1, 10) + parseInt(number2, 10);
}

function multiply (number1, number2) {
  return parseInt(number1, 10) * parseInt(number2, 10);
}

function factorial (number) {
  if (number === 0) {
    return 1;
  }
  else {
    return number * factorial(number - 1);
  }
}
```

Listing 3-7. Math module internals

This is the main functionality we want to expose from our module; it's just regular JavaScript at this point. We're yet to write any code to hook into Node's module system, but looking back at Listing 3-6 will give us a hint at how to do so.

There is an `exports` object available in scope, which is used to export functions from a module. Update **mmm.js** to make use of the `exports` object similar to Listing 3-8:

```
                                                     mmm.js (updated, excerpt)
exports.add = add;
exports.multiply = multiply;
exports.factorial = factorial;
exports.now = Date.now();

function add (number1, number2) {...}
```

```
function multiply (number1, number2) {...}

function factorial (number) {...}

function privateMethod () {...}
```

Listing 3-8. Math module exporting

We've removed the internals of the function implementation for clarity. The Node module framework uses the `exports` object during the initialization of the module. On the first three lines of the file, we are attaching the `add`, `multiply`, and `factorial` functions to the `exports` object. Remember, JavaScript is loosely typed, so developers are free to attach functions and values directly to `exports` using the dot (`.`) operator. There are some restrictions to the keys you can attach to `exports`, but as a rule of thumb, just avoid using any built-in `Object` function names such as `hasOwnProperty`. We've also attached the `now` property that we'll use a little later.

Only the values attached to `exports` will be available outside of the module. If you wanted some reusable code inside this module, but did not want it to be exposed outside this module, avoid attaching that function to `exports` and it will be unavailable. We've included `privateMethod` as an example. It isn't exported outside of **mmm.js** so it will only be usable inside this file.

Finally, in the same directory as `mmm.js`, create a simple test for this module:

test.js

```
var m = require('./mmm');

console.log(m.add(3,5));
console.log(m.multiply(4,5));
console.log(m.factorial(4));
```

Listing 3-9. Math module test

Enter `node test.js` in the terminal and you should see the results printing out. The very first line we're calling `require` and supplying a file path, so the `require` function will try to execute the file at that location. In **mmm.js**, we've declared a few simple functions and attached them to the available `exports` object. The `exports` object is used by the Node module framework to return a result object that's assigned to m. m has the `add`, `multiply`, and `factorial` function attached to it that, in turn, point to the functions inside **mmm.js**. This is how all the Node modules that you'll encounter in the ecosystem work.

Because the argument to `require` is a file path, a **package.json** file for this module is unnecessary; we have written a module for our own local use.

Caching

Now that we've written our own module, we should quickly touch on module caching. When you `require('./mmm')` in Listing 3-9, it runs the JavaScript inside the **mmm.js** file and returns an object. Under the hood in the Node module system, the result of `require` is cached after the first time it's called for a specific module. This means multiple calls to `require('./mmm')` will always return the same instance of the mmm module. Because the same module is often `required` many times in a single Node application, caching is used to mitigate the performance overhead. One important caveat is that the cache key used is based on the *resolved* file name. So if a program requires mmm multiple times, but the required path is different (`require("mmm")` versus `require('./othermodule/node_modules/mmm')`), it's enough to "break cache," and this would be treated as loading a new module.

This is easier to understand with a simple demonstration such as Listing 3-10:

```
var m = require('./mmm');

console.log('time after first require ' + m.now);

console.log(m.add(3,5));
console.log(m.multiply(4,5));
console.log(m.factorial(4));

setTimeout(function () {
  m = require('./mmm');
  console.log('time after second require ' + m.now);
}, 5000);
```

Listing 3-10. Module caching

If you run the updated test, you'll see that the time doesn't change, even though we used `setTimeout` and reran `require('/.mmm')`. now is set when "./mmm" is run, so why didn't it change when we ran it a second time with the second call to `require`? This is the Node module caching system in action. The module system knows that it has already loaded mmm from "./mmm" before, so the code to create it has no need to run a second time. In Listing 3-10, the line in **mmm.js** to set now only runs a single time, so now is set the first time the module is loaded with `require`. It's important to keep this in mind as you continue to create your own Node modules. A full explanation of module caching can be found here on the Node.js documentation.[15]

npm link

There is one more npm command that is worth covering now that we know how to write our own modules: `npm link`. Suppose we wanted to move mmm to a new folder and project so that we could work on it in isolation. One way to keep the module functional inside **test.js** is to change the path parameter of `require` to point to the new location.

Another option is to use the `npm link` command to set up a global symbolic link to the module. This will let you `require` the module as if it were installed in a project's local **node_modules** folder. Setting up an `npm link` is a two-step process.

npm link Step 1

First, move **mmm.js** into a new folder named **math-module** and open a terminal in the **math-module** directory. Next, create a **package.json** file now that we're going to use this module outside a single project. Do you remember the command to initialize a **package.json** without writing it by hand? When prompted for a module name, name it mmm. From within the **math-module** folder, run `npm link`. The response will be `/your/global/modules/path > /the/directory/you/ran/the/command/from`. This is telling us that there is a symlink created for the global Node modules folder to the **math-module** directory.

npm link Step 2

Go back to the folder in which **test.js** is stored. In that folder, enter `npm link mmm` in the terminal. Again, you will see path information alerting you to the location of the linked module. Looking back at Listing 3-9, the path we supplied to `require` is no longer valid. We are now treating the math module as if it were a community module that should be loaded from the **node_modules** folder. Remember, `require`

---

[15] http://nodejs.org/api/modules.html#modules_caching

can take several arguments, and one of them is a module name. We created a symlink in step 1 and named our module mmm in the corresponding **package.json** file. Let's update **test.js** to require our module by name:

test.js

```
var m = require('mmm');

console.log(m.add(3,5));
console.log(m.multiply(4,5));
console.log(m.factorial(4));
```

Listing 3-11. Link update for test script

After all the links are set up, try running `node test.js` again. It should work exactly the same as before. By setting up a link, we have separated the module we want to write from the application that's using it. This allows us to work on the module decoupled from the testing code. Because `npm link` is essentially just a symbolic link with some extra npm features, any changes you make to the math module going forward will continue to be reflected in **test.js**.

Summary

In this chapter, we discussed how Node's modules and npm work. We started by introducing npm, node's package manager that searches and loads packages from the npm registry. We examined the structure of the **package.json** file that npm uses to install packages. We also discussed the **node_modules** folder, which is where npm installs local modules, and how we can use `require()` to load modules. We finished by writing our own module that we can use in an example Node script.

In the next chapter, we're going to discuss Node's programming model.

Node's Programming Model

A language's programming model defines how developers write code, and can make or break a language. Since Node is just JavaScript, the rules of the language are the same; however, Node does adhere to a number of additional conventions that make code consistent across its core and third-party modules. In Chapter 2, you learned how to create a simple HTTP server in Node. The goal of this chapter is to help you better understand the code structure of that server so you can extend it to other Node applications.

The Event Loop

The most important concept to understand about JavaScript, and Node by extension, is that it is single-threaded. This means that JavaScript applications can only perform one task at a time. They can, however, give the *illusion* of being multi-threaded through the use of an event loop. Essentially, the JavaScript engine maintains several queues of unhandled tasks. These queues include things such as events, timers, intervals, and immediates. Each execution of the event loop, known as a cycle,[1] causes one or more tasks to be dequeued and executed. As these tasks execute, they

---

[1] https://github.com/joyent/node/issues/7703#issuecomment-44692636

can add more tasks to the internal queues. Each cycle is made up of smaller steps, known as **ticks**. An example of a tick would be the act of accessing an item from timer queue.

 Concurrent Execution

There are a few ways to achieve concurrent execution in JavaScript. The most common example is Web Workers, which execute code in separate threads. In Node, you can fork child processes using the `child_process` and `cluster` modules.

Listing 4-1 shows a simple example that executes across multiple event loop cycles:

```
console.log('one event loop cycle');

setTimeout(function() {
  console.log('different cycle');
}, 100);

console.log('same cycle');
```

Listing 4-1. Code that executes across multiple event loop cycles.

This example prints three strings to the console. The order in which the strings are logged speaks to the event loop cycle in which they are executed. The output of this code is shown in Listing 4-2:

```
$ node event-loop.js
one event loop cycle
same cycle
different cycle
```

Listing 4-2. Console output from running the code in Listing 4-1.

Notice that the `console.log()` inside the `setTimeout()` is executed last, despite being second in the source code. This happens because the `setTimeout()` function queues up the code to run in a future cycle.

The Illusion of Concurrency

The event loop allows JavaScript applications to appear multi-threaded when individual tasks run quickly. Unfortunately, it's all too simple to make this illusion come crashing down with a few lines of code. As an example, Listing 4-3 creates two intervals that repeatedly print to the console. One interval prints Task A, while the other prints Task B:

```
setInterval(function() {
  console.log('Task A');
}, 10);

setInterval(function() {
  console.log('Task B');
}, 15);
```

Listing 4-3. An example containing two interval tasks.

If these intervals were truly executing concurrently, any changes to one task would not affect the other. To prove this is not the case in JavaScript, Listing 4-4 introduces an infinite loop into Task B:

```
setInterval(function() {
  console.log('Task A');
}, 10);

setInterval(function() {
  while (true) ;
  console.log('Task B');
}, 15);
```

Listing 4-4. An infinite loop destroying the illusion of concurrency in JavaScript.

If you run this modified code, Task A is printed to the console after ten milliseconds, but then nothing else happens. When Task B runs for the first time, it enters into an infinite loop. This prevents control from ever being returned to the event loop, and therefore Task A never runs again. If these tasks were executing in separate threads or processes, Task A would continue to execute while Task B looped.

Asynchronous Coding

Node.js is practically synonymous with with asynchronous application design, particularly asynchronous I/O operations. As you learned in Chapter 2, I/O is extremely slow. Most languages perform **synchronous I/O** (also known as blocking I/O) which means that they begin some I/O operation (such as a disk read, network call, and so on) and then sit idle until the operation completes. Typically, languages that use blocking I/O calls are also multi-threaded; therefore, while one thread is idle, another thread can perform some meaningful work. Of course, as you've already seen, JavaScript is single-threaded. If Node were to block an I/O call, the entire application would come to a screeching halt until the I/O finished because there are no other threads available to perform work.

To avoid the performance penalties associated with blocking I/O, Node.js almost exclusively uses asynchronous non-blocking I/O. Under this paradigm, an application will initiate some long-running external operation such as I/O; however, instead of waiting for a response, the program will continue executing additional code. Once the asynchronous operation is finished, the results are passed back to the Node application for processing.

This seems simple enough in theory, but there is still one big unanswered question: how are the results of an asynchronous operation passed back to a Node application? There are a few ways it can be done. The three most popular ways in Node are callback functions, event emitters, and promises. There have been many passionate arguments fought over which way is the right way, but in the end it all comes down to personal preference. In the Node core, callback functions have been the primary winner, with event emitters coming in second. Promises have been fairly successful in third-party modules, and are used quite a bit in AngularJS, so we'll touch on them as well.

Callback Functions

Simply put, a callback function is a function that's invoked at the completion of an asynchronous operation with the results of the operation passed as function arguments. Listing 4-5 provides an example of asynchronous code that invokes a callback function:

```
var fs = require('fs');

fs.readFile('README.txt', 'utf8', function(error, data) {
  if (error) {
    return console.error(error);
  }

  console.log(data);
});
```

Listing 4-5. Asynchronously reading a file using a callback function.

This example utilizes the core `fs` module, which contains functions for working with the file system. We're using the `fs.readFile()` method to—as the name implies—read a file. `readFile()` takes three arguments: the name of the file, the character encoding used in the file, and a callback function that's invoked once the file is read. In this example, we're reading the file `README.txt` using UTF-8 character encoding.

The call to `readFile()` causes file system I/O to occur. Once the I/O completes, the `readFile()` callback function is invoked with two arguments. The first argument, `error`, represents any potential exceptions that occurred while reading the file. For example, if `README.txt` does not exist, `error` will contain an `Error` object. However, if the file exists and there are no problems reading the data, `error` will be `null` and `data` will be a string containing the contents of the file.

Calling Conventions

In order to make coding more consistent across Node projects, the community has adopted certain conventions. While not rules of the language, these are considered best practices, particularly on projects with more than a single developer. Two of the most universally accepted conventions are shown in Listing 4-5. The first is the idea that when passing a callback function as an argument, it should be the last argument. Adopting this convention makes your code read better, as you can see all the input arguments, followed by the continuation function.

Another calling convention shown in Listing 4-5 relates to error handling. Notice that `error` is the first argument to the `readFile()` callback. If an error can be passed to a callback function, Node convention dictates that it will be the first argument. This may seem arbitrary, but it makes error handling more of a priority for developers. Think about it like this: if the error argument came last, many developers would simply ignore it. In fact, if the error came last, you could write your callback function such that the error argument is omitted completely. By making the error come first, you're saying "hey, something could have gone wrong and you need to check for it."

There is another common convention related to method naming that's not shown in Listing 4-5 but is worth pointing out. As previously mentioned, asynchronous code is the norm not the exception in Node; however, synchronous code does have its place (initialization code, shell scripts, and so on). To help make code more understandable, many synchronous functions have the string `Sync` appended to their names. This is especially common in the `fs` module,[2] as there are synchronous and asynchronous versions of most methods. For example, Listing 4-5 used the `readFile()` method, but it could have been written using the synchronous `readFileSync()` method as shown in Listing 4-6:

```
var fs = require('fs');

try {
  var data = fs.readFileSync('README.txt', 'utf8');

  console.log(data);
} catch (error) {
  console.error(error);
}
```

Listing 4-6. Synchronous equivalent of Listing 4-5.

Exception Handling

Notice that the synchronous code in Listing 4-6 uses a `try...catch` statement to handle errors, while the asynchronous version does not. This is a key difference in asynchronous code that you absolutely must understand. When an asynchronous function call is made, program execution continues while the asynchronous call completes. During this time, the application's call stack changes.

A `try...catch` statement is incapable of catching asynchronously thrown errors because the error is not thrown inside the `try...catch`. An example illustrating

---

[2] http://nodejs.org/api/fs.html

this point is shown in Listing 4-7. In this example, if an error occurs while reading the file, the callback function will *rethrow* the error; however, because the callback function was invoked asynchronously, the `try...catch` is unable to handle the error:

```
var fs = require('fs');

try {
  fs.readFile('README.txt', 'utf8', function(error, data) {
    if (error) {
      throw error;
      return;
    }

    console.log(data);
  });
} catch (error) {
  console.error('Caught the error synchronously');
}
```

Listing 4-7. Attempting to catch an asynchronously thrown error.

You will notice throughout Node applications that `try...catch` statements are used sparingly. They are used with synchronous functions like `JSON.parse()`, but not much else. Node supports an asynchronous error-handling mechanism known as **domains,**[3] but they behave inconsistently and are listed as unstable in the official documentation. The generally preferred way of handling errors in Node is to pass them around using callback functions until you reach a place where it makes sense to handle them.

Callback Hell

One drawback to asynchronous code is that if you don't structure your code properly, you can wind up in hell—**Callback Hell**, to be specific. Callback Hell occurs when many callback functions are nested within each other. Consider the file reader from Listing 4-5. In that example, we merely tried to read a file, and if an error occurred we just printed it to the console and exited. But, what if we wanted to take extra precaution to ensure that certain error conditions were avoided completely?

---

[3] http://nodejs.org/api/domain.html

With a bit of extra code, we can verify that the file exists and that the filename corresponds to a file, not a directory or something else. Listing 4-8 shows how this is accomplished. Unfortunately, by adding calls to `fs.exists()` and `fs.stat()`, the function nesting level in this example has increased by two. Notice how the code becomes increasingly indented—the beginning of Callback Hell. In a non-trivial application, the indentation could easily reach a depth of greater than ten levels, leading to code that's difficult to read and maintain:

```javascript
var fs = require('fs');
var fileName = 'README.txt';

fs.exists(fileName, function(exists) {
  if (!exists) {
    return console.error('File does not exist');
  }

  fs.stat(fileName, function(error, stats) {
    if (error) {
      return console.error(error);
    } else if (!stats.isFile()) {
      return console.error('Not a file');
    }

    fs.readFile(fileName, 'utf8', function(error, data) {
      if (error) {
        return console.error(error);
      }

      console.log(data);
    });
  });
});
```

Listing 4-8. A small asynchronous program suffering from the beginnings of Callback Hell.

Luckily, Callback Hell can easily be avoided by structuring your code intelligently. First, notice that the indentation has not been increased when it can be avoided. Entire function bodies are not included in `if` statements. Instead, `if` statements are used to check for certain conditions, and if they are met the function returns. Second, we can use named functions instead of anonymous callback functions. Listing 4-9 shows how the previous example can be rewritten using named functions. Notice that Callback Hell is instantly vanquished using this approach, albeit at the expense of slightly more code[4]:

```
var fs = require('fs');
var fileName = 'README.txt';

function readCallback(error, data) {
  if (error) {
    return console.error(error);
  }

  console.log(data);
}

function statCallback(error, stats) {
  if (error) {
    return console.error(error);
  } else if (!stats.isFile()) {
    return console.error('Not a file');
  }

  fs.readFile(fileName, 'utf8', readCallback);
};

function existsCallback(exists) {
  if (!exists) {
    return console.error('File does not exist');
  }

  fs.stat(fileName, statCallback);
}

fs.exists(fileName, existsCallback);
```

Listing 4-9. A rewrite of Listing 4-8 to avoid Callback Hell.

Event Emitters

The second way to implement asynchronous code is via events. If you've done any client-side JavaScript development, you have certainly dealt with events and event-

---

[4] Another common way to avoid Callback Hell is to use a control flow module. The most popular of these is async. [https://github.com/caolan/async]

driven programming. Under this model, objects called **event emitters** create or publish events; for example, in the browser, an event could be a mouse click or key press. Elsewhere in the code, subscribers can listen for these events and react to them when they occur.

In Node applications, event emitters are created using the `EventEmitter` data type. The example in Listing 4-10 shows how events are created using `EventEmitter`s:

```
var events = require('events');
var EventEmitter = events.EventEmitter;
var emitter = new EventEmitter();

emitter.emit('start');
emitter.emit('count', 1);
emitter.emit('count', 2);
```

Listing 4-10. Creating several events using an `EventEmitter`.

The first line of this example imports the core `events` module, and the second line assigns the `EventEmitter` constructor to the variable `EventEmitter`. On the third line the constructor is called, and a new `EventEmitter` is created and stored in the `emitter` variable.

The last three lines of Listing 4-10 emit three events using the `emit()` method. The first argument to `emit()` is a string specifying the type of event being emitted. In this example, one `start` event and two `count` events are emitted. Any arguments following the event type are attached as arguments to the event. The `start` event does not have any arguments, but the `count` events each include a single numeric argument representing the current count. Please note that this example does not generate any output. We still need to listen for the events, but we'll tackle that soon.

Extending `EventEmitter`

It's also quite simple to create your own classes that extend the `EventEmitter` type. Listing 4-11 shows how this is accomplished. In this example, we'll create a counter that emits a new `count` once per second. Notice that the `EventEmitter` is called with the `Counter` object set as `this`. Note also that the inheritance relationship is set up using the `util.inherits()` method, which is part of the Node core:

```
var util = require('util');
var EventEmitter = require('events').EventEmitter;

function Counter() {
  var self = this;

  EventEmitter.call(this); // call EventEmitter constructor
  var count = 0;

  this.start = function() {
    this.emit('start');

    setInterval(function() {
      self.emit('count', count);
      ++count;
    }, 1000);
  };
}

util.inherits(Counter, EventEmitter); // setup inheritance
```

Listing 4-11. A `Counter` that inherits from `EventEmitter`.

The `Counter` type can then be instantiated using the code shown in Listing 4-12. In the next section, we'll learn how to listen for the events emitted from the `Counter` or any other event emitter.

```
var counter = new Counter();
```

Listing 4-12. Instantiating a `Counter` event emitter.

Listening for Events

In order for events to be useful, there must be at least one subscriber listening for them. To set up an event listener in Node, use the `on()`, `addListener()`, and `once()` methods. The `on()` and `addListener()` work in exactly the same manner: they create listeners for a specific type of event. We prefer `on()` over `addListener()` as it requires less characters. Listing 4-13 shows how `on()` is used to listen for the `start` and `count` events emitters from our `Counter` example. This example defines two listeners: one for `start` events and another for `count` events. The type of event that the listener responds to is denoted by the first argument passed to `on()`. Each time an event of the correct type is emitted, the callback function passed as the second argument is invoked. If the emitted event has any arguments associated with it, they are passed to the callback function:

```
var counter = new Counter();

counter.on('start', function() {
  console.log('start event');
});

counter.on('count', function(count) {
  console.log('count = ' + count);
});

counter.start();
```

Listing 4-13. Listening for events emitted by the `Counter`.

Recall that the counter's `start()` causes a `start` event to be emitted, followed by one `count` event per second. It's worth noting that `on()` does not work retroactively, so the listener will only respond to events that are emitted after the listener has been attached. Hence, if the listeners were attached after calling `start()`, there's a chance that events could be missed.

The `once()` method is similar to `on()` with one notable exception. After the `once()` callback function is invoked, the listener is removed. This makes `once()` good for handling one-time events. For example, our counter emits a single `start` event followed by potentially many `count` events. Therefore, we could use `once()` to listen for `start` events as shown in Listing 4-14. As an exercise, you are encouraged to experiment with using `once()` to listen for `count` events to verify that the listener is only invoked one time:

```
counter.once('start', function () {
  console.log('start event');
});
```

Listing 4-14. Setting up a one-time event listener using `once()`.

Exception Handling

The simplest way to deal with exceptions using EventEmitters is to emit an error event; however, you must take care as unhandled error events will cause your program to terminate. An example that emits an unhandled error is shown in Listing 4-15. This program crashes when it is run:

```
var EventEmitter = require('events').EventEmitter;
var emitter = new EventEmitter();

emitter.emit('error', new Error('our error is bad and we feel bad'));
```

Listing 4-15. An unhandled error event is emitted.

Luckily, error events can be handled like any other events. Listing 4-16 shows how an error event is handled using on():

```
var EventEmitter = require('events').EventEmitter;
var emitter = new EventEmitter();

emitter.on('error', function(error) {
  console.error(error.message);
});

emitter.emit('error', new Error('our error is bad and we feel bad'));
```

Listing 4-16. Handling an error event using on().

The uncaughtException Event

Node provides a global process object that's used to interact with the currently running process. When an error event is not caught, it causes an uncaughtException event to be emitted by the process object. Listing 4-17 shows how this type of event is handled:

```
var EventEmitter = require('events').EventEmitter;
var emitter = new EventEmitter();

process.on('uncaughtException', function(error) {
  console.error(error.message);
  process.exit(-1);
```

```
});

emitter.emit('error', new Error('our error is bad and we feel bad'));
```

Listing 4-17. Handling an `uncaughtException` event.

If an `uncaughtException` event is emitted, it signifies that something has gone terribly wrong with your application. At this point, your application is considered to be in an undefined state from which it may or may not be able to recover. In such a situation your application should not attempt to recover, and just shut down gracefully. In this example the application is terminated using `process.exit()`.

Promises

Promises are objects that represent a value that is yet to be known when the promise is created. A promise can be thought of as a contract associated with an asynchronous function. The asynchronous function returns immediately, but promises that a value will be available at some point in the future. In the past, promises were part of the Node core, but they were phased out in favor of callback functions. Many third-party modules have continued to support promises out of author preference, but they are now back in the core as of version 0.11.13.[5] Promises recently became a fully supported feature in theV8 engine, meaning that they are available in Node as well.

 Promises Are Only Supported in Node 0.11.13 and Later

If you're using a version prior to 0.11.13, the promise-related code in this section will fail to work. Instead, you'll encounter the error message `ReferenceError: Promise is not defined`.

When a promise is created, it's in a state known as *pending* or *unfulfilled*. The promise remains in this state until its associated asynchronous code has finished executing. If the asynchronous code completes successfully, the promise moves into the *fulfilled* state. But if the asynchronous call fails for some reason, the promise moves into the *rejected* state.

---

[5] http://stackoverflow.com/questions/21564993/native-support-for-promises-in-node-js

In code, a promise is created using the Promise constructor, as shown in Listing 4-18. Promise() takes one argument, a callback function that takes two arguments of its own. The callback arguments resolve and reject are functions. To fulfill the promise, you call the resolve() function. To reject the promise, you call reject(). You can pass whatever arguments you'd like to resolve() and reject(), but convention dictates that only Error objects should be passed to reject():

```
var promise = new Promise(function(resolve, reject) {
  var success = true;

  if (success) {
    resolve('promise fulfilled');
  } else {
    reject(new Error('promise rejected'));
  }
});
```

Listing 4-18. Creating a promise.

Listing 4-19 shows how promises are used with asynchronous code by returning to our file reader example. It looks a lot like the original file reader example; however, instead of printing messages to the console, we either fulfill or reject the promise based on the result of readFile():

```
var fs = require('fs');
var promise = new Promise(function(resolve, reject) {
  fs.readFile('README.txt', 'utf8', function(error, data) {
    if (error) {
      return reject(error);
    }

    resolve(data);
  });
});
```

Listing 4-19. Using promises with asynchronous code.

The next question is what can be done with the values passed to resolve() or reject()? That is where the promise's then() method comes into play. then() takes two arguments, a success callback function and a failure callback function. As you might expect, the success callback is invoked if the promise is fulfilled, while the failure callback is invoked if the promise is rejected. Listing 4-20 is a continuation of Listing 4-19 and illustrates how `then()` is used. This example simply prints the contents of the file on success or prints the error message on rejection:

```
promise.then(function(result) {
  console.log(result);
}, function(error) {
  console.error(error.message);
});
```

Listing 4-20. Example use of a promise's `then()` method.

It's worth pointing out that either of the callback functions passed to `then()` can be `undefined` without issue. For example, the call to `then()` shown in Listing 4-21 does not include a failure callback. In the event that the promise is rejected, nothing will happen:

```
promise.then(function(result) {
  console.log(result);
});
```

Listing 4-21. An example use of `then()` without a failure callback.

Promise Chaining

One of the upsides to promises is that they can be chained together. Listing 4-22 shows how chaining is accomplished using multiple calls to `then()`. In this example, when the promise is fulfilled the string THE END! is returned. That string is then available as the `result` argument in the chained `then()` call. Assuming the promise is fulfilled, the contents of the file will be printed followed by the string THE END!:

```
promise.then(function(result) {
  console.log(result);
  return 'THE END!';
}).then(function(result) {
  console.log(result);
});
```

Listing 4-22. Chaining promises using `then()`.

You can also use the `catch()` method to handle rejections in a promise chain. The example in Listing 4-23 shows how `catch()` is used. The code will behave as though the `catch()` callback were passed as the second callback to `then()`, but is more convenient for chaining. In the event that the promise is rejected, the `catch()` callback will display the error message.

```
promise.then(function(result) {
    console.log(result);
    return 'THE END!';
}).catch(function(error) {
    console.error(error.message);
});
```

Listing 4-23. Promise chaining using the `catch()` method.

You can even interleave `then()` and `catch()` in a chain. The example in Listing 4-24 prints the contents of the file or the error message, depending on what happens with the original promise. The final `then()` will print THE END! regardless of what happens:

```
promise.then(function(result) {
    console.log(result);
}).catch(function(error) {
    console.error(error.message);
}).then(function() {
    console.log('THE END!');
});
```

Listing 4-24. Promise chaining that interleaves `then()` and `catch()`.

Summary

This chapter has covered the basics of Node's programming model. You've been introduced to the event loop, callback functions, event emitters, and promises. You've also learned how to handle exceptions in an asynchronous environment. It might seem difficult or strange at first, but you'll find it fairly easy to pick up after a little practice. In the next chapter, you'll learn how to apply the techniques learned in this chapter to the core Node modules.

Chapter 5

Core Modules

In Chapter 3, you learned about Node's module system and the `require()` function. Then, Chapter 4 taught you how to write code in the Node way. Along the way, you've also seen a few examples that used the `http` and `fs` core modules. This chapter brings all the previously discussed material together, explaining how to use some of Node's core modules in detail. Before we start, it's worth pointing out that we'll only scratch the surface of the Node core—it's **far** too large to cover in a single chapter; however, after completing this chapter, you should have adequate knowledge to understand the Node documentation.[1]

Command Line Arguments

Reading arguments from the command line is extremely simple in Node. All command line arguments passed to a Node application are available via the `process.argv` array. Note that the first two elements of this array are the `node` executable, followed by the name of the invoked JavaScript file. This means that the actual application arguments begin at `process.argv[2]`. Listing 5-1 shows how command line arguments are accessed and printed to the console using the `forEach()` method. To run

---

[1] http://nodejs.org/api/

this example, save the code in a file named `argv-demo.js`, and run `node argv-demo foo bar baz`:

```
process.argv.forEach(function(value, index, args) {
  console.log('process.argv[' + index + '] = ' + value);
});
```

Listing 5-1. Accessing command line arguments using `process.argv`.

Working with the File System

As you've already seen in a few examples, the `fs` module allows you to access the file system. If you've been a client-side JavaScript developer in the past, you know how frustrating it's been to have nonexistent or inconsistent APIs for working with the file system. Node, being a complete server-side implementation, makes this frustration a thing of the past.

__filename and __dirname

Any file in a Node application can determine its absolute location using the `__filename` and `__dirname` variables. `__filename` and `__dirname` are strings, and, as their names imply, they specify the file being executed and the directory containing the file. Listing 5-2 shows an example that uses `__filename` and `__dirname`. The output from running this code is shown in Listing 5-3. Your output will differ depending on where you run the code on your machine:

```
console.log('Currently executing file is ' + __filename);
console.log('It is located in ' + __dirname);
```

Listing 5-2. Using `__filename` and `__dirname` to print file paths.

```
$ node file-paths.js
Currently executing file is /home/node/file-paths.js
It is located in /home/node
```

Listing 5-3. Example output from running the code in Listing 5-2.

It is worth noting that __filename and __dirname are **not** global variables. Instead, they are local variables that are defined in every file. Therefore, if your project consists of multiple files, these values will be different in each file.

The Current Working Directory

Node applications have a concept of a current working directory. This is the directory that's used as the baseline when working with relative file paths. At any time during program execution, you can access the current working directory using the pro-cess.cwd() method. This method takes no arguments, and returns a string representing the application's working directory.

You can also change the current working directory using the process.chdir() method. This method takes a single argument, a string representing the directory in which to change. If a problem occurs—for example, if the target directory does not exist—chdir() throws an exception.

Listing 5-4 shows how the current working directory is inspected and changed. This example displays the current working directory, and then attempts to move to the / directory. If an error occurs, it is logged to stderr. Finally, the new working directory is printed to the console:

```
console.log('Starting in ' + process.cwd());

try {
  process.chdir('/');
} catch (error) {
  console.error('chdir: ' + error.message);
}

console.log('Current working directory is now ' + process.cwd());
```

Listing 5-4. Displaying and changing the current working directory.

Reading Files

The simplest way to read a file in a Node application is via the fs module's read-File() and readFileSync() methods. Both of these methods take a filename to read as their first argument. An optional second argument can be used to specify additional options such as the character encoding. If the encoding is not specified, the contents of the file are returned in a `Buffer` (a Node data type used to store raw binary data).

The synchronous call, `readFileSync()`, returns the contents of the file or throws an error if something goes wrong. The asynchronous call, `readFile()`, takes a callback function as its final argument. The callback function takes two arguments, a possible error object and the file contents. The application in Listing 5-5 using `readFile()`, in conjunction with `__filename`, to read its own source code. The equivalent synchronous code using `readFileSync()` is shown in Listing 5-6:

```
var fs = require('fs');

fs.readFile(__filename, function(error, data) {
  if (error) {
    return console.error(error.message);
  }

  console.log(data);
});
```

Listing 5-5. An example application that reads its own source code.

```
var fs = require('fs');
var data;

try {
  data = fs.readFileSync(__filename);
  console.log(data);
} catch (error) {
  console.error(error.message);
}
```

Listing 5-6. The synchronous equivalent of Listing 5-5.

When you run one of these examples, you'll notice that it displays a `Buffer` object as a series of raw bytes. While this is a true representation of the file contents, it is not particularly user-friendly. There are two ways to view the data as a string. The first is to call `toString()` on the `data` variable. This will return the `Buffer` contents as a UTF-8 encoded string. The second approach is to specify UTF-8 encoding using the optional second argument, as shown in Listing 5-7. This will cause the data to be returned as a string instead of a `Buffer`.

```
var fs = require('fs');

fs.readFile(__filename, {
  encoding: 'utf8'
}, function(error, data) {
  if (error) {
    return console.error(error.message);
  }

  console.log(data);
});
```

Listing 5-7. Setting the encoding type during a file read.

Writing Files

Files can easily be written using the `writeFile()` and `writeFileSync()` methods. These methods are the counterparts of `readFile()` and `readFileSync()`. These methods take a filename as their first argument, and the data to write (as a string or `Buffer`) as their second argument. The third argument is optional, and is used to pass additional information such as the encoding type. Unlike the `readFile()` variations, these methods default to using UTF-8 encoding. `writeFile()` takes a callback function as its last argument. A potential error object is the only argument passed to the callback. `writeFileSync()` does not return a value, but throws an error if necessary. Listing 5-8 shows how a file is written using `writeFile()`.

```
var fs = require('fs');
var data = 'some file data';

fs.writeFile(__dirname + '/foo.txt', data, function(error) {
  if (error) {
    return console.error(error.message);
  }
});
```

Listing 5-8. Writing data to a file using `writeFile()`.

By default, `writeFile()` will create a new file, or overwrite an existing file with the same name. This behavior can be modified by passing a `flag` value using the optional third argument. For example, passing the flag `wx` causes an error to be thrown if the file already exists, while the `a` flag causes data to be appended to an existing file instead of overwriting. A full list of available flags is included in the fs documentation,[2] and an example use of the wx flag is shown in Listing 5-9:

```
var fs = require('fs');
var data = 'some file data';

fs.writeFile(__dirname + '/foo.txt', data, {
  flag: 'wx'
}, function(error) {
  if (error) {
    return console.error(error.message);
  }
});
```

Listing 5-9. Setting the flag option when called writeFile().

Streams

A **stream** is a mechanism for moving data between two points. A stream can be thought of as a simple garden hose. The hose is connected to a water source. When the source pushes water into the hose, it flows through to the other end of the hose. At this point, the water can be used by a sprinkler or some other consumer.

Node utilizes streams in much of its core, such as files and sockets. Streams are attractive because they allow an application to process data in small pieces, instead of handling all the data at once. Unfortunately, streams are also a common source of confusion, as Node has implemented several types of stream APIs. This section will explain streams in their simplest form.

Readable Streams

Readable streams are sources of data. These streams emit data, close, end, and error events, which are used to process the data stream. When a new piece of data known as a **chunk** becomes available, the stream emits a data event with the actual data passed as a Buffer. The close event is optional, and can be emitted when the underlying source of the data stream (such as a file), is closed. Once the stream has sent all of its data, the end event is emitted. After an end event is emitted, no more

---

[2] http://nodejs.org/api/fs.html#fs_fs_open_path_flags_mode_callback

data events should be emitted. If anything goes wrong, the stream emits an error event.

Readable File Streams

As a good example of working with a readable stream, we turn to the fs.createRead-Stream() method. This method opens a file as a readable stream. Compare this behavior to readFile(), which reads the entire contents of a file and stores it in memory. If your application needs to process many potentially large files simultaneously (for example, a web server), memory usage and garbage collection can become a problem when using readFile().

createReadStream() returns a readable stream based on the filename passed in as an argument. Listing 5-10 uses createReadStream() to display the contents of a file named foo.txt. Notice that the data event handler converts the data chunk to a string and then displays it using process.stdout.write(). The console.log() method was not used here because it appends an additional new line to the string that it displays.[3] If console.log() was used to display an input file that required multiple chunks, it would be displayed with extra line breaks sprinkled throughout. process.stdout represents the standard output stream of the current process. This is a writable stream that will be covered shortly:

```
var fs = require('fs');
var stream = fs.createReadStream('foo.txt');

stream.on('data', function(data) {
  var chunk = data.toString();

  process.stdout.write(chunk);
});

stream.on('end', function() {
  console.log();
});
```

---

[3] https://github.com/joyent/node/blob/master/lib/console.js#L53

```
stream.on('error', function(error) {
  console.error(error.message);
});
```

Listing 5-10. Displaying the contents of a file using a readable stream.

Writable Streams

Writable streams are destinations—or sinks—for data. Data is sent to a writable stream by calling its `write()` method. Once all the desired data has been written, the stream's `end()` method is used to signal the end of the stream. You've seen an example of a writable stream in Listing 5-10 when `process.stdout.write()` was invoked. Like readable streams, writable streams also emit `close` and `error` events that behave in the same fashion.

Handling Back Pressure

A writable stream can only handle so much data at one time, as underlying buffers may become full. Once this limit is reached the stream is saturated, and any additional data written to the stream can cause problematic or unpredictable behavior. **Back pressure** is how the writable stream signals its source to stop sending data.

Back pressure is implemented via the `write()` method's Boolean return value. If this value is `false`, the source should not write any more data to the stream. This gives the writable stream time to process the data that has already been written. Once the stream is ready to receive more data, it emits a `drain` event. The source can detect this event and begin sending data again.

Writable File Streams

Writable streams associated with file descriptors are created using the `fs.create-WriteStream()` method. Listing 5-11 shows how a writable file stream is created. In this example, a readable file stream is used to read data from a file. The data from the readable stream is then sent to the writable stream automatically using the `pipe()` method. Essentially, this code performs a file copy:

```
var fs = require('fs');
var readStream = fs.createReadStream('foo.txt');
var writeStream = fs.createWriteStream('bar.txt');

readStream.pipe(writeStream);
```

Listing 5-11. Piping a readable file stream into a writable file stream.

pipe() is a convenient method that allows the output of one stream to be connected to the input of another stream. This saves the developer the hassle of handling a variety of stream-related events, such as drain.

The Standard Streams

Node applications are connected to three standard streams by default. These streams are stdin, stdout, and stderr, and are accessible via the process object. stdin is a readable stream that's employed to gather user input. stdout and stderr are writable streams that are used to display output and errors respectively. The console.log() and console.error() family of methods are simple wrappers around calls to process.stdout.write() and process.stderr.write().

When a Node application runs, the stdin stream is in a paused state by default; however, you can read data from stdin by unpausing the stream and handling data events. Listing 5-12 shows how data is read from stdin. In this example, stdout is used to create a prompt for the user's name. Then, stdin is unpaused using the readable stream resume() method. When the user types in their name and presses Return, a data event is emitted. This triggers the handler, which greets the user by name and then returns stdin to a paused state:

```
process.stdin.once('data', function(data) {
  process.stdout.write('Hello ' + data.toString());
  process.stdin.pause();
});

process.stdout.write('What is your name?  ');
process.stdin.resume();
```

Listing 5-12. Working with the standard streams.

Web Programming

Node.js is probably most famous for developing web applications: a web server is featured on the project's home page. This section will focus on HTTP servers specifically. If you're interested in more generic TCP/IP programming, you'll want to check out the net core module.[4]

Creating a Server

Listing 5-13 shows the web server example from the Node.js home page. We've examined this code sample before, but in this chapter we're going to dive in more thoroughly. HTTP server functionality is defined in the http and https modules. In this case we're creating an insecure HTTP server. Creating an HTTPS server is a similar process but requires a bit more work, which we'll revisit later.

As you likely know, HTTP is a request-response protocol. Clients request specific resources from the server, and the server processes the request and sends back an appropriate response. The server in Listing 5-13 executes the createServer() callback each time a request is received from a client. The req argument contains information about the client and the requested resource. The res argument, on the other hand, contains information and methods regarding the response.

The writeHead() method is used to write the status code and any optional response headers. As shown in Listing 5-13 the headers are specified using an object, where the object keys specify the header names and the object values represent the header values. Data is written using zero or more res.write() calls. After all the data has been written, the server completes the connection with a single **mandatory** call to res.end(). For added convenience, res.end() supports the same arguments as res.write(). This means that the entire response can be written via res.end(), as shown in Listing 5-13. This basic server sends back a single response header, Content-Type, a 200 response status code, and the body, Hello World\n:

```
var http = require('http');
http.createServer(function (req, res) {
  res.writeHead(200, {'Content-Type': 'text/plain'});
```

---

[4] http://nodejs.org/api/net.html

```
  res.end('Hello World\n');
}).listen(1337, '127.0.0.1');
console.log('Server running at http://127.0.0.1:1337/');
```

Listing 5-13. A very simple HTTP server.

Figure 5.1 shows what a response from this server looks like in Chrome. Chrome's developer tools have been used to inspect the HTTP request and response. The "Hello World" response body clearly shows in the main browser window. Notice the 200 OK status code and Content-Type response header whose value is set to text/plain. Note also that a number of other response headers have been included that we did not specify in our application logic. Node will add a number of response headers by default if the application does not include them.

Figure 5.1. The response from the server in Chrome's developer tools

The final step to starting the server is calling the listen() method. This causes the server to begin accepting connections on port 1337. The second argument is optional and is used to specify the host to which the server will respond. This is useful on machines that have multiple network interfaces. Once the server is successfully listening on the port, a listening event is emitted. You can provide an optional callback to listen() that will handle the listening event.

Routes

The server in Listing 5-13 is extremely limited because it responds to every request in the exact same way. A real server would likely need to perform different actions depending on the request method (also known as a **verb**) and URL. The combination of an HTTP verb and requested URL is known as a **route**. In the previous examples, the same response was returned for every route. Listing 5-14 shows an updated server that supports two routes with an additional handler that returns a 404 status code for unmatched requests. Notice that the requested URL is available via `req.url`, while the HTTP verb is found in `req.method`:

```
var http = require('http');

http.createServer(function(req, res) {
  if (req.url === '/' && req.method === 'GET') {
    res.writeHead(200, {'Content-Type': 'text/html'});
    res.end('Hello <strong>home page</strong>');
  } else if (req.url === '/account' && req.method === 'GET') {
    res.writeHead(200, {'Content-Type': 'text/html'});
    res.end("Hello <strong>account page</strong>");
  } else {
    res.writeHead(404, {'Content-Type': 'text/html'});
    res.end();
  }
}).listen(1337);
```

Listing 5-14. An HTTP server with support for multiple routes.

Accessing Request Headers

Headers are an important part of HTTP transactions. For example, cookies, which are responsible for maintaining state in web applications, are sent from the client to the server in the `Cookie` request header. Similarly, when a server sets a cookie, it does so via the `Set-Cookie` response header. You've already seen how easy it is to set response headers. Node makes it just as simple to obtain the values of request headers—they're available in `req.headers`. To make matters even simpler, Node lowercases the header names, so there's no need to test for both `Host` and `host`. For example, to read the value of the `Cookie` request header, you would check `req.headers.cookie`. If the header name has a hyphen in the name (`User-Agent`, for example), you would use `req.headers['user-agent']`. The example in Listing 5-15 reports the value of the `User-Agent` header:

```
var http = require('http');
http.createServer(function (req, res) {
    res.end('Your user agent is ' + req.headers['user-agent']);
}).listen(1337, '127.0.0.1');
console.log('Server running at http://127.0.0.1:1337/');
```

Listing 5-15. An example of accessing HTTP request headers.

Summary

This chapter has introduced the basics of some of Node's core modules. Specifically, this chapter has gone on a whirlwind tour of the command line, the file system, streams, and web servers. Unfortunately, a complete overview of the entire Node core is beyond the scope of this book, but the reader is encouraged to explore the complete documentation.[5]

---

[5] http://nodejs.org/api/

Building the Node Server

We've covered everything you need to dive into creating a real Node server in the preceding chapters. This chapter will focus on building a subset of the Node server for the human resources application we're using to demonstrate the MEAN stack.

Server Plan

Before you start writing any code, you need to have a basic idea of what your web server should do. For this subset example, our server will need to do two tasks: view employee information as a list, and for an individual. The server must also be able to send static resources such as CSS, client-side JavaScript, images, and HTML files. We should strive to make the various employee resources RESTful rather than use SOAP/WSDL[1]. As we delve further into the development of our Human Resources application, you'll find that hooking in different front-end frameworks such as Angular is much easier with a RESTful API that's simple to consume. The RESTful design pattern also lines up cleanly with the employee operations we require for our application, namely create, retrieve, update, and delete (CRUD). We should

---

[1] http://en.wikipedia.org/wiki/Web_Services_Description_Language

have the static resources segmented out into their own folder and break the code up into logical and reusable pieces.

Structuring the Application

Below is the file structure of the application. The files and folders listed here will be referenced frequently, so keep Listing 6-1 handy:

```
|____database
| |____employees.json
|____index.js
|____lib
|____node_modules
| |____colors
|____package.json
|____public
| |____home.html
| |____style.css
```

Listing 6-1. Final directory structure for Node example application.

In general, the **lib** folder is where local, project-specific modules are located. Inside the **public** folder, we'll store our static resources. To keep it simple for this example, we'll use **employees.json** as a database that we can query. You can see the **node_module** is present, and we already have the `colors` module installed.

Getting Started

Do you remember the npm command used to start a new Node project? Create a new directory and open the terminal window in that directory. Within that folder, initialize a new node application using the correct npm command. After that, install `colors` and make sure the **package.json** file is created and updated. Next, create the **index.js** file in the root of the directory.

Finally, we'll write the stub server that you've seen several times throughout this book:

```
var http = require('http');

http.createServer(function (req, res) {
```

```
// A parsed url to work with in case there are parameters
var _url;

// In case the client uses lower case for methods.
req.method = req.method.toUpperCase();
console.log(req.method + ' ' + req.url);
res.end('The current time is ' + Date.now())

}).listen(1337, '127.0.0.1');

console.log('Server running at http://127.0.0.1:1337/');
```

Listing 6-2. Server skeleton

Listing 6-2 creates a server and begins listening on port 1337. If you make requests to `localhost:1337/`, you should see information being logged into the console, indicating that the server is listening. You should notice that the server never responds in this state. Can you spot why? It's because we have yet to do anything with the `res` object; specifically, `res.end()` is never called. `res.end()` is what ends and sends a response to the incoming request. We will fill in the correct responses as the server becomes more fleshed out.

About `req` and `res`

The `req` and `res` objects often seen in Node servers are short for "request" and "response." The `req` object in this example is an `http.ClientRequest` object. You can find more information about this object in the Node.js documentation.[2] The related `res` object is an `http.ServerResponse` object, for which the documentation for this object is also found in the Node.js documentation[3]. Going into the details of these objects is outside the scope of this book. For now, try to remember that "`req`/request" is the incoming request and "`res`/response" is the response the server builds and eventually sends. If you have questions about methods, properties, or events on these objects, we encourage you to consult the Node.js documentation links specified.

---

[2] http://nodejs.org/api/http.html#http_class_http_clientrequest
[3] http://nodejs.org/api/http.html#http_class_http_serverresponse

Routing

The most fundamental feature of any web server is the ability to route requests. Looking back at our plan for the server, there are mainly three routes we are concerned with:

1. one for retrieving a list of employees
2. one for retrieving a specific employee
3. a general catchall route for static files

In addition, we only support GET requests for this example server, so we should respond properly if the client tries to make a non-GET request:

```
http.createServer(function (req, res) {
  // A parsed url to work with in case there are parameters
  var _url;

  // In case the client uses lower case for methods.
  req.method = req.method.toUpperCase();
  console.log(req.method + ' ' + req.url);

  if (req.method !== 'GET') {
    res.writeHead(501, {
      'Content-Type': 'text/plain'
    });
    return res.end(req.method + ' is not implemented by this
➥server.');
  }

  if (_url = /^\/employees$/i.exec(req.url)) {
    // return a list of employees
    res.writeHead(200);
    return res.end('employee list');
  } else if (_url = /^\/employees\/(\d+)$/i.exec(req.url)) {
    // find the employee by the id in the route
    res.writeHead(200);
    return res.end('a single employee');
  } else {
    // try to send the static file
    res.writeHead(200);
    res.end('static file maybe');
  }
}).listen(1337, '127.0.0.1');
```

Listing 6-3. Node server with primitive routing

First, we sure that the method is a GET request. If it isn't, the correct status code to respond with is 501. We use `res.writeHead` and pass two arguments. The first argument is the status code that will be returned to the client. The second is the response headers. In this example, we're only supplying `"Content-Type"` to be plain text.

If the incoming method is a GET request, we want to try to route the request. First, we want to see if the request is for `"/employees"`. The regular expression runs against `req.url` and looks for a match. If there is one, `_url` will have a value, execute the first `if` block, and respond with `"employee list"`. If `req.url` doesn't match the first regular expression, we try a second regular expression checking for `"/employees/a_number"`. In that case, the server will respond with `"a single employee"`. Finally, if the requested URL fails to match either of those regular expressions, we'll assume it's a static file. The code will check the file system to locate the file and then send it. If the file does not exist, the correct status code to send is a 404.

For both of the employee routes, we have to query a database. Rather than pollute **index.js** with database querying logic, we're going to write a simple database module. Remember, for this example the database will be a JSON file.

Database Module

The database module should encapsulate the logic required to retrieve a list of employees and for looking up a single employee based on their ID. You may recall in previous chapters, we noted that database queries are I/O and should be non-blocking. The JavaScript pattern for non-blocking I/O is to supply a `callback` function that is executed when the I/O is complete.

Create an **employees.js** file in the **lib** folder and an **employees.json** file in the **database** folder:

```
var employeeDb = require('../database/employees');

exports.getEmployees = getEmployees;
exports.getEmployee = getEmployee;

function getEmployees (callback) {
```

```
    setTimeout(function () {
      callback(null, employeeDb);
    }, 500);
}

function getEmployee (employeeId, callback) {
  getEmployees(function (error, data) {
    if (error) {
      return callback(error);
    }

    var result = data.find(function(item) {
      return item.id === employeeId;
    });

    callback(null, result);
  });
}
```

Listing 6-4. Simple database module

This pattern should look familiar from the chapter about modules. We export two functions, one to obtain a list of employees (`getEmployees`) and one to fetch a single employee (`getEmployee`). Both of these functions take `callback` as a parameter. That function that will be executed when the I/O is complete.

If you remember back to when we discussedthe `require` keyword, you'll recall thatit accepts many different files and paths. One option is to pass a path to a JSON file. In Listing 6-1 under the **database** folder, we have an **employees.json** file stored. Copy Listing 6-5 into **database/employees.json**.

```
[
    {
      "id": "1000003",
      "name": {
        "first": "Colin",
        "last": "Ihrig"
      },
      "address": {
        "lines": ["11 Wall Street"],
        "city": "New York",
        "state": "NY",
```

```
      "zip": 10118
    }
  },
  {
    "id": "1000021",
    "name": {
      "first": "Adam",
      "last": "Bretz"
    },
    "address": {
      "lines": ["2 Market Square","(Market Square)"],
      "city": "Pittsburgh",
      "state": "PA",
      "zip": 15222
    }
  }
]
```

Listing 6-5. Example **employees.json** file

`var employeeDb = require('../database/employees');` will load the JSON file into memory as a regular JavaScript collection that can be referenced from the functions in this file. Again, to simulate a query to a real database, we've inserted some delay with `setTimeout` in the `getEmployees` function.

The `getEmployee` function takes two parameters: a callback function and an employee ID. First, we call the `getEmployees` function and pass an anonymous function as the `callback` parameter. After 3,000 milliseconds, the callback function will be executed by the `getEmployees` functionand pass the caller `error` and `data` arguments. If there's an `error`, we want to execute the `callback` function and bubble this error up to the calling function. This is an extremely common pattern, so it's worth memorizing. If there is no error, we want to iterate over **data** and try to locate an employee with an ID equal to `employeeId`. Finally, execute `callback` and pass back any errors and the **employee** object from the "database."

In Node, the common callback convention is that the first argument to a callback function should be the error object, or `null` if there were no errors. Similarly if a function requires a callback function, just as with both of our employee functions, the last argument in the arguments list should be the callback function. You'll find this to be common practice throughout the Node community.

The `find` Method

A quick note about the `find` method. It is in the spec for ECMAScript 6 but is currently unavailable in the Node runtime as of Node version 0.10.32. For this example, you can add a polyfill for the `Array.find` method. A **polyfill** is a term used to describe code that enables future JavaScript features in environments that are yet to support it. You can also write an additional method in **lib/employees** that locates an element in an array based on an ID. This bit of code will be removed once a true database is introduced, so don't feel obligated to spend much time on it.

Querying the Database

The logic to query the ad hoc database is now encapsulated in **lib/employees.js**. Let's update the **index.js** file to load the new module into memory and use the exported methods:

```
var http = require('http');
var employeeService = require('./lib/employees');

http.createServer(function (req, res) {
  // A parsed url to work with in case there are parameters
  var _url;
  (...)

  if (_url = /^\/employees$/i.exec(req.url)) {
    // return a list of employees
    employeeService.getEmployees(function (error, data) {
      if (error) {
        // send a 500 error
      }
      // send the data with a 200 status code
    });
  } else if (_url = /^\/employees\/(\d+)$/i.exec(req.url)) {
    // find the employee by the id in the route
    employeeService.getEmployee(_url[1], function (error, data) {
      if (error) {
        // send a 500 error
      }

      if (!data) {
        // send a 404 error
```

```
    }

    // send the data with a 200 status code
  });
 } else {
    // try to send the static file if it exists,
    // if not, send a 404
 }
}).listen(1337, '127.0.0.1');
```

Listing 6-6. Incorporating the employee database module

In Listing 6-6, the employee database module is loaded with `var employeeService = require('./lib/employees');`. `employeeService` is an object that has the methods defined in **lib/employees.js**. The `getEmployees` function is called if the incoming URL is `"/employees"`, and `getEmployee` is called if the incoming URL is `"/employees/a_number"` with `"a_number"` being passed to `getEmployee` as the employeeId.

Remember back to the function definitions of the `employeeService` module; both require callback functions that will be executed when the I/O is completed. We supply anonymous functions as input parameters to both function calls. When the database query is completed, execution will continue inside the callback functions.

You'll notice that the response logic has been replaced with comments about what *should* happen when various conditions are met. Looking at the comments, it should be clear that there's an opportunity to write another module that handles sending responses to the client.

Response Generator

We are going to create another module that handles sending responses to the client. Create a file called **lib/responseGenerator.js** to encapsulate the response logic.

Looking at the comments about responses, we can see that four different responses; a 200 with JSON, a 404, a 500, and a file response. This module should expose four distinct methods to respond accordingly:

```javascript
var fs = require('fs');

exports.send404 = function (response) {
  console.error("Resource not found");

  response.writeHead(404, {
    'Content-Type': 'text/plain'
  });
  response.end('Not Found');
}

exports.sendJson = function (data, response) {
  response.writeHead(200, {
    'Content-Type': 'application/json'
  });

  response.end(JSON.stringify(data));
}

exports.send500 = function (data, response) {
  console.error(data.red);

  response.writeHead(500, {
    'Content-Type': 'text/plain'
  });
  response.end(data);
}

exports.staticFile = function (staticPath) {
  return function(data, response) {
    var readStream;

    // Fix so routes to /home and /home.html both work.
    data = data.replace(/^(\/home)(.html)?$/i,'$1.html');
    data = '.' + staticPath + data;

    fs.stat(data, function (error, stats) {

      if (error || stats.isDirectory()) {
        return exports.send404(response);
      }

      readStream = fs.createReadStream(data);
      return readStream.pipe(response);
```

```
    });
  }
}
```

Listing 6-7. The response generator

`send404`, `sendJson`, and `send500` essentially do the same task. Data (if there is response data) and a response object are passed in, the proper `Content-Type` header is set based on what the response payload will be, and `end` is called to write the payload and finish the response. The `response` parameter will be the `res` argument in **index.js**, which, if you remember, is an `http.ServerResponse` object.

`staticFile` accepts a single argument, `staticPath`. That argument can be thought of as a mount point, a file under which all the static content resides on the file system. A function is returned that accepts a `data` and a `response` object, just like the other function in this file. `staticFile` retrieves information about the file located at `path`. If the file doesn't exist or is a directory, we reuse the `send404` function.

Otherwise, we create a read stream based on the filepath and pipe that into the response. The `response` object (an `http.ServerResponse` object) implements the Writable stream interface.[4] This allows streams to be piped directly into the response without additional development. The stream-and-pipe approach is ideal in this circumstance because there is no processing on the files before they're transmitted, so there's no need to buffer the full file before sending it back to the client. This drastically reduces the amount of memory required to serve static files.

Putting It Back Together

The response generator module encapsulated the logic required to send responses for this example server. Let's update the **index.js** file to use the new module:

```
var http = require('http');
var employeeService = require('./lib/employees');
var responder = require('./lib/responseGenerator');
var staticFile = responder.staticFile('/public');

http.createServer(function (req, res) {
```

---

[4] http://nodejs.org/api/stream.html#stream_class_stream_writable

```
  // A parsed url to work with in case there are parameters
  var _url;

  // In case the client uses lower case for methods.
  req.method = req.method.toUpperCase();
  console.log(req.method + ' ' + req.url);

  if (req.method !== 'GET') {
    res.writeHead(501, {
      'Content-Type': 'text/plain'
    });
    return res.end(req.method + ' is not implemented by this
➥server.');
  }

  if (_url = /^\/employees$/i.exec(req.url)) {
    employeeService.getEmployees(function (error, data) {
      if (error) {
        return responder.send500(error, res);
      }
      return responder.sendJson(data, res);
    });
  } else if (_url = /^\/employees\/(\d+)$/i.exec(req.url)) {then
➥added
    employeeService.getEmployee(_url[1], function (error, data) {
      if (error) {
        return responder.send500(error, res);
      }

      if (!data) {
        return responder.send404(res);
      }

      return responder.sendJson(data,res);
    });
  }
  else {
    // try to send the static file
    res.writeHead(200);
    res.end('static file maybe');
  }
}).listen(1337, '127.0.0.1');

console.log('Server running at http://127.0.0.1:1337/');
```

Listing 6-8. Final example server

Listing 6-8 is the final **index.js** file to make our server completely functional. The new response generator module has been loaded into the code as `responder`, and we use this module throughout the route logic to send the proper responses.

As a last exercise, put some static HTML and CSS in the two files under **public**. Be sure to load the **style.css** file in the **home.html** file. We'll leave it up to you to decide what HTML and CSS you want to write.

Pointing your browser to `"localhost:1337/home"` should display the contents of **home.html** and download the **style.css** file from the **public** directory. Pointing a browser to `http://localhost:1337/employees/1000003` will net a server response with employee data from **employees.json**.

The server will respond to the routes described in the routing section and send back valid JSON responses. It will also respond to requests for static files that are stored under the **public** directory. We encourage you to experiment with these files to better understand how everything fits together.

Up to this point, we have been discussing these pieces (modules, I/O, events, streams, and so on) in isolation. I trust that this exercise gave you a better understanding of how all the pieces connect and how to stand up a rudimentary Node web server. In the Express chapters, we'll revisit these files and learn how leveraging a framework can drastically reduce the amount of boilerplate code required to set up a simple server.

Summary

This chapter focused on building a subset of the Node server for the human resources application that we'll be using to demonstrate the MEAN stack throughout this book. We started by building a skeleton structure for our app, then added basic functionality to cover routing, querying a database and sending a response. We'll be refactoring this functionality in later chapters.

In the next chapter, we;re going to introduce MongoDB.

7

MongoDB Introduction

Almost all web applications depend on some sort of database for persisting information. Databases are primarily either relational or NoSQL. Relational databases, the
de facto standard for years, are identified by their use of SQL. The NoSQL family
of databases, as their name suggests, do not use SQL, and have risen to prominence
in recent years, mainly due to the perceived ease of use and speed. The MongoDB
documentation provides a very good comparison of (Mongo-specific) NoSQL commands to SQL.[1] The next three chapters will discuss MongoDB, one of the most
popular NoSQL databases, while relational databases will be explored in Chapter
10.

NoSQL Databases

The name NoSQL is a bit generic, referring to a number of data store types. Essentially, NoSQL represents any data store that does not use SQL. Some example types
of NoSQL databases are document stores, object stores, and key/value stores. Ex-

---

[1] http://docs.mongodb.org/manual/reference/sql-comparison/

amples of NoSQL implementations are Redis[2], Memcached[3], Cassandra[4], and, of course, MongoDB. None of these follow the table-based setup of relational databases.

NoSQL databases are generally faster than relational databases because they don't typically follow a predefined schema or enforce data consistency as strictly as their relational cousins. This means that NoSQL data stores are usually suited to prototyping, and to social media applications that don't require the data to be perfectly consistent at all times. For example, if you miss an entry on your Facebook newsfeed, it's likely to be no big deal. On the other hand, you'd probably want your bank account to accurately reflect the amount of money you deposit into it, and for this reason a relational database is preferable.

History of MongoDB

Development began on MongoDB in 2007 at a company named 10gen. Mongo was originally designed as a component in a planned PaaS (Platform as a Service) offering. Then in 2009, MongoDB was open-sourced. Mongo became so successful that 10gen changed its name to MongoDB Inc. to more closely associate the company name with its flagship product. Since its release, Mongo has been used at many high-profile companies including Craigslist, Foursquare, eBay, and *The New York Times*. According to db-engines.com,[5] MongoDB is the most popular NoSQL database at the time of writing, and the fifth most popular database overall.

MongoDB falls into the document store class of NoSQL databases. Mongo stores data in binary JSON (BSON) formatted documents.[6] Mongo's native use of JSON provides a simple and convenient interface for JavaScript applications. Mongo installations also come with several tools such as an interactive shell, data import and export utilities, and statistics-reporting applications.

Installing MongoDB Locally

MongoDB runs on many platforms, including Windows, OS X, and the most popular flavors of Unix. Current and previous releases for all platforms can be downloaded

---

[2] http://redis.io/

[3] http://memcached.org/

[4] http://cassandra.apache.org/

[5] http://db-engines.com/en/ranking

[6] http://www.mongodb.com/json-and-bson

from Mongo's downloads page.[7] The binary distributions found on this page are the official versions; however, Mongo can also be installed via package managers[8] such as Homebrew. Regardless of how you choose to install MongoDB, you should reference the installation guide for your particular platform.[9]

Once installation is complete, verify that everything is installed by running the command shown in Listing 7-1. mongod is the primary daemon process used by MongoDB, and this command returns the version currently installed. If it is installed properly, you should see output similar to what is shown in Listing 7-2. In this particular case, Mongo 2.6.3 is installed.

```
mongod -version
```

Listing 7-1. Verifying that MongoDB is installed

```
db version v2.6.3
2014-07-27T13:57:07.359-0400 git version: nogitversion
```

Listing 7-2. Example version output from Listing 7-1

Cloud Hosting

A number of companies will host MongoDB instances in the cloud for you. This saves you the hassle of setting up and maintaining Mongo yourself. Many of these companies will even host your database for free if it's under a certain size, making it an ideal solution for prototypes. As with all cloud services, you'll pay an increasing amount of money as your resource requirements increase. By hosting your data in the cloud, it is easily accessible from anywhere in the world.

A list of MongoDB-approved cloud partners is available on mongodb.com.[10] The examples throughout the remainder of this book use MongoLab[11] as the cloud-hosting provider for MongoDB. MongoLab provides a free sandbox environment with 0.5GB of storage, which is more than enough for the examples in this book.

---

[7] http://www.mongodb.org/downloads
[8] http://www.mongodb.org/downloads#packages
[9] http://docs.mongodb.org/manual/installation/
[10] https://www.mongodb.com/partners/cloud
[11] https://mongolab.com/

Heroku Integration

MongoLab integrates quite easily with Heroku[12] applications, which is what we'll use for cloud hosting of Node.js applications in the book examples. If you plan to follow along with the sections related to Heroku, make sure that you sign up for a free account[13] and install the Heroku toolbelt,[14] a set of command line tools for working with Heroku.

To add MongoLab to a Heroku application, run the following command. This will create everything you need to access a MongoLab-hosted database:

```
heroku addons:add mongolab
```

Listing 7-3. Command to add MongoLab to a Heroku application

At this point, MongoLab should be listed as an add-on in your Heroku project, as shown in Figure 7.1. By clicking on the `MongoLab` text, you will be taken to a page resembling Figure 7.2. This page contains information about your application's database, including its name, your username, a command for connecting using the Mongo shell, and a URI for connecting using a driver. In this example, the database name and username are both `heroku_app21015781`. In the next chapter, you'll learn how to access your database from a Node application using the provided URI.

---

[12] http://www.heroku.com
[13] https://signup.heroku.com/dc
[14] https://toolbelt.heroku.com/

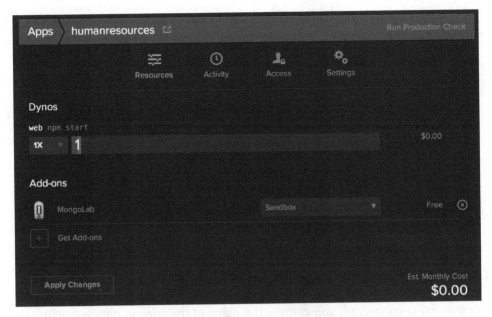

Figure 7.1. MongoLab integration with a Heroku application

Figure 7.2. MongoLab page showing database information

The MongoDB Shell

The Mongo shell program, `mongo`, is one of the command line utilities installed with MongoDB by default. If you're using MongoLab, you can utilize the `mongo` command shown in Figure 7.2 to connect to your database. If you are running Mongo locally, you'll have to first start the Mongo daemon, `mongod`, as it accepts the incoming connections from `mongo`. By default, `mongo` attempts to connect to port 27017 on `localhost`, but this can be configured using the `--port` and `--host` flags. Assuming that you are running locally, the `mongo` command's output is shown in Listing 7-4. Notice the > character on the last line of output. This is the `mongo` command prompt.

Permission Granted

You must have the proper permissions to access Mongo's `/data/db` directory. If you run into permission errors, you might want to check out this relevant Stack Overflow question.[15]

```
$ mongo
MongoDB shell version: 2.6.3
connecting to: test
>
```

Listing 7-4. Connecting to MongoDB using `mongo`

Once `mongo` is connected, you can see the name of the current database using the `db` command, as shown in Listing 7-5. In this case, we are connected to the default `test` database:

```
> db
test
```

Listing 7-5. The `db` command displays the name of the current database

To change to a different database, issue the **use** command followed by the name of the database to switch to. For example, to switch to the `presidents` database, issue the command shown in Listing 7-6. This command will work even if the `presidents` database is yet to be created. You can verify that the change worked properly using the `db` command. It is worth noting that Mongo will only create the database once data is added:

```
> use presidents
switched to db presidents
```

Listing 7-6. The **use** command switches between databases

---

[15] http://stackoverflow.com/questions/7948789/mongodb-mongod-complains-that-there-is-no-data-db-folder

To view all the available databases, use the `show dbs` command as shown in Listing 7-7. If you've been trying these examples in order, you'll notice that the `presidents` database is absent, as no data was added.

```
> show dbs
admin   (empty)
local   0.078GB
```

Listing 7-7. List all available databases using the `dbs` command

Inserting New Data

`db` is not just a command for showing the name of the current database. It is also the root object of the database, which you can use to manipulate data. For example, supposing we want to add Bill Clinton to our database of presidents. First, issue the `use presidents` command to switch to the `presidents` database. Next, issue the command shown in Listing 7-8 to insert Bill Clinton. This command adds the object `{name: 'Bill Clinton'}` to the `people` collection of the `presidents` database. Since the `presidents` database doesn't technically exist yet, Mongo creates it now. Mongo is also kind enough to create the `people` collection for us. Notice that the `WriteResult` returned by this operation verifies that one object has been created in the database via the `nInserted` field. You can also verify that the `president` database and `people` collection now exist using the `show dbs` and `show collections` commands respectively.

```
> db.people.insert({name: 'Bill Clinton'})
WriteResult({ "nInserted" : 1 })
```

Listing 7-8. Adding data to a MongoDB database

Multiple items can be added in one `insert()` call by passing in an array of objects. An example of this is shown in Listing 7-9. Notice that the resulting `BulkWriteResult` specifies that two objects have been inserted:

```
> db.people.insert([{name: 'George H Bush'},
                     {name: 'George W Bush'}])
BulkWriteResult({
  "writeErrors" : [ ],
  "writeConcernErrors" : [ ],
```

```
      "nInserted" : 2,
      "nUpserted" : 0,
      "nMatched" : 0,
      "nModified" : 0,
      "nRemoved" : 0,
      "upserted" : [ ]
})
```

Listing 7-9. Adding multiple pieces of data with one call to insert()

Retrieving Data

Now that data has been added to our database, we need some way of reading it back.
This is accomplished using the collection's find() method. Returning to our presidents example, Listing 7-10 shows how all the presidents can be retrieved at once.
Within these results it's worth pointing out the _id field. MongoDB assigns this
field to every object it stores. It's a unique identifier for the object in question:

```
> db.people.find()
{ "_id" : ObjectId("53d58ad9ec6dce1f6c577082"), "name" : "Bill
➥Clinton" }
{ "_id" : ObjectId("53d58ee05a0f7ff4e38b8ba3"), "name" : "George H
➥Bush" }
{ "_id" : ObjectId("53d58ee05a0f7ff4e38b8ba4"), "name" : "George W
➥Bush" }
```

Listing 7-10. Retrieving all items in a collection using find()

These results are nice but in most cases you'll want to apply some search criteria,
instead of returning every item in the collection. find() supports this functionality
by allowing a criteria object to be passed as an argument. Listing 7-11 shows how
a search can be performed for all presidents named Bill. In this example, the search
criteria specifies that the name field must match the regular expression /^Bill/ (a
string beginning with Bill). A full list of the query operators is available in the Mongo
query documentation.[16] Note that if you wanted a more exact query for Bill Clinton,
you could use db.people.find({name: 'Bill Clinton'}).

---

[16] http://docs.mongodb.org/manual/reference/operator/query/

```
> db.people.find({name: {$regex: '^Bill'}})
{ "_id" : ObjectId("53d58ad9ec6dce1f6c577082"), "name" : "Bill
➥Clinton" }
```

Listing 7-11. Applying search criteria to find()

Limiting the Size of the Result Set

There are two main ways to limit the size of the result set returned by find(). The first way is to use findOne() instead of find(). findOne() is used in the same fashion, but returns just a single match. Listing 7-12 shows how findOne() is used to select one of the presidents named George Bush:

```
> db.people.findOne({name: {$regex: '^George'}})
{ "_id" : ObjectId("53d58ee05a0f7ff4e38b8ba3"), "name" : "George H
➥Bush" }
```

Listing 7-12. Performing a search using findOne()

The second approach is to chain the limit() method to the find() method. limit() takes a number representing the maximum result set size as an input argument. Listing 7-13 shows how limit() is used to restrict the result set size to two:

```
> db.people.find().limit(2);
{ "_id" : ObjectId("53d5a5965a0f7ff4e38b8ba5"), "name" : "Bill
➥Clinton" }
{ "_id" : ObjectId("53d5a59d5a0f7ff4e38b8ba6"), "name" : "George H
➥Bush" }
```

Listing 7-13. Restricting the result set size using limit()

Updating Data

Data is updated using the collection's aptly named update() method. update() takes a query object as its first argument. This object specifies which items should be updated, and uses the same syntax as find(). The second argument to update() is another object that specifies how the values should be updated. update() supports a third, optional object argument. This object supports these properties:

- upsert: a Boolean value that defaults to false. If this is true, update() will create a new document if no existing items match the query criteria.

▪ `multi`: a Boolean value that defaults to `false`. If this is set to `true`, `update()` will modify all documents that match the query criteria.

▪ `writeConcern`: a document that defines the write behavior of the update. For more information on this parameter, see the write concern documentation.[17]

A simple example of `update()` is shown in Listing 7-14. In this example, Bill Clinton is renamed William Clinton. This update also adds a new `terms` field to the document to specify the number of presidential terms served. It's an example of NoSQL's flexibility compared to relational databases. At runtime, NoSQL databases can define new fields on an individual piece of data. In a relational database this would violate the schema of the table. Notice that the results indicate that one document was matched and updated, while no documents were upserted:

```
> db.people.update({name: 'Bill Clinton'}, {$set: {name: 'William
➥Clinton', terms: 2}})
WriteResult({ "nMatched" : 1, "nUpserted" : 0, "nModified" : 1 })
```

Listing 7-14. Modifying existing data using `update()`

Deleting Data

The final CRUD operation is delete. Data is deleted from a collection using the `remove()` method. `remove()` takes a `find()` style query object as it's first argument. A second, optional object argument supports two fields: `justOne` and `writeConcern`. If `justOne` is set to `true`, the removal will be limited to a single document. This defaults to `false`, meaning that all matches are removed. The `writeConcern` parameter is a document that behaves in the same fashion as `update()`'s `writeConcern`.

The example in Listing 7-15 shows how one of the presidents with the last name Bush can be removed from the collection. Notice that the results specify only *one* item was removed, despite two presidents matching the search criteria:

```
> db.people.remove({name: {$regex: 'Bush$'}}, {justOne: true})
WriteResult({ "nRemoved" : 1 })
```

Listing 7-15. Deleting data using `remove()`

---

[17] http://docs.mongodb.org/manual/core/write-concern/

If you've been following along with all the examples, your database should now look like Listing 7-16 after issuing a `find()`. Notice that Bill Clinton has been renamed and the `terms` property has been added, while George H Bush has been deleted:

```
> db.people.find()
{ "_id" : ObjectId("53d58ee05a0f7ff4e38b8ba4"), "name" : "George W
➥Bush" }
{ "_id" : ObjectId("53d58ad9ec6dce1f6c577082"), "name" : "William
➥Clinton", "terms" : 2 }
```

Listing 7-16. State of the `people` collection after manipulating data

Deleting Collections

Entire collections can be removed from the database using the collection's `drop()` method. Listing 7-17 shows how the `people` collection is dropped:

```
> db.people.drop()
true
```

Listing 7-17. Deleting the `people` collection using `drop()`

In Listing 7-18, the show collections command verifies that the collection no longer exists:

```
> show collections;
system.indexes
```

Listing 7-18. Displaying the available collections after calling `drop()`

Deleting Databases

It is possible to delete entire databases and all underlying data using the `dropDatabase()` method. Listing 7-19 shows how this is done:.

```
> db.dropDatabase()
{ "dropped" : "presidents", "ok" : 1 }
```

Listing 7-19. Deleting a database using `dropDatabase()`

This should be used with caution. You should double check that you're using the correct database before issuing `dropDatabase()`.

Summary

This chapter has introduced the basic concepts of MongoDB. You've learned how to get up and running with MongoDB, both locally and using a cloud hosting provider. You have also learned about the basic operations supported by the `mongo` shell. For a more comprehensive dive into Mongo's shell, we'd encourage you to browse the documentation.[18]

In the next chapter, you'll learn how to work with MongoDB from within Node.js applications. There are two modules primarily used for this task. The first is the MongoDB native driver.[19] The second is a module named Mongoose, which operates at a slightly higher level of abstraction than the native driver.

---

[18] http://docs.mongodb.org/manual/
[19] http://mongodb.github.io/node-mongodb-native/

Chapter 8

Interacting with MongoDB Using Mongoose

The previous chapter covered the basics of MongoDB: what it is, how to set it up, and how it can be useful. We'll assume that by this point you have a MongoDB instance up and running somewhere. We're going to use the instance we've created, but you should create your own so that you have the freedom to experiment on your own. If you're yet to do so, you can create a free MongoDB instance at MongoLab.[1]

In this chapter, we're going to cover the nuts and bolts of working with MongoDB. If you remember previous chapters, we used the term CRUD (create, retrieve, update, and delete). CRUD operations cover the majority of data interactions in most computer systems. When you understand the basic CRUD features of MongoDB, you'll be surprised at how much you can accomplish with very little code.

For this chapter, we're going to keep all of our code in a single file for clarity. We'll just keep appending and editing the same file, and end up with a database priming script for future use in this book.

---

[1] https://mongolab.com/welcome/

Mongoose Node Module

During our conversation about modules, we said that most common problems already have a module that's been created to solve the problem; interacting with a MongoDB instance is no exception. The standard Node module used for database operations is Mongoose.[2] It is very unlikely that you'll work on a Node server that communicates with a MongoDB and *not* use Mongoose. While Mongoose is the de facto module for interfacing with a MongoDB instance, there are other options. A native driver[3] is available for Node that is a port of the Ruby version. It is much more low-level than Mongoose and as a result, can be much more performant in certain situations.

For ease of use and community adoption, all of our examples will use the Mongoose module.

Mongoose exposes all the MongoDB features in an intuitive and JavaScript-friendly interface. There are calls for all the querying features MongoDB supports, as well as defining schemas and instantiating models from the database.

An important point to remember throughout this chapter is that MongoDB is the actual database that stores and retrieves data. Mongoose is the Node module that encapsulates the interactions with a MongoDB instance.

Schemas

Using Mongoose, everything starts with a schema. A schema maps to a MongoDB document or collection and is a set of rules and instructions for creating models. You can think of a Mongoose schema as a table definition if you have experience with traditional relationship-based databases such as MySQL.

At its core, a schema is like any other JavaScript object—a key-value pair. The `key` is the property name and the `value` is a Mongoose `SchemaType`. When a document is retrieved from the database, Mongoose attempts to convert the value to the related `SchemaType` and then return a model object. The available `SchemaTypes` are:

- `String`
- `Number`

---

[2] http://mongoosejs.com/
[3] https://github.com/mongodb/node-mongodb-native

- Date
- Buffer
- Boolean
- Mixed
- ObjectId
- Array

It is also possible to declare custom SchemaTypes if the built-in ones fail to suit your needs. The majority of the SchemaTypes should be fairly self-explanatory; most of them map directly to native JavaScript types; however, Mixed and ObjectId merit some further discussion.

Mixed Schema Type

The Mixed schema type is essentially a wildcard. Any value can be associated with a schema type listed as Mixed. This flexibility comes with a trade-off, however; it is difficult to maintain. Because Mongoose has no reliable way to compare changes to the value, the developer is responsible for alerting Mongoose any time the value changes. Using Mixed is best avoided, unless you're really unsure what data is going to be used for the particular key.

ObjectID Schema Type

It is worth repeating that MongoDB is not a relational database. There isn't a concept of foreign keys or many-to-many relationships. MongoDB is a database to store documents, generally JSON objects. That being said, an ObjectId schema type allows you to store MongoDB unique identifiers in memory. This, combined with some other schema options, allows you to reference sub-documents from other documents.

 Mongoose Is Not MySQL

When you first realize that you can refer to other documents like a relational database, you will be tempted to try to make MongoDB work like MySQL. Avoid this for your own sanity. Trying to combine aspects of both databases ends up making work in MongoDB much more difficult. You'll spend many hours trying to make MongoDB work like SQL, and it just won't.

Example Mongoose Schema

We'll use listing 8-1 for the rest of our discussion of Mongoose schemas. We're going to declare two schemas: one for a team and one for an employee.

```
var mongoose = require('mongoose');
var Schema = mongoose.Schema;
var TeamSchema = new Schema({
  name: {
    type: String,
    required: true
  }
});

var EmployeeSchema = new Schema({
  name: {
    first: {
      type: String,
      required: true
    },
    last: {
      type: String,
      required: true
    }
  },
  team: {
    type: Schema.Types.ObjectId,
    ref: 'Team'
  },
  image: {
    type: String,
    default: 'images/user.png'
  },
  address: {
    lines: {
      type: [String]
    },
    postal: {
      type: String
    }
  }
});
```

Listing 8-1. A basic employee Mongoose Schema

Schema is a constructor that takes a key-value pair object that describes our schema. The team schema is defined to store only the name of the team.

The employee schema is more interesting. Every employee document is going to have a name object with a first and last key. Both of those values are required and must be strings. The team key is how we can create a reference to another document/schema. The Schema.Types.ObjectId indicates that the value for team is going to be a MongoDB unique identifier and the ref key alerts Mongoose what model to use when this value is populated from the database. This will become clearer as we discuss models next.

The image key indicates that the value will be a string; if the value is absent, images/user.png will be used instead. address consists of an array of strings for line and a string for postal. We want to support internationalization, so we'll be better served using a String instead of a number.

Looking at the completed schema, you'll notice that it reads very easily. It is quite clear at a glance how our documents are going to be structured in the database. Remember, a schema tells Mongoose how data is going to be sent in and out of our database. Suppose we want to add city to address in the future. With a document storage database such as MongoDB, that would be a simple change. We'd add city to EmployeeSchema, and now city would be available to read and write for any Employee documents.

This is only the tip of the iceberg for Mongoose schemas. You can build very advanced and powerful schemas working with all the different options provided by Mongoose. For further reading, check out the Schemas section on the official Mongoose documentation page.[4]

Mongoose Models

We've mentioned models a few times, so let's now examine what models are and how we can use them. Instances of a model represent documents in the MongoDB database. When you execute a query, the resultant document is fed through the proper schema and a model is returned and ready for use. Most of the time you'll be interacting with models, rather than schemas, when working with Mongoose.

---

[4] http://mongoosejs.com/docs/guide.html

Let's update Listing 8-1 and insert a few teams into our database:

```
[...]
var db = mongoose.connection;
var dbUrl = 'mongodb://username:password@ds043917.mongolab.com:43917
➥/humanresources';

var TeamSchema = new Schema({
  name: {
    type: String,
    required: true
  }
});
var Team = mongoose.model('Team', TeamSchema);

db.on('error', function () {
  console.log('there was an error communicating with the database');
});

mongoose.connect(dbUrl, function (err) {
  if (err) {
    return console.log('there was a problem connecting to the
➥database!' + err);
  }

  console.log('connected!');
  var team = new Team({
    name: 'Product Development'
  });

  team.save(function (error, data) {
    if (error) {
      console.log(error);
    } else {
      console.dir(data);
    }

    db.close();
    process.exit();
  });
});
```

Listing 8-2. Writing a team into the database

Before moving forward, be sure to set up a MongoDB instance with MongoLab as per the setup instructions in Chapter 7. The dbUrl in Listing 8-2 is for demonstration purposes only, and will need to be updated to point to your MongoLab database instance.

We've moved some of the original code around for brevity and to emphasize adding specific items to the database. We establish a connection to the database and then set up some event listeners to the mongoose.database object for error events. Inside of the mongoose.connect callback, we instantiate a new Team model and assign the name key.

The line var Team = mongoose.model('Team', TeamSchema); essentially tells Mongoose that any time we want to create a Team model, it needs to adhere to the TeamSchema. mongoose.model() returns a function that can be considered a constructor. Inside the "open" event callback, we use the Team constructor to create an instance of a team and set name.

Assuming the connection to the database is correct, you should see { __v: 0, name: 'Product Development', _id: 53c32948e385c35d71ad6797 } or similar logged to the console. This means that there's now one Team document stored in the database with the name'Product Development.' You should notice the two additional keys in the result of the save operation: __v and _id. __v is an internal key that Mongoose uses to keep track of versions and changes to the document that this model represents. _id is the auto-generated unique identifier (ObjectId) for this document inside MongoDB.

Our solution is okay if we only want a single team, but what if we wanted to add three or four teams in a row? Let's refactor to insert several teams with one command:

```
[...]

mongoose.connect(dbUrl, function () {
  console.log('connected!');

  Team.create([{
    name: 'Product Development'
  }, {
    name: 'Dev Ops'
  }, {
    name: 'Accounting'
```

```
}], function (error, pd, devops, acct) {
  if (error) {
    console.log(error);
  } else {
    console.dir(pd);
    console.dir(devops);
    console.dir(acct);

    db.close();
    process.exit();
  }
});
});
```

Listing 8-3. Inserting multiple teams into the database

`Team.create` allows us to create several new documents in a single command. This is much more convenient than doing several document `saves` in a row. It's worth noting that this is *only* a convenience method rather than a true bulk insert. The underlying Mongoose implementation still loops through each element and inserts them one at a time.

Creating More Documents

Let's add some employees to our teams. We certainly *can* add employees and teams separately to each other, but remember back to our `EmployeeSchema`: we have a `team` key that stores `Schema.Types.ObjectId` values. While MongoDB has no concept of foreign keys, we can retrieve documents from different collections with a single query using Mongoose.

The `team` key is specified to store `Schema.Types.ObjectId`, which represents the primary identifier of MongoDB documents. The `ref` key in `EmployeeSchema` instructs Mongoose to find a document inside the `Team` collection with the unique ID (`_id`) value equal to the value stored in `team`. In this way, we can simulate a foreign key relationship; however, it is different to an SQL foreign key.

Traditional SQL databases enforce referential integrity, which means that you're unable to create a relationship from one table to another without the keys from both tables existing and being valid. In MongoDB, there is no concept of referential integrity because there are no foreign keys. So any `ObjectId` value can be stored in the `team` key and there will be no complaint from MongoDB. The same rules apply to deletes. If all our `Employee` documents have their `team` value set to the `_id` associated with the Dev Ops team, the Dev Ops team could be freely deleted at any time. Think of references more as query shortcuts than traditional foreign-key relationships from SQL.

Because this script is becoming more complicated with several callbacks, we'll do a little refactoring and break each of our steps into functions and call them one at a time. Remember, each step is asynchronous, so we should plan on passing callback functions as parameters that will be called when the database activity is complete:

```
[...]

var EmployeeSchema = new Schema({...});

var Employee = mongoose.model('Employee', EmployeeSchema);
[...]
function insertTeams (callback) {
  Team.create([{
    name: 'Product Development'
  }, {
    name: 'Dev Ops'
  }, {
    name: 'Accounting'
  }], function (error, pd, devops, acct) {
    if (error) {
      return callback(error);
    } else {
      console.info('teams successfully added')
      callback(null, pd, devops, acct);
    }
  });
}

function insertEmployees (pd, devops, acct, callback) {
  Employee.create([{
    name: {
      first: 'John',
      last: 'Adams'
    },
    team: pd._id,
    address: {
      lines: ['2 Lincoln Memorial Cir NW'],
```

```
      zip: 20037
    }
  }, {
    name: {
      first: 'Thomas',
      last: 'Jefferson'
    },
    team: devops._id,
    address: {
      lines: ['1600 Pennsylvania Avenue', 'White House'],
      zip: 20500
    }
  }, {
    name: {
      first: 'James',
      last: 'Madison'
    },
    team: acct._id,
    address: {
      lines: ['2 15th St NW', 'PO Box 8675309'],
      zip: 20007
    }
  }, {
    name: {
      first: 'James',
      last: 'Monroe'
    },
    team: acct._id,
    address: {
      lines: ['1850 West Basin Dr SW', 'Suite 210'],
      zip: 20242
    }
  }], function (error, johnadams) {
    if (error) {
      return callback(error);
    } else {
      console.info('employees successfully added');
      callback(null, {
        team: pd,
        employee: johnadams
      });
    }
  })
}
```

```
mongoose.connect(dbUrl, function (err) {
  if (err) {
    return console.log('there was a problem connecting to the
➥database!' + err);
  }
  console.log('connected!');

  insertTeams(function (err, pd, devops, acct) {
    if (err) {
      return console.log(err)
    }
    insertEmployees(pd, devops, acct, function (err, result) {
      if (err) {
        console.error(err);
      } else {
        console.info('database activity complete')
      }

      db.close();
      process.exit();
    });
  });
});
```

Listing 8-4. Inserting employees

Listing 8-4 looks very different to Listing 8-3. We've created two new functions:
insertTeams and insertEmployees. After establishing a connection to the database,
we want to call insertTeams and pass a callback function. After the teams have
been inserted, we want to call insertEmployees and pass the results of insertTeams,
as well as a callback into insertEmployees. After the employees have been inserted,
we'll execute the final callback, log the results to the console, close the database
connection, and exit the process. We'll have a use for result in the next step. For
now, just think of it as a data store that we'll pass around to use in different functions
that can change as database activity is completed.

Simple Queries

Now that our database has some data in it, let's write a few simple queries. A common database query is to retrieve a document by its ID:

```
function retrieveEmployee (data, callback) {
  Employee.findOne({
    _id: data.employee._id
  }).populate('team').exec(function (error, result) {
    if (error) {
      return callback (error);
    } else {
      console.log('*** Single Employee Result ***');
      console.dir(result);
      callback(null, data);
    }
  });
}
[...]
insertEmployees(pd, devops, acct, function (err, result) {

    retrieveEmployee(result, function (err, result) {
        if (err) {
            console.error(err);
        } else {
            console.info('database activity complete')
        }

        db.close();
        process.exit();
    });
});
```

Listing 8-5. Retrieving a single employee

The `retrieveEmployee` function uses the `findOne`, `populate`, and `exec` functions attached to the `Employee` model. `findOne` accepts a key-value pair as an argument. The logic indicates that we want to return a single `Employee` document with an `_id` equal to `data.employee._id`. The `populate` function takes several parameters, but for our purposes we only need to supply `team` because that's the additional document we want to populate. This is where the `team` key in `EmployeeSchema` comes into play. Finally, `exec` runs the query against the database.

After running this, you should see the "John Adams" document logged out to the console. Notice that the `team` key has been populated with a complete `Team` document.

Suppose we wanted to find all the employees in our database whose first name starts with a "J." Let's add another function to return all the employees with this criteria:

```
function retrieveEmployees (data, callback) {
  Employee.find({
    'name.first': /J/i
  }, function (error, results) {
    if (error) {
      return callback(error);
    } else {
      console.log('*** Multiple Employees Result ***')
      console.dir(results);
      callback(null, data);
    }
  });
}
[...]
retrieveEmployee(result, function (err, result) {

    retrieveEmployees(result, function (err, result) {
        if (err) {
            console.error(err);
        } else {
            console.info('database activity complete')
        }

        db.close();
        process.exit();
    });
});
```

Listing 8-6. Retrieving an employee by name

The `Employee.find` method can take several distinct arguments; it is the primary entry point for database querying. In this example, we're indicating that we want all the Employee documents from the database with a first name that starts with "J," and the search should be case insensitive. When `retrieveEmployees` is executing in our `async.waterfall`, the employees whose first name start with "j" should now be logged to the console.

Updating

Oops! We set one of our employee's names to "John Adams" when we really meant "Andrew Jackson." Let's write a basic function to update that single employee. Back in the `insertEmployees` function, we started passing around a `data` object to the subsequent waterfall functions. The `data` object has a single employee and single team attached to it; let's use that in our update function:

```javascript
function updateEmployee (first, last, data, callback) {
    console.log('*** Changing names ***');
    console.dir(data.employee);

    var employee = data.employee;
    employee.name.first = first;
    employee.name.last = last

    employee.save(function (error, result) {
        if (error) {
            return callback(error);
        } else {
            console.log('*** Changed name to Andrew Jackson ***');
            console.log(result);
            callback(null, data);
        }
    });
}
[...]
retrieveEmployees(result, function (err, result) {

    updateEmployee(result, function (err, result) {
        if (err) {
            console.error(err);
        } else {
            console.info('database activity complete')
        }

        db.close();
        process.exit();
    });
});
```

Listing 8-7. Updating an employee

`data.employee` is still an `Employee` model from `insertEmployees`. Inside `updateEmployee` we change the values of `name.first` and `name.last`, and then call `save`. You'll see when we've logged out the result that the data has changed in the database.

Summary

It is impossible to cover every aspect of a new database in a few pages. We hope this section of the book will serve as a primer and a springboard for further learning and experimentation, and encourage you to check out both MongoDB[5] and Mongoose[6] on your own.

One task we left out of this example was removing documents from the database. It is good practice to clean out any old or bad data before you start priming a new database. We encourage you to write two functions that delete all the employees and teams from the database before we start inserting anything.

[5] http://www.mongodb.org/
[6] http://mongoosejs.com/index.html

Chapter

9

Using MongoDB and Mongoose in Our Sample App

In Chapter 6, we began work on our example human resources application. At the time, Node was unfortunately the only technology that had been introduced, so the application in Chapter 6 only consisted of a Node HTTP server returning hard-coded employee data from a JSON file. Now that we have a good understanding of MongoDB and the Mongoose module, we can update the example application to use a database.

This chapter will build on the server from Chapter 6. We're going to assume that you have the example application code on your local machine already. We'll also assume that you have run `npm install`, and can successfully connect to the server using a browser. For example, you should be able to view the employee listing shown in Figure 9.1 by visiting the URL http://127.0.0.1:1337/employees.[1]

---

[1] http://127.0.0.1:1337/employees

```
[
    {
        "id": "1000003",
        "name": {
            "first": "Colin",
            "last": "Ihrig"
        },
        "address": {
            "lines": [
                "11 Wall Street"
            ],
            "city": "New York",
            "state": "NY",
            "zip": 10118
        }
    },
    {
        "id": "1000021",
        "name": {
            "first": "Adam",
            "last": "Bretz"
        },
        "address": {
            "lines": [
                "46 18th St",
                "St. 210"
            ],
            "city": "Pittsburgh",
            "state": "PA",
            "zip": 15222
        }
    },
]
```

Figure 9.1. Output data from the example application

Adding Mongoose Models

We're going to begin by creating two Mongoose models for working with our Mon-goDB instance. The first step is to install the `mongoose` module and save it to the project's `package.json` using the command shown in Listing 9-1:

```
npm install --save mongoose
```

Listing 9-1. Install `mongoose` and add it to `package.json`

Once that is finished, create a directory named `models` in the root of the application. This is where our model files will be saved. Inside the `models` directory, add two files: `employee.js` and `team.js`. As the name implies, `employee.js` will store the model related to employee data. We're also going to introduce the concept of employee teams, which is what will be stored in `team.js`.

The Employee Model

The code for the employee model is shown in Listing 9-2. After importing the `mongoose` model, a new schema is created. According to this schema, each employee has:

- an `id` (separate from Mongo's `_id` property) that acts as a primary key
- a name object
- an address
- a team designation
- a profile picture

The `team` is simply a reference to an instance of the `Team` model, which we'll be creating soon. On the final line of Listing 9-2, a model is created from the schema and exported:

```
var mongoose = require('mongoose');
var Schema = mongoose.Schema;
var EmployeeSchema = new Schema({
  id: {
    type: String,
    required: true,
    unique: true
  },
  name: {
    first: {
      type: String,
      required: true
    },
    last: {
      type: String,
      required: true
    }
  },
  team: {
    type: Schema.Types.ObjectId,
    ref: 'Team'
  },
  image: {
```

```
    type: String,
    default: 'images/user.png'
  },
  address: {
    lines: {
      type: [String]
    },
    city: {
      type: String
    },
    state: {
      type: String
    },
    zip: {
      type: Number
    }
  }
});

module.exports = mongoose.model('Employee', EmployeeSchema);
```

Listing 9-2. Mongoose employee model

The profile picture stored in `image` is simply a string that denotes the URL of an image file. If a profile picture is unspecified, use the default image shown in Figure 9.2. For now, you can ignore the profile picture. We'll revisit this in Chapter 13, when we incorporate Express into our example app.

Figure 9.2. Default profile picture

The Team Model

In most companies, employees work in teams. To capture this requirement, we're introducing the concept of teams into our application. Code for the Team model is shown in Listing 9-4. Notice that this code uses the mongoose-post-find and async modules. These will need to be installed using the following command:

```
npm install --save async mongoose-post-find
```

Listing 9-3. Installing and saving async and mongoose-post-find

The Team schema is simple. It only consists of a team name and an array of team members. The interesting code surrounds the TeamSchema.plugin() call. plugin() allows a Mongoose schema to utilize a plugin in order to extend built-in functionality. This is where mongoose-post-find is integrated to enable post find() and findOne() hooks. These hooks are functions that are run when find() and findOne() are called, and are able to modify the results before returning to the calling function. These hooks update Employee documents to assign them to the correct team.

```
var mongoose = require('mongoose');
var postFind = require('mongoose-post-find');
var async = require('async');
var Schema = mongoose.Schema;
var TeamSchema = new Schema({
  name: {
    type: String,
    required: true
  },
  members: {
    type: [Schema.Types.Mixed]
  }
});

function _attachMembers (Employee, result, callback) {
    Employee.find({
        team: result._id
    }, function (error, employees) {
        if (error) {
            return callback(error);
        }
```

```
        result.members = employees;
        callback(null, result);
    });
}


// listen for find and findOne
TeamSchema.plugin(postFind, {
    find: function (result, callback) {
        var Employee = mongoose.model('Employee');

        async.each(result, function (item, callback) {
            _attachMembers(Employee, item, callback);
        }, function (error) {
            if (error) {
                return callback(error);
            }

            callback(null, result)
        });
    },
    findOne: function (result, callback) {
        var Employee = mongoose.model('Employee');

        _attachMembers(Employee, result, callback);
    }
});

module.exports = mongoose.model('Team', TeamSchema);
```

Listing 9-4. Mongoose team model

Populating the Database

Now that our models are ready, we can populate our database. First, remove the
`database` directory as we'll no longer need the hard-coded JSON database. Next,
create a file in the `lib` directory named `connection.js`. This file, shown in Listing
9-5, will establish a database connection and register our Mongoose models. We've
also added a `SIGINT` handler that will shut down the Mongo connection and the
Node process when the user presses `Control+C`:

```
var mongoose = require('mongoose');
var dbUrl = 'mongodb://your_mongo_connection_url';

mongoose.connect(dbUrl);

// Close the Mongoose connection on Control+C
process.on('SIGINT', function() {
  mongoose.connection.close(function () {
    console.log('Mongoose default connection disconnected');
    process.exit(0);
  });
});

require('../models/employee');
require('../models/team');
```

Listing 9-5. MongoDB connection code

Next, we're going to create a script that will populate the database with a set of data. In the root of the project, create a directory named bin. Inside this, create a file named populate_db.js. The contents of this file are shown in Listing 9-6. This script is quite long, but fortunately it's relatively uncomplicated.

We're going to use the async module to execute a number of asynchronous database operations without falling into Callback Hell—see the async.series() call near the end of the script. We begin by deleting any existing Employee and Team documents, ensuring that we start with a clean slate.

Next, we populate the database with the employee and team information stored in the data variable. The final step is to add employees to teams. This is done in the updateEmployeeTeams() function. For the sake of simplicity, we'll add everyone to the same team. Once this is done, we close the database connection and exit.

```
var async = require('async');
var mongoose = require('mongoose');
require(process.cwd() + '/lib/connection');
var Employee = mongoose.model('Employee');
var Team = mongoose.model('Team');

var data = {
  employees: [
    {
```

```
      id: '1000003',
      name: {
        first: 'Colin',
        last: 'Ihrig'
      },
      image: 'images/employees/1000003.png',
      address: {
        lines: ['11 Wall Street'],
        city: 'New York',
        state: 'NY',
        zip: 10118
      }
    },
    {
      id: '1000021',
      name: {
        first: 'Adam',
        last: 'Bretz'
      },
      address: {
        lines: ['46 18th St', 'St. 210'],
        city: 'Pittsburgh',
        state: 'PA',
        zip: 15222
      }
    },
    {
      id: '1000022',
      name: {
        first: 'Matt',
        last: 'Liegey'
      },
      address: {
        lines: ['2 S Market Square', '(Market Square)'],
        city: 'Pittsburgh',
        state: 'PA',
        zip: 15222
      }
    },
    {
      id: '1000025',
      name: {
        first: 'Aleksey',
        last: 'Smolenchuk'
      },
```

```
      image: 'images/employees/1000025.png' /* invalid image */,
      address: {
        lines: ['3803 Forbes Ave'],
        city: 'Pittsburgh',
        state: 'PA',
        zip: 15213
      }
    },
    {
      id: '1000030',
      name: {
        first: 'Sarah',
        last: 'Gay'
      },
      address: {
        lines: ['8651 University Blvd'],
        city: 'Pittsburgh',
        state: 'PA',
        zip: 15108
      }
    },
    {
      id: '1000031',
      name: {
        first: 'Dave',
        last: 'Beshero'
      },
      address: {
        lines: ['1539 Washington Rd'],
        city: 'Mt Lebanon',
        state: 'PA',
        zip: 15228
      }
    }
  ],
  teams: [
    {
      name: 'Software and Services Group'
    },
    {
      name: 'Project Development'
    }
  ]
};
```

```javascript
var deleteEmployees = function(callback) {
  console.info('Deleting employees');
  Employee.remove({}, function(error, response) {
    if (error) {
      console.error('Error deleting employees: ' + error);
    }

    console.info('Done deleting employees');
    callback();
  });
};

var addEmployees = function(callback) {
  console.info('Adding employees');
  Employee.create(data.employees, function (error) {
    if (error) {
      console.error('Error: ' + error);
    }

    console.info('Done adding employees');
    callback();
  });
};

var deleteTeams = function(callback) {
  console.info('Deleting teams');
  Team.remove({}, function(error, response) {
    if (error) {
      console.error('Error deleting teams: ' + error);
    }

    console.info('Done deleting teams');
    callback();
  });
};

var addTeams = function(callback) {
  console.info('Adding teams');
  Team.create(data.teams, function (error, team1) {
    if (error) {
        console.error('Error: ' + error);
    } else {
        data.team_id = team1._id;
    }
```

```
      console.info('Done adding teams');
      callback();
  });
};

var updateEmployeeTeams = function (callback) {
  console.info('Updating employee teams');
  var team = data.teams[0];

  // Set everyone to be on the same team to start
  Employee.update({}, {
    team: data.team_id
  }, {
    multi: true
  }, function (error, numberAffected, response) {
    if (error) {
        console.error('Error updating employe team: ' + error);
    }

    console.info('Done updating employee teams');
    callback();
  });
};

async.series([
  deleteEmployees,
  deleteTeams,
  addEmployees,
  addTeams,
  updateEmployeeTeams
], function(error, results) {
  if (error) {
      console.error('Error: ' + error);
  }

  mongoose.connection.close();
  console.log('Done!');
});
```

Listing 9-6. Script for populating the database

You can run this script using the command shown in Listing 9-7. It's simple enough, but we can go one step farther. Update the `scripts` entry in the **package.json** file, as shown in Listing 9-8. Note, if there are any other entries in `scripts`, you should take care to avoid overwriting them. This allows `populate_db.js` to be run using the command `npm run populate`.

```
node bin/populate_db.js
```

Listing 9-7. Command used to run the `populate_db.js` script

```
"scripts": {
  "populate": "node ./bin/populate_db"
}
```

Listing 9-8. Adding the `populate_db.js` script to the `package.json`

Accessing the Database

After running `npm run populate` at least once, the database should be ready for use by our application. Next, we'll update the application code to use the database. Replace the contents of `lib/employees.js` with the code shown in Listing 9-9. We are maintaining the existing module interface, but using Mongoose to retrieve data instead of hard-coded JSON:

```
var mongoose = require('mongoose');
var Employee = mongoose.model('Employee');

exports.getEmployees = getEmployees;
exports.getEmployee = getEmployee;

function getEmployees (callback) {
  Employee.find().sort('name.last').exec(callback);
}

function getEmployee (employeeId, callback) {
  Employee.findOne({
    id: employeeId
  }).populate('team').exec(callback);
}
```

Listing 9-9. Employee route handlers

Notice that we're using the `sort()`[2] method to order the results in both functions. `sort()` orders by one or more fields in ascending order, unless the field name is prefixed with a `"-"`. `sort()` can also accept an object as its argument. For more details on usage, refer to the documentation.

The final step is to update `index.js` to establish a database connection for our app. This is a simple one-line change. After the line that reads `var colors = require('colors');`, add the code shown in Listing 9-10 on the third line of **index.js**:

```
require('./lib/connection');
```

Listing 9-10. Establishing a database connection in `index.js`

Our application should be completely configured to work with Mongo. Now when you visit http://127.0.0.1:1337/employees,[3] you should see a response containing Mongo's `_id` property as shown in Figure 9.3.

---

[2] http://mongoosejs.com/docs/api.html#query_Query-sort
[3] http://127.0.0.1:1337/employees

```json
{
    "__v": 0,
    "_id": "53fa2ec5db067f00007e950b",
    "id": "1000003",
    "team": "53fa2ec5db067f00007e9511",
    "address": {
        "city": "New York",
        "state": "NY",
        "zip": 10118,
        "lines": [
            "11 Wall Street"
        ]
    },
    "image": "images/employees/1000003.png",
    "name": {
        "first": "Colin",
        "last": "Ihrig"
    }
},
```

Figure 9.3. Example data from the MongoDB example application

Summary

This chapter has continued the development of our human resources example application. In this chapter, we have replaced a hard-coded JSON database with a Mongoose implementation that accesses a MongoDB back end. The next time we revisit our example app, we'll be transitioning from Node's core http module to the much more powerful Express framework. Before we jump into Express, though, Chapter 10 is going to explore SQL databases as an alternative to MongoDB.

Chapter

10

Alternatives to Mongo

MongoDB is a fantastic technology, but it is far from being the only option when it comes to adding a data store to your applications. There are a number of NoSQL alternatives such as Redis[1], CouchDB[2], and Cassandra[3]. Alternatively, you could turn to a relational database management system such as MySQL,[4] Oracle[5], or SQL Server[6]. Using a relational database will require you to understand SQL, but picking up the basics of SQL is relatively easy. This chapter explores MySQL as a free, relational alternative to MongoDB. Technically, this deviates from the MEAN stack, but we feel strongly about exploring popular and viable alternatives.

---

[1] http://redis.io/
[2] http://couchdb.apache.org/
[3] http://cassandra.apache.org/
[4] http://www.mysql.com/
[5] https://www.oracle.com/database/index.html
[6] http://www.microsoft.com/en-gb/server-cloud/products/sql-server/

Relational Databases and SQL

Relational databases are still hugely popular, despite the rise of NoSQL alternatives. According to the db-engines.com rankings,[7] the four most popular databases—Oracle, MySQL, SQL Server, and PostgreSQL[8]—are all relational databases. So if this book were to ignore relational databases, we'd be doing a huge disservice to our readers. Many people—the authors of this book included—actually prefer relational databases due to SQL's simplicity, guaranteed data consistency, and extensive support of data joins.

In relational databases, data is stored in a collection of tables. Tables can be thought of as a 2x2 grid of data. Columns in the grid are fields that every table entry must have, and represent the table's schema. The rows in a table, known as records or **tuples**, are the data values that must conform to the schema.

An example table is created using the SQL `CREATE` command shown in Listing 10-1. This command creates a table named `Presidents`. All records in this table must have `Id`, `Name`, and `Terms` fields in order to conform to the defined schema. The `Id` field is an unsigned integer that cannot be `null`, and whose value is automatically incremented by 1 each time a new record is added. The `AUTO_INCREMENT` property makes the `Id` field ideal for use as a primary key. A **primary key** is one or more fields that uniquely identify a record in a table. The other fields in the table are used to store the presidents' names and number of terms served.

```
CREATE TABLE Presidents (
  Id INT UNSIGNED NOT NULL AUTO_INCREMENT,
  Name VARCHAR(100) NOT NULL,
  Terms INT UNSIGNED NOT NULL,
  PRIMARY KEY(Id)
);
```

Listing 10-1. An SQL command to create a `Presidents` table

---

[7] http://db-engines.com/en/ranking
[8] http://www.postgresql.org/

Use an Online SQL Playground to Try These Examples

As an alternative to installing MySQL on your machine, you can use an online SQL playground such as SQL Fiddle.[9] Heroku and other PaaS providers also provide convenient cloud hosting of MySQL databases. We're using Heroku's ClearDB MySQL Database add-on, which can easily be added to your application using the command `heroku addons:add cleardb`.

The next step is to populate the `Presidents` table with data. In SQL, this is done using the `INSERT` command. Listing 10-2 shows an example `INSERT` command that adds two records to the `Presidents` table. The (`Name, Terms`) part of the command lists the field names and their expected order in the `VALUES` section. As you might expect, the `VALUES` section provides the data to be inserted. Notice that the name and number of terms are provided, but the `Id` field is not. This is where the `AUTO_INCREMENT` flag used during the table creation is extremely convenient.

```
INSERT INTO Presidents (Name, Terms) VALUES
  ('Bill Clinton', 2),
  ('George W Bush', 2);
```

Listing 10-2. An SQL command to insert values into the `Presidents` table

To retrieve data from a relational database, use the SQL `SELECT` command. The simplest incarnation of this command, which retrieves everything from the `Presidents` table, is shown in Listing 10-3. The result of this command is shown in Table 10.1.

```
SELECT * FROM Presidents;
```

Listing 10-3. An SQL command to retrieve values from the `Presidents` table

Table 10.1. Presidents table after inserting data

ID	Name	Terms
1	Bill Clinton	2
2	George W Bush	2

[9] http://sqlfiddle.com/

The SELECT command supports a wide range of options. For example, assume that we only wanted to select the name and number of terms served for the presidents whose first name is Bill. Listing 10-4 shows the SQL command to accomplish this. Notice that the command specifically requests the Name and Terms fields instead of the * wildcard. This command also uses a WHERE clause to only select records where the Name field matches the regular expression Bill %. SQL uses the % character as a wildcard. In more familiar syntax, this regular expression would be /Bill */. The results of this query are shown in Table 10.2. For a full overview of the supported SELECT options, see the MySQL SELECT documentation.[10]

```
SELECT Name, Terms FROM Presidents WHERE Name LIKE 'Bill %';
```

Listing 10-4. An SQL command to retrieve presidents named Bill

Table 10.2. Selecting presidents whose first name is Bill

ID	Name	Terms
1	Bill Clinton	2

The SQL UPDATE command is used to modify existing records. A basic example update is shown in Listing 10-5 where the command renames President George W Bush to his father's name.

```
UPDATE Presidents SET Name = 'George H Bush' WHERE Name = 'George W
➡Bush';
```

Listing 10-5. Example SQL UPDATE command

The final CRUD operation to cover is delete. To remove records from a table, use the DELETE command. The simplest version of this command, shown in Listing 10-6, removes all records from a table:

```
DELETE FROM Presidents;
```

Listing 10-6. Removing all records from the Presidents table

---

[10] http://dev.mysql.com/doc/refman/5.7/en/select.html

You can also remove records more selectively using SELECT style clauses. For example, to remove all presidents whose last name is Bush, use the command shown in Listing 10-7:

```
DELETE FROM Presidents WHERE Name LIKE '% Bush';
```

Listing 10-7. Removing all presidents whose last name is Bush

To delete the table itself, use the DROP command as shown in Listing 10-8. The only problem with this command is that it will cause an error if the table does not exist for whatever reason. To work around this, include IF EXISTS in the command, as shown in Listing 10-9.

```
DROP TABLE Presidents;
```

Listing 10-8. Example DROP TABLE command.

```
DROP TABLE IF EXISTS Presidents;
```

Listing 10-9. DROP TABLE command using IF EXISTS

The mysql Module

Now that we've covered the basics of relational databases and SQL, it's time to see how to access MySQL from Node applications. There is no built-in support for MySQL, but the mysql[11] module is extremely popular. In fact, it is even referenced in the MySQL documentation.[12] To install the mysql module, use the command shown in Listing 10-10:

```
npm install mysql
```

Listing 10-10. Installing the mysql module

---

[11] https://github.com/felixge/node-mysql
[12] http://dev.mysql.com/doc/ndbapi/en/ndb-nodejs-setup.html

Connecting to a Database

The first step to working with MySQL is establishing a connection. By this point, you should have either installed MySQL,[13] or provisioned cloud hosting. Next, connect to your database using the code shown in Listing 10-11. There are a few items to point out here. First, the mysql module is imported, then the createConnection() method is used to create a connection object. The connection string passed to createConnection() includes the username and password (if required), the host and port, and the database name. These will all vary depending on your setup.

After calling createConnection(), you must still call the connection's connect() method. This method is asynchronous and its callback takes a possible error condition as an argument. If everything is established correctly, the error argument should not be set, and you should be connected to your database.

```
var mysql = require('mysql');
var connection =
 mysql.createConnection('mysql://user:secret@localhost:3306/dbname');

connection.connect(function(error) {
  if (error) {
    return console.error(error.message);
  }

  console.log('successfully connected!');
});
```

Listing 10-11. Connecting to a MySQL database

It is worth pointing out that createConnection() also accepts an object argument instead of a connection string. For example, the same connection could have been established using the call shown in Listing 10-12:

```
var mysql = require('mysql');
var connection = mysql.createConnection({
  host: 'localhost',
  port: 3306,
```

---

[13] http://dev.mysql.com/doc/refman/5.7/en/installing.html

```
    user: 'user',
    password: 'secret',
    database: 'dbname'
});
```

Listing 10-12. Calling `createConnection()` with an object instead of a connection string

Connection Pooling

In a production server, it is inefficient to establish a new connection each time the application needs to access the database. Alternatively, you can create a pool of connections to be shared among all incoming requests. Each time the application needs to connect to the database, it can request a connection from the pool. If no connections are available, the request will be placed in a queue. Once a connection is available, it is allocated to perform some work. Once its work is finished, the connection is returned to the pool for future use.

Creating a connection pool is very similar to creating individual connections. An example that creates a connection pool is shown in Listing 10-13. The connection pool is created using the `createPool()` method, which is very similar to `createConnection()`; however, it accepts several additional parameters: `connectionLimit`, `queueLimit`, and `waitForConnections`. `connectionLimit` sets the maximum size of the pool and defaults to 10. `queueLimit` sets the maximum size of the connection backlog queue size and defaults to no limit. `waitForConnections` is a Boolean that defaults to `true`. If `waitForConnections` is `true`, requests are added to the queue if no connections are available. Otherwise, the callback is invoked immediately with an error.

```
var mysql = require('mysql');
var pool = mysql.createPool({
  host: 'localhost',
  user: 'username',
  password: 'secret',
  database: 'dbname',
  connectionLimit: 20,
  queueLimit: 100,
  waitForConnections: true
});
```

```
pool.getConnection(function(error, connection) {
  if (error) {
    return console.error(error.message);
  }


  console.log('successfully obtained connection!');
});
```

Listing 10-13. Creating a connection pool

Note that the connection's `connect()` method is not called. Instead, the pool's `getConnection()` method is used to obtain a connection. The connection passed as the second argument to the callback will already be in the connected state, meaning that there is no need to call `connect()`.

The final point worth mentioning in this example is that the code will not terminate on its own. Because a pool of open connections has been established, the program is not able to exit single-handedly. Instead, you can terminate the program using **Control-C**. If you are bothered by this behavior, force the program to exit using `process.exit(0)`.

Closing Connections

Non-pooled connections are closed using the `end()` and `destroy()` methods. `end()` closes the connection gracefully, meaning that any queued queries are allowed to execute. `destroy()`, on the other hand, immediately shuts down the underlying socket, killing anything that is currently in progress.

Pooled connections are closed using the `release()` and `destroy()` methods. `release()` returns the connection to the pool, while `destroy()` shuts down the connection and removes it from the pool. If a connection is destroyed, the pool will replace it. Listing 10-14 shows an updated version of Listing 10-13, which acts responsibly and releases the connection back to the pool:

```
var mysql = require('mysql');
var pool = mysql.createPool({
  host: 'localhost',
  user: 'username',
  password: 'secret',
  database: 'dbname'
```

```
});

pool.getConnection(function(error, connection) {
  if (error) {
    return console.error(error.message);
  }

  console.log('successfully obtained connection!');
  connection.release();
});
```

Listing 10-14. Releasing a pooled connection

Executing Queries

The query() method of a connection object is used to send SQL commands to MySQL. query() takes two arguments. The first is an SQL string, while the second is a callback function that takes error and results object as arguments. Listing 10-15 shows an example that creates the familiar Presidents table using the query() method:

```
var mysql = require('mysql');
var pool = mysql.createPool({
  host: 'localhost',
  user: 'username',
  password: 'secret',
  database: 'dbname'
});

pool.getConnection(function(error, connection) {
  if (error) {
    return console.error(error.message);
  }

  var sql = 'CREATE TABLE Presidents (' +
            'Id INT UNSIGNED NOT NULL AUTO_INCREMENT,' +
            'Name VARCHAR(100) NOT NULL,' +
            'Terms INT UNSIGNED NOT NULL,' +
            'PRIMARY KEY(Id))';

  connection.query(sql, function(error, results) {
    connection.release();
```

```
    if (error) {
      return console.error(error.message);
    }

    console.log('successfully created table!');
  });
});
```

Listing 10-15. Creating the `Presidents` table using the `query()` method

A more complete example is shown in Listing 10-16. It uses the `Presidents` table created in Listing 10-15, so make sure that table exists first. The example in Listing 10-16 inserts data into the table, reads the data back using a `SELECT` command, and then drops the table:

```
var mysql = require('mysql');
var pool = mysql.createPool({
  host: 'localhost',
  user: 'username',
  password: 'secret',
  database: 'dbname'
});

pool.getConnection(function(error, connection) {
  if (error) {
    return console.error(error.message);
  }

  var insertSql = 'INSERT INTO Presidents (Name, Terms) VALUES' +
            '(\'Bill Clinton\', 2),' +
            '(\'George W Bush\', 2)';

  connection.query(insertSql, function(error, results) {
    if (error) {
      connection.release();
      return console.error(error.message);
    }

    var selectSql = 'SELECT * FROM Presidents';

    connection.query(selectSql, function(error, results) {
      if (error) {
        connection.release();
```

```
      return console.error(error.message);
   }

   console.log('results of SELECT:');
   console.log(JSON.stringify(results, null, 2));

   var dropSql = 'DROP TABLE IF EXISTS Presidents';

   connection.query(dropSql, function(error, results) {
      connection.release();

      if (error) {
         return console.error(error.message)
      }

      console.log('table dropped!');
     });
    });
   });
});
```

Listing 10-16. Inserting data, reading it back, and then deleting a table

The output of Listing 10-16 is shown in Listing 10-17 below. Notice that the results of the SELECT query are returned as an array of objects. Although not shown in this example, it is worth inspecting the output of non-SELECT queries, as they often include useful information such as the number of rows affected.

```
$ node mysql-exercise.js
results of SELECT:
[
  {
    "Id": 1,
    "Name": "Bill Clinton",
    "Terms": 2
  },
  {
    "Id": 2,
    "Name": "George W Bush",
    "Terms": 2
```

```
    }
]
table dropped!
```

Listing 10-17. Result of executing the code in Listing 10-16

Summary

This chapter has shown how relational databases can be used with Node.js applications. More specifically, it explored how the `mysql` Node module is used to interact with a MySQL database. After completing this part of the book, you should feel a little more comfortable interacting with most types of databases. There is still a lot more to learn about relational databases. If you're interested in learning more, the MySQL documentation[14] is a good place to start.

The next part of the book moves away from databases and towards web server software. You've already learned about Node's core `http` module. The next part, which focuses on the Express framework, raises the level of abstraction in an effort to increase developer productivity.

---

[14] http://dev.mysql.com/doc/

Chapter 11

Introduction to Express

We touched on Express earlier, but now we're going to really dive into it. Express[1] is a Node module that provides a thin web application framework around the core Node modules discussed in Chapter 5. As of this writing, it is the most starred module on the npm registry.

A Google search for "getting started with Node" will almost always lead you to installing and using Express. It is a very mature and community-tested framework. The first version of Express (1.0.0) was released in November 2010 after going through several beta and release candidate versions. The lead developer of Express from beta though version 3 was TJ Holowaychuk who worked alongisde a few key members of the GitHub community. After version 3, Holowaychuk became less involved with its daily development, handing the reins to a group of core GitHub community members. In July 2014, Holowaychuk handed ownership of Express to a Node startup company named StrongLoop. StrongLoop continues to keep Express open source, and the majority of the core community still work with StrongLoop on the steady development of Express.

---

[1] http://expressjs.com/

A framework is only as successful as who use it. Express is used by companies such as MySpace, Apiary.io, Ghost, and Persona, a Mozilla-backed sign-in system. Express was also used as the foundation for PayPal's open-source KrakenJS framework,[2] while StrongLoop uses Express for its LoopBack project.[3] The complete list of featured companies using Express can be found on its website[4]. The list does not account for any internal/enterprise applications, personal web projects, or APIs being built on top of the Express framework.

In this chapter, we're going to discuss the basis of Express—the "E" of the MEAN stack. Express provides request routing, a static file server, view engine integration, and a plethora of community modules. Express is a very thin layer that sits on top of the the core modules discussed in previous chapters. Working with a thin framework means that the code you write is never too far away from the core features of Node. Pipes and streams are still very easy to access in an Express application. You also have direct access to the `ClientRequest` and `ServerResponse` core Node objects. Behind all the trappings, an Express application still boils down to `http.createServer(...)`.

We've demonstrated and even built a few web servers that were very basic and only required a few lines of JavaScript. If we can create a web server in only four or five lines, why should we even use a framework? It might be easier to write all our own code than try to learn another framework. Looking back at the code we wrote in Chapter 6, there are a few issues that make it apparent why a framework is the right way to go, namely:

- maintainability
- module integration
- solution structure

Maintainability is going to be an issue in trying to write an entire Node web server using only the built-in modules. We only created two real routes and there's a fair amount of code already. We have route parameters working, but what if we wanted to have multiple route parameters? We're also without support for any concept of query-string parameters or different HTTP verbs. We could implement all of these

---

[2] http://krakenjs.com/
[3] http://strongloop.com/node-js/loopback/
[4] http://expressjs.com/resources/applications.html

features ourselves just using the core Node modules, but that would be inefficient. Implementing simple cookie logic could be several hundred lines of code, and that's only one small feature out of many that a complete web server needs. It just isn't practical to write a whole web server using only core Node modules with everything a modern-day web server is expected to do.

A second issue with our home-rolled server solution is modules. Modules are one of the biggest driving forces in the Node ecosystem. What if you wanted to use a server-side templating engine or a CSS precompiler? There are several Node options available, but incorporating them with this current solution would be very tedious. If we insist on only using the core modules, we are going to limit ourselves because integrating many community modules will be difficult. Our server will end up being lines and lines of JavaScript spaghetti code.

A third issue is that without a framework, your solution is completely unstructured. Frameworks typically provide you with two big advantages. The first is all the tools, functionality, and community that come with using a framework. The second is that using frameworks provides a foundation to structure your solution. A framework gives you tools, but also provides a blueprint for how to think about and structure a solution. After all, a web server is a solved problem at this point; there really is no need to reinvent the wheel.

A drawback of using a thin framework such as Express is that you still need to have a reasonable understanding of the core modules discussed in Chapter 5. You also need an understanding of how web servers are supposed to work with regard to routes, status codes, and headers. Express, like any framework, isn't an "easy button" for development. There are still challenges and problems that require solving. Aspects such as cookie management, user authentication, and caching are open to the developer to implement. Again, there are Express modules on the npm registry that help solve these problems, but they don't come built into Express and still require integration code.

The Building Blocks of Express

An Express server can be broken down into three building blocks: the router, routes, and middleware. Everything else are just refinements and further abstractions.

Router

The core of any web server is robust request routing. If you think about the server-client request life cycle, it essentially boils down to: the client requests a resource, the server tries to locate the resource and if it's found, respond in a way that the client is expecting. Without a structured way to handle and route requests, your web server will do very little.

The core `http` module has no concept of resource routing. We had to write a regular expression for each route. When the request came into the `http` server, we had to check `req.path` against different regular expressions in `if else` blocks. In addition, we had to add catchall logic to try to find CSS and HTML static files. It was fairly tedious with only a few routes; imagine spanning that out into a production-ready server. By contrast, Express provides an easy-to-use and expressive routing interface.

Generally creating a route is as simple as `app.get('/employees/:id', function(res, res, next){...});`. This creates a route in the routing table that will match `GET` requests and have a URI of `/employees/employee_id`. When the match occurs, the associated function will execute and send a response to the client. We'll cover more specifics and features about route declarations in a moment.

Route Lookup

The order in which routes are added to the router is very important. When a request comes into the web server, the URI is run through the routing table. The first match in the table is the code that is going to execute. If there is a second matching route further down the route table, it will not be executed unless you do some internal re-routing. Even if the second route is technically more specific, the first match will always be the one that runs.

Static Files

A web server must have a simple way to serve static files. The average website can have hundreds of static files all being served from the web server. There has to be a way to alert the router that files in a specified directory do not need to be individually added to the routing table, and should be retrieved from the file system when requested.

With Express, this is accomplished with `express.static(directory)`. This essentially creates a rule in the routing table to look for files in **directory** and, if they are found, serve the files. If they are not found, it will continue down the routing table and try to match fileson another route. There will be a more complete example later in this chapter on static files, but it was important to introduce `static` here in the routing section.

Middleware

Middleware is any JavaScript function that has the function signature `function (req, res, next)`. A single Express route can have as many middleware functions associated with it as needed. Every middleware function is executed in order from left to right. Middleware functions can be used in any part of the request life cycle right up until the response is sent back to the client. A request is considered complete when a middleware function sends a response to the client. A middleware function that completes a request is sometimes referred to as a **handler**. A middleware function could be used to set a cookie or header, check a user log in status, compress JavaScript, and thousands of other purposes.

Middleware Breakdown

Let's examine each of the parameters in a middleware function for a better idea of what they are used for. The `req` parameter is the incoming request object. It is the same `http.ClientRequest` that we discussed in Chapter 6. By the time it reaches our middleware functions, it has been augmented by Express to provide additional functionality. It has new methods such as `accepts()`, `get()`, and `is()`. It also exposes several new properties such as `path`, `host`, `xhr`, and `cookies`. For the full list that Express adds to the `http.ClientRequest` object, check out the documentation.[5]

The `res` object is the response object. If you recall in Chapter 6, we discussed that `res` is an `http.ServerResponse` object augmented by Express, just like the `req` object. Express adds `cookie()`, `redirect()`, `send()`, and many other useful response functions documented on the Express API documentation page.[6]

Finally, the `next` parameter is a callback function provided by the Express framework. This is useful for middleware functions that have asynchronous activity. Simply call `next()` when the code is complete to alert Express that this middleware function is done. If the middleware is responsible for sending a response with

---

[5] http://expressjs.com/4x/api.html#req.params
[6] http://expressjs.com/4x/api.html#res.status

res.send, there's no need to call next. For every other non-terminating middleware function, you must call next only once.

 Notes about next

Just like every other callback function in Node, next has the signature of next(error). If you try to pass data to another function with next, you'll trigger the Express error handler. As a general rule, any truthy value passed into next will be treated as an error, preventing any further middleware functions from executing for the current request. The one exception to the truthy rule is passing the string "route" to next. Passing "route" causes the Express router to skip to the next middleware function or next matching route, assuming any exist. While this technique can be useful at times, it can create routing scenarios that are difficult to trace and debug, so it should be used sparingly.

When your Express app becomes more complicated, you'll eventually need to pass data from one middleware function to another. Most people's first instinct is to try to pass data via next, but that will cause an error. Each new request receives a new copy of req and res at the beginning of the route. These objects are passed by reference to each middleware function, and any changes you make to req or res will be available to every downstream middleware function. res.locals is the built-in Express container that is useful for passing data from one function to the next. You can also create your own data container on either req or res, such as res.myData.

It's very important to always execute next in middleware functions that don't send responses. If you forget to do this, the response will just hang and never respond. Even if there is no asynchronous code in the function, you still must call next to keep the request flowing through the route.

Routes

A route can be thought of as consisting of an HTTP verb and a path. The HTTP verb, or method, is generally one of four: GET, POST, PUT, and DELETE. A GET request is used to get data from a web server. It is the most common type of request today, and is used for both static content and dynamic information from the web server. A POST request is the second-most common HTTP verb and is used to send data to a web server. DELETE and PUT requests are far from common, but are gaining popularity as more and more browsers support them. DELETE is used to delete information from a web server and PUT is generally used to update existing data on a server.

There are a few other HTTP verbs defined,[7] but the four listed are the ones on which we'll be focusing our attention. The most important difference in HTTP verbs is how data is passed around. In a GET request, data is passed either in the URI or as query-string parameters. For POST methods, there is a payload or body attached to them. This allows POST requests to send much more information in the request compared to GET requests. The DELETE method generally lacks a body, similar to GET requests. Finally, PUT methods have a payload, just like POST.

The second half of an HTTP request is the uniform resource identifier, or URI. Every request web browsers make is to some URI; www.google.com, for example, is a URI that goes directly to the Google home page resources. URIs use two distinct mechanisms for passing parameter data to the web server: query-string parameters and route parameters.

In Express route definitions, we combine the HTTP verb and a pattern to match incoming URI requests. The pattern compontent is refered to a path. For example, a typical Express path with route parameters looks like this: /teams/:teamName/employees/:employeeId.

As an example, suppose we had a running Express server and pointed a browser at /teams/nodeTeam/employees/15?mode=short. The default behavior of a browser is to send GET requests, so the browser would issue a request to our running Express server that was a GET request for the resource located at /teams/nodeTeam/employees/15?mode=short. If we combine the verb and path concepts, we have a route definition that would look like GET "/teams/:teamName/employees/:employeeId". This route would match our request that we sent from the browser.

When the request comes into the Express router, the route parameters :teamName and :employeeId will be parsed from the incoming URI and made available via req.params.teamName and req.params.employeeId. The Express router will look this route up in the routing table and if there is a match, the corresponding code will be run and a response sent. The query-string part of the URI is *not* used in routing decisions.

---

[7] http://www.w3.org/Protocols/rfc2616/rfc2616-sec9.html

Optional Parameters

In the previous example, all the route parameters are required because, without them, the client request will match nothing in our routing table. Suppose we wanted to allow clients to request all the employees on a team? Well, we could make the `:employeeId` parameter optional. The assumption would be that without the this parameter, we should return all the employees on the `teamName team`. If we postfix a parameter with `?`, it becomes optional. The updated path parameter would become `/teams/:teamName/employees/:employeeId?`.

So there would be a match on this route path for both of these URIs: `/teams/node-Team/employees` and `/teams/nodeTeam/employees/15`. While optional route parameters can sometimes be helpful, they can also create routing bugs that are difficult to trace. If one developer created a route that matched on the path pattern `/teams/:teamName/employees/:employeeId?` and another developer created another route with the path `/teams/:teamName/employees`, both patterns will both match requests to `/teams/javaScriptTeam/employees`. If there are two different routes set up, which one will the router use? Remember one of the key points from the router section: the first route that's registered will be the entry in the route table that is used. Rather than rely on the ordering of routes, it's generally better to avoid optional route parameters if they create confusion.

Finally, it is possible to have multiple optional parameters in a single route path. Suppose we wanted to expand on our previous example and allow both `:teamName` and `:employeeId` to be optional. This would allow users to obtain information about a team or single employee all from the same route definition. It we update our working example, the path value would become `/teams/:teamName?/employees/:employeeId?`. Now users can make requests to `/team/node`, `/team/employees/15`, and `/team/node/employees/15`. All three of these URIs would be covered by our updated path parameter. In general, this is not a recommended approach as it is hard to document and unclear what the response will be based on a variety of parameter options.

Other Route Options

Express also allows regular expressions to be used as URIs. When using regular expressions for routes, the developer is responsible for handling any route parameters. Let's rewrite `"/teams/:teamName/employees"` as a regular expression. `/^\/teams\/(\w+)\/employees$/i` would be the equivalent URI definition. When using regular expressions, you'll need to create capture groups using () to have access to that value in any middleware functions.

It is worth mentioning here that, under the hood, Express converts all route definitions to regular expressions. This shouldn't be too surprising if you revisit Chapter 6 and look at how we set up our routes when we wrote our simple Node server.

Putting It Together

We've covered the building blocks of an Express app: the router, middleware functions, static file server, and basic route explanations. Let's put everything together with a very simple code example. Let's create a small Express web server that uses everything we've covered up to this point:

```
var express = require('express');
var app = express();

// Route one
app.get('/teams/:teamName/employees/:employeeId', function (req, res
➥, next) {
  console.log('teamName = ' + req.params.teamName);
  console.log('employeeId = ' + req.params.employeeId);
  res.send('path one');
});

// Route two
app.get('/teams/:teamName/employees', function (req, res, next) {
  console.log('setting content type');
  res.set('Content-Type', 'application/json');
  res.locals.data = 100 ;
  next();
}, function (req, res, next) {
  console.log('teamName = ' + req.params.teamName);
  console.log(res.locals.data);
  res.send('path two');
});

// Route three
app.get(/^\/groups\/(\w+)\/(\d+)$/, function (req, res, next) {
  console.log('groupname = ' + req.params[0]);
  console.log('groupId = ' + req.params[1]);
  res.send('path three');
});
```

```
var server = app.listen(1337, function() {
  console.log('Server started on port 1337');
});
```

Listing 11-1. Creating a simple Express application

Listing 11-1 is a summation of most of the topics covered in this chapter. The first two lines create the Express application. `app.use(express.static(__dirname + '/public'));` sets up our static file server. We'll go into more detail about `app.use` in the next chapter. Remember, that line adds an entry into the routing table to look for files in the **public** directory.

The first two `app.get` lines establish the routes we've been discussing throughout this chapter. As you can see, we have access to the route parameters via `req.params`. The final `app.get` line illustrates using regular expressions as the path parameter of `app.get`.

Route two shows an example of multiple middleware functions in a single route. When the route matches, Express will execute the first function in the Express lane. In this example, we're going to log some information, set the `"Content-Type"` header, attach a value to `res.locals`, and then call `next()`. Remember, you always have to call `next()` unless you're ending the response with `res.send()` or some other termination function. After calling `next()`, Express will advance to the next middleware function; log the data from `req.params.teamName`, log the value attached to `res.locals.data`, and then send a simple JSON object.

Route three illustrates using regular expression parameters. The parentheses around the different path segments create regular expression capture groups. We access each value by index via `req.params[index]`. Regular expression capture groups are numbered and start at index 0. 0 correlates to the `(\w+)` capture group and 1 correlates to `(\d+)`.

The last few lines create a server and start listening on port 1337. The neat thing about `app.listen` is that it's identical to the `server.listen` function we used when we wrote a server using pure Node.

Try any of the following URIs in a browser to test the different routes and the results:

- `/teams/javascript/employees/15` — Should return "`path one`" and log `teamName = javascript employeeId = 15` to the console.

- `/teams/javascript/employees` — Should return "`path two`" and log `setting content type teamName = javascript`. If you examine the response headers with via `curl` or the development tools in your browser, you should see the correct Content-Type header.

- `/groups/accounting/142` — Should return "`path three`" and log `groupname = accounting groupId = 142` to the console.

The code in Listing 11-1 above should demonstrate how much easier this small Express web server will be to maintain and debug than a Node server that only uses the core modules. It is much easier to read, requires less code, and has more features. Remember, even though Express is a framework, the underlying core modules are never too far from reach.

Generating an Express App

If you remember back to Chapter 4, about modules, sometimes it's best to install modules globally because they provide a command line interface that would be useful outside of a specific project. Let's now install the `express-generator` module globally. Once the install is complete, create an empty directory and run `express` from the command line.

Let's run through a high-level explanation of what the express generator does for us. (We'll go into much more detail in the next chapter about the actual *contents* of these files.) You'll notice that the generator creates several folders and files, giving developers a reasonable and predictable project structure to work in. The generator also creates a **package.json** file with some dependencies pre-filled in.

`app.js` is the main entry point for the application and where logic for the web server resides. Remember our static file server that was configured to look inside the **public** folder? The **public** folder was created and seeded with subfolders for images, JavaScript files, and style sheets. We'll have a use for those folders later.

Inside the **routes** folder are several files for declaring and attaching routes to the Express app. This is a good pattern to follow. For a complete web server there could be thousands of routes, making the **app.js** file completely unmaintainable. It would also be difficult to work in a team because that file would constantly be changing.

Jade

The **views** folder is set up to take advantage of Jade,[8] a Node server-side templating language. While we won't be using Jade in this book, it is worth mentioning. Jade is a templating engine, but it's also a higher order language. You write your views in the Jade language that are then compiled into raw HTML, allowing you to write much more HTML with fewer characters. It also ensures that the HTML on your web page is never broken nor incorrect. The compiler will throw errors if you try to create invalid HTML.

Summary

Listing 11-1 is an Express app that is completely abstracted away from directly using the `http` module. It allows us to declare routes in a simple and uniform way. It provides a robust router, a built-in static fill server, and a programming pattern we can follow to add more features and routes. It also promotes code reuse and modularity with the concept of middleware functions.

Even though we can create a whole web server without directly using the `http` module or any of the other core modules, they aren't far from the surface. Both `req` and `res` are core Node objects and `app.listen` is the same as `server.listen`.

This chapter demonstrated the basics of an Express application. In the next chapter, we'll go into detail about the Express app we generated in this chapter and discuss the architecture of a typical Express web server.

---

[8] http://jade-lang.com/

12

Architecture of an Express Application

In the previous chapter, we generated our first Express application. At the time of writing, Express was in version 4 so that's the version this book will be discussing. The Express generator gives developers a great place to start building a new web server. It provides a few simple routes, Jade templating integration, cookie and body parsing, and static file serving. In this chapter, we'll cover the important files and concepts of the generated Express application. This will give you a strong understanding of the architecture of the Express ecosystem, as well as the interactions in many of the framework's moving parts.

Starting the Server

The first thing you'll probably notice is that if you run `node app.js`, nothing happens. The generator created a **bin** folder with a **www** file inside of it. The intention is to use this to start the server instead of **app.js**. To start your server, run `node bin/www`. You can also run `npm start` as well because that command has been entered into **package.json**. Once the server is running, point a web browser to `localhost:3000` and you should be greeted with a simple welcome page.

One thing worth mentioning right away is the addition of the **bin** folder and **www** file. Very generally speaking, a Node convention is to put files that are intended to be run from the command line inside a **bin** folder. The **www** file in the generated application serves as the entry point for the Node application. The **www** file in this example requires in **app.js** and starts the Express server.

app.js

Even though we don't start the server with `node app.js`, **app.js** still houses the majority of the server logic. Quickly glancing at the file, you should see a few familiar concepts as well as some new items. Notice also the several instances of `app.use`. We mentioned it in passing in the previous chapter, but let's now discuss it in more detail.

app.use

`app.use` registers a middleware function that will be called on every request that comes into the web server. It's useful for tasks that you need to happen on every request. Remember, `app.use` just adds entries to the routing table. The same order rules for other routes are in effect for `app.use` statements as well. The statements will execute in the order in which they are registered, top to bottom, every time a new request comes in.

Suppose you wanted to print a message to the console for every request that comes into the server. You would use something like the code in Listing 12-1 and log the request information in that middleware. There really is very little to `app.use`. It's just a way to register a middleware function that runs on every request, regardless of the HTTP verb or URI.

```
app.use(function (req, res, next) {
  console.log(req.method + ' ' + req.url);
  next();
});
```

Listing 12-1. A simple request logger

The additional logic exposed by `app.use` is the optional first argument known as a **mount path**. It defaults to / if no path argument is specifically provided. Suppose we only wanted to log requests for the API segment of our web server. We could change Listing 12-1 to use a mount point:

```
app.use('/api', function (req, res, next) {
    console.log('/api logger');
    console.log(req.method + ' ' + req.url);
    next();
});
```

Listing 12-2. Logging API requests

As this is yet to be a complete example, don't be alarmed if you receive 404 errors when testing. They are more demonstrative of syntax and concepts rather than end-to-end examples. By the end of this chapter, you will have built a funcional Express server.

By adding /api to the argument list, we have changed the requests we want to log. With Listing 12-2, only requests that start with /api will be logged. This is one way to only run certain middleware for specific segments of the routing table. Suppose you wanted to track the number of calls to /api resources clients are making. This would be a great way to track just those specific /api requests.

cookieParser

So far, we've been writing all our own middleware functions. Remember, one of the reasons to use a framework such as Express is for access to ready-made modules. Our generated Express app comes with several of the most common Express middleware functions pre-installed. We're going to examine cookieParser in detail to better understand how most community middleware functions are written. The cookieParser middleware function essentially turns the "Cookie" header into a usable JavaScript object.

The code for cookieParser can be found in **node_modules/cookie-parser/index.js**. The first element you should notice is the signature of the exported function: it is a function that returns a function. This is a very common pattern because it allows options to be passed into the middleware function. In the cookieParser example, we can pass secret and opt arguments.

By returning a function from another function, we've created a closure. In this example, the cookieParser is returning an Express middleware function. The inner cookieParser function has access to the original values of opt and secret passed in the first time the outer cookieParser is called. For example, if we included the cookieParser middleware like this: app.use(cookieParser('cookie-secret')), every request will go through the cookieParser middleware. When this line of code is executed the first time Express server is starting, cookieParser() will return a middleware function. secrete will be cookie-secrete and the inner returned function will have access to secrete.

The returned function has the signature function (req, res, next) {...}, just like every other middleware function we've examined. This function also demonstrates the concept of editing and attaching values to req and res and using those values elsewhere. secret, cookies, and signedCookies will be attached to every request (req) that executes this middleware function, and will be available to every downstream middleware function. Finally, after all the logic, next is called to keep the request moving through the server.

Feel free to examine other middleware functions being registered with app.use such as bodyParser.json and bodyParser.urlencoded. You'll find that they all follow the same pattern.

Static Files Revisited

With app.use and the middleware pattern under our belts, we can revisit static file serving and have a better explanation of how it works. Let's examine the line in **app.js** that sets up the static file server:

```
app.use(express.static(path.join(__dirname, 'public')));
```

Listing 12-3. Express default static file server

First we're using app.use, which takes an optional mount point and a middleware function. Since all our static content resides under **public**, we don't need a mount point in this case, and the default value of / is fine.

express.static is a function that takes a root argument, an optional options argument, and returns a middleware function; this is the same pattern we saw in cookieParser. path is one of the core Node modules and it is used for path and directory logic. Rather than simply passing 'public' to express.static, we're going to concatenate the current directory, which is available globally with __dirname, and 'public' for the complete path. It's good practice to use path in this way to help avoid any file system differences between distinct operating systems.

Finally, a middleware function is returned and registered with app.use that will try to locate static files saved under the **public** directory. If they are found, it will serve them. If they are not found, it will continue looking from top to bottom for a matching route in the routing table.

Error Handling

Any time you pass a truthy value into next, you are alerting Express that there has been an error. We mentioned this in the last chapter, but what does that really mean? Switch back to **app.js** and you should see a function similar to Listing 12-3.

```
app.use(function(err, req, res, next) {
    res.status(err.status || 500);
    res.render('error', {
        message: err.message,
        error: err
    });
});
```

Listing 12-4. Express error handler

What makes this an error handler and not just a normal middleware function? Technically, it is a middleware function because we've registered it via app.use, but look at the function signature: err, req, res, next. This middleware function expects an err argument as the first parameter whereas other middleware functions expect a request object as the first parameter. The truthy value you pass into next becomes the err value in the Express error handling function. In the default error handling function, we are using res.render to render the error template and pass information about the error into the view.

There are a few well established rules for dealing with errors in programming and JavaScript is no exception. While any truthy value passed into next will get sent to the error handler, you should make a habit of passing true Error objects rather than strings. Error objects include the execution stack which can often be invaluable in tracing error conditions. Simply passing "there was an error" into next won't be very helpful when your Express app is running in production.

If this were a production system, we would want to record the error into something permanent like a database or a log file. We might also want to send out email alerts or even restart the server depending on the error severity. The default error handler is a good place to start and you should treat it as essentially a stub to fill out with more robust error handling.

Error Handling in Practice

Let's write a quick middleware function demonstrating how to hook into the Express error-handling middleware and demonstrate a common pattern in Express servers. We'll reference some of the code we wrote back in Chapter 8. Let's assume for this example that we have an open connection to our MongoDB, and that we have properly defined an `Employee` model. In this middleware function, we're going to look up an employee by their ID, which has been passed into the Express server via a route parameter.

```
function retrieveEmployee (req, res, next) {
  Employee.findOne({
    _id: req.params.employeeId
  }).exec(function (error, employee) {
    if (error) {
      return next(error);
    }
    res.locals.employee = employee;
    return next();
  });
}
```

Listing 12-5. Using Express error handler

Let's revisit the `retrieveEmployee` function from Chapter 8 and refactor it to be an Express middleware function. In this version, we're going to look up the employee by the ID supplied in the route parameter named `employeeId`. If there's an error looking up the employee, such as the connection being closed or the database unreachable, `error` will be an `Error` object. That the employee is not in the database isn't necessarily considered to be an error. If there is an error, we will call `next` and pass `error`. Otherwise, we'll attach the resulting employee to `res.locals`, call `next`, and continue the request life cycle.

When you call `next(error)`, the error handler will take over and the error-handling logic will execute. When you do this, you generally do *not* want the remainder of the route to execute because the code is in an unexpected error state. Calling `next` with an error will short-circuit the currently running route and skip right to the error-handling function; however, it is critical that you remember to call `return next(error)`. Simply calling `next` is not enough to stop executing the current middleware function. Only `return` can stop function execution.

In Listing 12-4, if you omitted `return` from the `return next(error)` statement, you would introduce a bug that's difficult to track down. In the case where there was an error, the error handler would execute and respond with the error page. After that, execution would continue down the file, try to attach `employee` to `res.locals.employee`, and then call `next` again. This would eventually lead to the server trying to send a second response for a request that already had a response from the error handler. It is good practice to always put `return` in front of a callback, just to be sure.

app.set

`app.set` gives us a common place to read and write application-wide settings. For example, running `app.set('title', 'Express Server');` will assign the server setting `title` to `Express Server`. You can get these values back using `app.get('title')`. When rendering views, you can access the application settings via `settings`.

Most of the settings are for the developers' use; however, Express does use this mechanism internally to manage internal settings such as `views`, `view engine`, `jsonp callback name`, and several others documented here.[1]

If you check out **app.js** again, you'll notice that the example has set the `view engine` to `jade` and the `views` to use the **views** directory. Internally, Express references these values and treats them as configuration options. You'll often see several `app.set` calls near the top of a server file.

---

[1] http://expressjs.com/4x/api.html#app-settings

Router Object

You'll notice in **app.js** that there are no route registrations via `app.get`. This is because the generated app takes advantage of the `Router` object.

The `Router` object is like a mini Express application that can only execute middleware and perform routing. It lacks the other features the full Express application has, and is a kind of middleware that can be required and used by the main Express application.

In our previous examples when we registered a route with `app.get`, we were referring to the built-in `Router` object that every Express application has attached to it.

The small `Router` objects allow developers to break route registration away from **app.js** into one or more files. This drastically cleans up the main server file so that it is solely initialization code and moves the bulk of the logic into modular files.

Using the `Router` Object

In **app.js**, you would have noticed `app.use('/users', users);`. If we look in **/routes/users.js**, we'll see a nice example of how to work with the `Router` object.

First, we receive a reference to the `Router` object via `express.Router();` and from there, it has the exact same interface that we've been working with when using **app**. You can register routes and middleware, even include additional `router.use` commands.

Two interesting points about **users.js**; first, we export the router at the end of the file. Just as with any other Node object, we export items that we want to have access to in other files. Second, the only route registered is `GET /`, which sends `"respond with a resource"`. But if you start the server and point a web browser to /, you'll see the Express landing page rather than `"respond with a resource"`. So what's going on here?

If you flip back over to **app.js**, it should become clear. `app.use('/users', users);` is setting up a mount point under /users and any route that starts with /users should use the `users` middleware function. We exported the router from **users.js** that had only a single route attached to it.

If you make a request to /users, you should see "respond with a resource" printed to the screen with no styling. When the GET request for /users comes into the server, it will match on the /users mount point. /users will be stripped from the path and become /. Execution will continue into the registered middleware. The registered middleware is an Express router and has a single route set up for /, so that is the code that will execute and send the desired response.

Being able to break route registration like this really helps in sharding responsibilities across different endpoints. It also helps to cut down on changes to **app.js**, and prevents teams from overwriting each other and creating code conflicts.

Exercise

To tie together everything we've covered in this chapter, let's make the request to /users actually send back some user data and the current time. Instead of just sending back JSON, lets send some simple HTML as well. In the example code, we're going to simulate a database request again with setTimeout; however, if you're feeling ambitious, we encourage you to use some of the code from the MongoDB chapters to communicate to your MongoDB instance.

For this example, we want to perform a few tasks:

1. Simulate database interaction to obtain a list of users (again, if you are feeling ambitious go ahead and communicate to your MongoDB).

2. Take the results of the database interaction and generate a simple HTML document with which to respond.

3. Add a reference to a local CSS file to illustrate using app.use(express.static(path.join(__dirname, 'public')));.

Refer to Listing 12-6 for a complete solution.

Simulating Database Interaction

By now you should be very familiar with simulating database calls using setTimeout. To keep our code readable, change the single route in **routes/users.js** to have two middleware functions. Normally, we'd want to separate these calls into different files and modules. For step 1, write a setTimeout function to simulate database activity. Make sure that your code is set up to pass the array of users into the next middleware function.

Generating the HTML

In the second middleware function, attach a timestamp to the result object. After you have the timestamp, set a header named X-Special-Header to "MEAN Stack". Lastly, send the response back to the client. You'll find the complete answer in Listing 12-6. Try to solve this without looking at the answer using what we've covered in this chapter and the Express documentation.

routes/users.js

```
var express = require('express');
var router = express.Router();

/* GET users listing. */
router.get('/', function(req, res, next) {
  setTimeout(function() {
    res.locals.users = [{
      first: 'Abraham',
      last: 'Lincoln'
    }, {
      first: 'Andrew',
      last: 'Johnson'
    }, {
      first: 'Ulysses',
      last: 'Grant'
    }];
    return next();
  }, 1000)
}, function (req, res, next) {
  res.locals.time = Date.now();
  res.set({
    'X-Special-Header': 'MEAN Stack'
  });

  var view = '<!DOCTYPE html><html lang="en">'
  + '<head><link rel="stylesheet" href="/stylesheets/style.css")'
  + '<body><h1>User Output</h1><table>';
  for (var i = 0, length = res.locals.users.length; i < length; i++)
➥{
    var user = res.locals.users[i];
    view += '<tr><td>' + user.first + '</td><td>' + user.last +
```

```
➥ '</td></tr>';
  }

  view += '</table></body></html>';

  res.send(view);
});

module.exports = router;
```

Listing 12-6. User response

Listing 12-6 illustrates several of the Express principles that we've covered in the last couple chapters. We've passed two different middleware functions into router.get. In the first middleware function, we are simulating database access with setTimeout. After one second, the callback will run and we'll attach three users to res.locals.users. There are two points to keep in mind in this step; first, we only want to call next when this step is done. If we called it outside of the setTimeout function, execution would go to the next piece of middleware, sending a response before it was truly ready. The second point is that we cannot pass data to another function with next. Passing any truthy value into next will initiate the error handler; instead, we must attach values to req and res to move data from one middleware function to the next.

In the second middleware function, we use res.set to set the X-Special-Header to "MEAN Stack". res.set is an Express method attached to res that enables developers to easily set headers in a response. Next, we build a string of HTML (stored in view) that will be the response for this request. Notice the reference to /stylesheets/style.css. This will engage the static file server set up with app.use(express.static(path.join(__dirname, 'public'))) in **app.js**. Remember, the parameter to express.static tells Express where to start looking for static files.

Next, we iterate over the list of users attached to res.locals.users employing a simple for loop and fill the HTML table with information. Finally, we use res.send(view) to end the request life cycle and send a response back to the client. res.send has a few nice features that make sending responses with it much more convenient than using the core http module. res.send will try to automatically set the correct Content-Type based on the data being sent. It will also set the Content-Length header as well.

If you open the developer tools in your preferred web browser and make a request to the /user route, you can see all the headers that Express has set for us. Note that the Content-Type and Content-Length have both been set automatically, as shown in Figure 12.1. You should also see two requests—one for users and one for style.css.

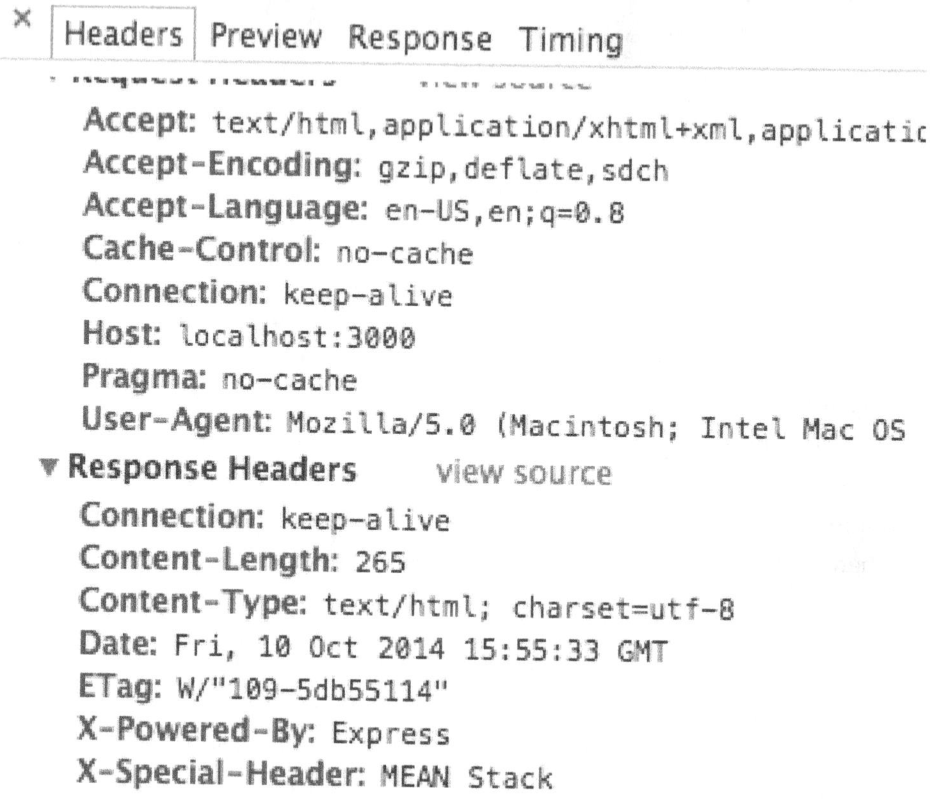

```
 ×  | Headers | Preview  Response  Timing

    Accept: text/html,application/xhtml+xml,applicatic
    Accept-Encoding: gzip,deflate,sdch
    Accept-Language: en-US,en;q=0.8
    Cache-Control: no-cache
    Connection: keep-alive
    Host: localhost:3000
    Pragma: no-cache
    User-Agent: Mozilla/5.0 (Macintosh; Intel Mac OS
 ▼ Response Headers        view source
    Connection: keep-alive
    Content-Length: 265
    Content-Type: text/html; charset=utf-8
    Date: Fri, 10 Oct 2014 15:55:33 GMT
    ETag: W/"109-5db55114"
    X-Powered-By: Express
    X-Special-Header: MEAN Stack
```

Figure 12.1. Network Inspector

Summary

In this chapter, we learned about more of the internal workings of an Express application. As you can see, working with a Node framework is much easier and maintainable than working directly with the http module. In just a few lines, we built a nearly feature-complete web server without reaching down into the core Node modules once.

The Express routing logic is very expressive and allows developers to register routes with both strings and regular expressions. Express also has a specific `Router` object that is a slimmed down Express application, enabling developers to break apart route registration into separate files to keep the main server file clean.

The functions in Express routes are called middleware and they all have the same function signature. There are many middleware functions available in the open-source community that solve many common web development problems, easily plugging into Express servers.

In the next chapter, we're going to continue building our human resources style application and combine the three technologies we've covered to this point: Express, Node, and MongoDB.

13

Using Express in Our App

This chapter revisits the example Human Resources application that was started in Chapter 6 and continued in Chapter 9. Up to this point, we've created a Node application that communicates with a MongoDB store. We used Node's `http` module to write a custom implementation for a router. Now that we have the more powerful Express router at our disposal, we're going to replace our `http` code.

If we were starting a new application from scratch, we would likely want to use a scaffolding generator, such as Yeoman[1] (which has a MEAN stack generator[2]); however, since we're updating our existing application, we're going to modify everything by hand.

Updates to package.json

The first step in our migration to Express is to update the **package.json** file. We need to install Express and several pieces of middleware. We can install all the necessary modules using the command in Listing 13-1:

---

[1] http://yeoman.io/

[2] http://meanjs.org/generator.html

```
npm install --save body-parser cookie-parser debug express morgan
➥serve-favicon
```

Listing 13-1. Installing Express and other required middleware

We can also remove the `colors` and `array.prototype.find` modules, which we have no need for anymore. This can be done using the command shown in Listing 13-2:

```
npm remove --save colors array.prototype.find
```

Listing 13-2. Removing modules that are no longer required

We're also going to add a `start` entry to the `scripts` object. This will allow us to easily start our server using the command `npm start`. Add the entry shown in Listing 13-3. Note that this command depends on `bin/www`, which is yet to exist. We'll be adding it very soon.

```
"start": "node ./bin/www"
```

Listing 13-3. Adding the `start` entry in the `scripts` object

The complete and updated `package.json` can be seen in Listing 13-4.

```
{
  "name": "example-server",
  "version": "0.1.0",
  "description": "HR application server.",
  "main": "index.js",
  "scripts": {
    "test": "echo \"Error: no test specified\" && exit 1",
    "start": "node ./bin/www",
    "populate": "node ./bin/populate_db"
  },
  "author": "Peter Pluck",
  "license": "ISC",
  "dependencies": {
    "async": "^0.9.0",
    "body-parser": "^1.6.7",
    "cookie-parser": "^1.3.2",
    "debug": "^2.0.0",
```

```
    "express": "^4.8.7",
    "mongoose": "^3.8.15",
    "mongoose-post-find": "0.0.2",
    "morgan": "^1.2.3",
    "serve-favicon": "^2.1.1"
  }
}
```

Listing 13-4. The pdated **package.json** file

The npm start Script

The next step is to create a file named **www** in the project's **bin** directory. The contents of **www** are shown in Listing 13-5. This code starts our server, which is defined in the project's **index.js** file. The server listens on port 3000 by default, but that value can be overwritten by setting an environment variable named PORT. For example, if you wanted the server to listen on port 4000, use the command PORT=4000 npm start.

```
var debug = require('debug')('example-server');
var app = require('../');

app.set('port', process.env.PORT || 3000);

var server = app.listen(app.get('port'), function() {
  debug('Express server listening on port ' + server.address().port);
});
```

Listing 13-5. The bin/www script

Notice that the **debug** module is used to display a message. By default, if you run npm start, nothing will be displayed. To enable the debug message, set the process's DEBUG environment variable to example-server.

Defining Routes

The next step is to create the Express routes that will process incoming requests. Create a **routes** directory in the root of the project. This is where we'll place all our route files. Inside the **routes** directory, create two files: **employees.js** and **teams.js**.

Employee Routes

The contents of **routes/employees.js** are shown in Listing 13-6. We are supporting the following routes:

- GET /employees — returns all employees, sorted by last name

- GET /employees/:employeeId — returns information for a single employee, whose employee ID is passed through the employeeId parameter

- PUT /employees/:employeeId — used to update an existing employee; the employee ID is passed through the employeeId parameter, while the employee data is passed in the request body

```javascript
var express = require('express');
var mongoose = require('mongoose');
var Employee = mongoose.model('Employee');
var Team = mongoose.model('Team');
var router = express.Router();

router.get('/employees', function(req, res, next) {
  Employee.find().sort('name.last').exec(function(error, results) {
    if (error) {
      return next(error);
    }

    // Respond with valid data
    res.json(results);
  });
});

router.get('/employees/:employeeId', function(req, res, next) {
  Employee.findOne({
    id: req.params.employeeId
  }).populate('team').exec(function (error, results) {
    if (error) {
      return next(error);
    }

    // If valid user was not found, send 404
    if (!results) {
      res.send(404);
    }
```

```
    // Respond with valid data
    res.json(results);
  });
});

router.put('/employees/:employeeId', function (req, res, next) {
  // Remove this or mongoose will throw an error
  // because we would be trying to update the mongo ID
  delete req.body._id;
  req.body.team = req.body.team._id;

  Employee.update({
    id: req.params.employeeId
  }, req.body, function (err, numberAffected, response) {
    if (err) {
      return next(err);
    }

    res.send(200);
  });
});

module.exports = router;
```

Listing 13-6. The contents of routes/employees.js

Team Routes

The team routes are stored in routes/teams.js, whose contents are shown in Listing 13-7. The following team routes are supported:

- GET /teams — displays all the teams stored in the database, sorted by team name

- GET /teams/:teamId — displays information regarding a single team; the team's ID is passed through the teamId parameter, and must match the associated MongoDB _id property

```
var express = require('express');
var mongoose = require('mongoose');
var Team = mongoose.model('Team');
var router = express.Router();

router.get('/teams', function (req, res, next) {
```

```
Team.find().sort('name').exec(function (error, results) {
    if (error) {
      return next(error);
    }


    // Respond with valid data
    res.json(results);
  });
});

router.get('/teams/:teamId', function (req, res, next) {
  Team.findOne({
    _id: req.params.teamId
  }, function (error, results) {
    if (error) {
      return next(error);
    }


    res.json(results);
  });
});

module.exports = router;
```

Listing 13-7. The contents of **routes/teams.js**

Update index.js

The final step in our upgrade to Express is the conversion of the **index.js** file. The modified contents of **index.js** are shown in Listing 13-8. There is a lot happening in this file, so we'll explain it in smaller pieces.

 Commonly Known as ...

> The two most common names for the application's main file are **index.js** and **app.js**. **app.js** is probably more common in Express applications, but the two are used fairly interchangeably.

The file begins by importing Express, `path`, and some middleware. Next, we establish a database connection, import the application's routes, and initialize the `app` variable. Then we set up some of the middleware. Notice that the `favicon` middleware is commented out. This is because there is no favicon in our project. If your project has one, uncomment this line.

The last five calls to `app.use()` are what really contains our application-specific code. By `use()`ing the `employees` and `teams` variables, we're adding our routes to the router. The next step is a call to `app.use()` that sets up a generic 404 route. This is used to return a 404 on any requests not handled by our routes.

The final two `app.use()` calls are responsible for handling errors. You'll notice that only one error handler is employed in development, where it's used to send back additional error data. The final handler is utilized in non-development settings, and only returns a status code.

```
var express = require('express');
var path = require('path');
var favicon = require('serve-favicon');
var logger = require('morgan');
var cookieParser = require('cookie-parser');
var bodyParser = require('body-parser');

require('./lib/connection');
var employees = require('./routes/employees');
var teams = require('./routes/teams');

var app = express();

// app.use(favicon(__dirname + '/public/favicon.ico'));
app.use(logger('dev'));
app.use(bodyParser.json());
app.use(bodyParser.urlencoded({ extended: true }));
app.use(cookieParser());
app.use(express.static(path.join(__dirname, 'public')));

// application routes
app.use(employees);
app.use(teams);

// catch 404 and forward to error handler
app.use(function(req, res, next) {
  var err = new Error('Not Found');

  err.status = 404;
  next(err);
```

```
});

// error handlers

// development error handler
// will print stacktrace
if (app.get('env') === 'development') {
  app.use(function(err, req, res, next) {
    res.status(err.status || 500);
    res.send({
      message: err.message,
      error: err
    });
  });
}

// production error handler
// no stacktraces leaked to user
app.use(function(err, req, res, next) {
  res.status(err.status || 500);
});

module.exports = app;
```

Listing 13-8. The modified contents of `index.js`

Summary

This chapter has continued the development of our Human Resources example application. In this chapter, we migrated from a custom `http`-based server to a more flexible and scalable Express-based application. At this point, we have a fairly solid back end for our HR application. Shortly, we'll be turning our attention to the front end, which is built using AngularJS. First, however, we're going to take a whirlwind tour of Hapi, an Express alternative developed at Walmart Labs.

14

Alternative Server Frameworks

With a language as popular as JavaScript, there are bound to be differences in opinion on how to solve any problem— from something as simple as loop optimization to the more complex, such as the best way to simulate classical object-oriented inheritance. The passion and drive to perform tasks the best way followed JavaScript enthusiasts into the Node community, and is evident when looking at the available web server frameworks. A few quick Google searches and you'll see that the list of available frameworks is quite large, while a search for "framework http" on npm[1] nets you page after page of various web server frameworks. There are far too many options to name here without doing any of them a disservice.

In this chapter we're going to focus on hapi, an alternative to the Express framework. We'll look at hapi because it's the second-most popular Node framework, and it's very different from Express.[2]

---

[1] https://www.npmjs.org/search?q=framework%20http
[2] Full disclosure: both authors are currently employed by Walmart and have contributed to hapi and several of the modules it relies on.

hapi Overview

The hapi server framework[3] has an active and growing community, as well as many big name supporters. At the time of writing, hapi is the second-most starred server framework on the npm registry and is quickly becoming more popular. hapi's approach is to be configuration-centric instead of development-centric. This allows developers to focus more on business logic than the nuts and bolts of a web server and an evergrowing list of middleware functions.

Just as Express's list of users is impressive, so is hapi's. Some of the big names currently using hapi in production include OpenTable, PayPal, Beats Music, and Walmart; you can check out the website for a full list of companies using hapi.[4] Walmart has an extra incentive to see hapi succeed, as the main contributors built hapi while working for Walmart's research and development division.

hapi offers all the same high-level features that Express does. It has a robust routing system, integration options for templating languages, and an easy-to-use static file server. It also supports a solid plugin system and provides built-in input validation.

Express Comparison

There are numerous differences between Express and hapi. The main logical component in Express is the middleware function. A route consists of a series of one or more middleware functions, and eventually a function that sends a response to the client. The majority of middleware logic that developers have to write in Express are configuration options in hapi. A route in hapi consists of a path, an HTTP method, and a single handler function. Everything else is handled via a configuration object passed into the router.

Let's revisit the code from Listing 12-6 and rewrite it using hapi in Listing 14-1:

```
var Hapi = require('hapi');
var server = new Hapi.Server('localhost', 3000);

server.route({
  method: 'GET',
```

---

[3] http://hapijs.com/
[4] http://hapijs.com/community

```
    path: '/users',
    config: {
      handler: function (request, reply) {
        var result = {};
        setTimeout(function () {
          result.users = [{
            first: 'Abraham',
            last: 'Lincoln'
          }, {
            first: 'Andrew',
            last: 'Johnson'
          }, {
            first: 'Ulysses',
            last: 'Grant'
          }];
          result.time = Date.now();

          return reply(result).header('X-Special-Header', 'MEAN
  ➥Stack');
        }, 3000);
      }
    }
});

server.start();
```

Listing 14-1. Example hapi route

In Listing 14-1, `server` is the hapi server object. To add a route, we execute the `route` method and pass a series of options. `method` and `path` are used to set up the matching rules for the router. The `config` option is where all the other configuration for this route will reside. The `handler` function is what's responsible for sending a reply to the client. `request` is the incoming request and `reply` is a function that sends a response. It is worth noting that the `request` object is *not* the built-in Node request object. It is a hapi-specific request object. The Node request object is available via `request.raw.req`.

What if we wanted to cache the response from Listing 14-1? With Express, a developer would have to write logic to set the proper headers instructing the browser to cache the response. If you had several dozen routes with different cache requirements, you'd have to add a `setCache`-type middleware for each route. In hapi, the cache headers are controlled via a setting defined with the route configuration.

```
server.route({
  method: 'GET',
  path: '/users',
  config: {
    handler: function (request, reply) {
      //...
    }
  },
  cache: {
    expiresIn: 30000
  }
});
```

Listing 14-2. hapi cache headers

Route Configuration

The `cache` option exposes several methods for setting the `"Cache-Control"` header. In Listing 14-2, we are setting the cache header to expire in 30,000 milliseconds. Additionally, hapi will not set the cache headers if there's an error. In Express, there'd be a few lines of development required for removing the cache headers to avoid caching error pages. Check out hapi's API site for a complete list of configuration options.[5] It can be a little overwhelming at first, but before trying to implement any big functionality, review the documentation and you might find that all you need is to add an additional configuration to the server or route.

As a second example, what if you wanted to validate the outgoing response before sending it back to the client? Using Express, you would have to write additional code to achieve this. With hapi, you can simply update the route configuration to include response validation. In addition to the response, you can also validate the incoming headers, the query string, and the route parameters. You might use a simple function and write your own validation rules, or use another of the hapijs modules: Joi.[6]

Joi is a stand-alone validation module that can been hooked right into any hapi route configuration. It is a very powerful and expressive validation module that

---

[5] http://hapijs.com/api
[6] https://github.com/hapijs/joi

pairs nicely with hapi, because any configuration that exposes validation accepts
a Joi configuration object as well as validation function. Here's an example:

```
var joi = require('joi');

server.route({
  method: 'GET',
  path: '/users',
  config: {
    handler: function (request, reply) {
      reply(request.query);
    },
    validate: {
      query: joi.object().keys({
        page: joi.number().integer().min(1).max(10),
        number: joi.number().integer().min(1).max(5)
      })
    }
  }
});
```

Listing 14-3. Joi example

In Listing 14-3, we are tapping into the `validate` option of the route config, and
setting `validate.query` to a Joi schema. By setting `validate.query`, hapi will validate the query-string parameters before the handler is run. If the validation fails,
the server will respond with a 400 status code and an object representing the validation errors. Expressed in words, the Joi schema enforces that `page` is an integer
between one and ten. It also enforces that `number` is an integer between one and
five. Finally, `joi.object().keys()` prevents any extra values in the query string.
Only `page` and `number` will be allowed in this route. Joi is well beyond the scope of
this book, so we strongly encourage you to checkout Joi and validation on your own.

Routing

The order that routes are registered with Express is very important. The first one
that matches is the route that is executed. It is also possible to register the same
route multiple times. And finally, with Express you can match on pattern A, execute
some code, and if a response hasn't been sent, match a second time on pattern B
before responding to the client.

hapi uses a deterministic routing table. This means that the order in which routes are registered has no influence on how they're handled. The routes are sorted from most specific to least specific as the routing table is created in the framework. hapi will throw an error if developers try to register the same route multiple times. Additionally, the router will only ever match *one* route and execute a single handler. These route-handling differences essentially eliminate all the routing bugs sometimes found in Express applications that are difficult to trace.

As a simple specificity example, suppose we had two routes with paths `"/file.txt"` and `"/file.{ext}"`. Between those two paths, `"/file.txt"` is more specific because it has no parameters, so a request for `"/file.txt"` would match the first route and that handler would be used. `"/file.txt"` would match both paths, but the more specific would be the winner in this example and that handler would run.

Built-in Capability

Express is billed as being thin and unopinionated and, for the most part, that's true. You can wire in almost any module into the Express ecosystem and build a feature-complete web server. Building items such as server-side caching or user authentication into an Express server requires several modules often written by different developers, communicating perfectly and staying in sync. Indeed, many Express applications do this successfully.

hapi, by contrast, has these features out of the box. hapi has a server-side cache engine that can be used to store values in memory, or in a redis or MongoDB instance. If your server requires authentication, there are configuration options for that as well. All a developer needs to do is configure the authentication for the specific routes that require it. If basic authentication is not enough, or if you want to use social logins, there are several hapi plugins that add more flexible user authentication. The majority of those plugins require no development, just additional configurations and plugin modules. We'll talk more about plugins shortly in this chapter.

Events

One of the common praises of hapi is that it is "Node-like." Besides supporting pipes and streams natively, there are many server events that developers can hook into. The main `server` object inherits from `Events.EventEmitter`. Because it uses a core Node object, we already know how to interact with it.

Suppose we wanted to log every response that the server sends. In Express, this would require some development and middleware functions placed strategically in the router. In hapi, we can listen for the `response` event and log information about the response.

```
server.on('response', function (event) {
    console.log(event.info.received);
});
```

Listing 14-4. Logging server events

Listing 14-4 easily allows us to execute logic after the hapi server has sent a response to the client. There are several other events that can be listened for that provide logging and performance benchmarking. These events aren't used for control flow, or to extend the functionality of the hapi server; they are just ways to observe different events that the server emits.

Extension points, by contrast, provide structured hooks to extend and alter the standard hapi request lifecycle.[7] Suppose we wanted to write a log file to the file system after authentication on a particular web resource occurred. In Express, you would add another middleware function that would write the file and then execute next. With hapi, you can use the `onPostAuth` extension point.

```
server.ext('onPostAuth', function (request, next) {
    require('fs').writeFile('log' + Date.now() + '.txt', 'Successful
➥authentication!', next);
});
```

Listing 14-5. onPostAuth extension point

Obviously this is a contrived example, but it demonstrates the concept of extension points. This function writes a file after every `onPostAuth` event. The nice part about using events rather than middleware functions is that the function only needs to be written and declared once. There's no need to go looking for the different places that might use the equivalent Express middleware. In addition, as long as you've properly set up the listener, this logic can reside in any file in the project because it is event driven.

---

[7] http://hapijs.com/api#request-lifecycle

Plugins

hapi has a robust plugin system. A **plugin** can be thought of as a bundled subset of server functionality. A plugin can add new routes and additional events, and provide support for higher-order languages such as Stylus and Less CSS—almost anything a completely new server can do. The plugin architecture is one reason why hapi is so attractive.

Plugine allow a server to have its logic segmented across many different modules. Let's expand on that with an example. Suppose you are working with a team that is building a new web server. You want to expose data such as an API that a smartphone phone can consume for native apps, but you also want to serve a website. Working with Express, this could be complicated.

The API team would want routes set up one way and the front-end developers would want them set up another. The front-end team would want to add middleware functions for compiling templates and serving static assets, something for which the API has no need. Juggling the needs and designs of two teams both working on the same server would be trying, as well as require great coordination.

With hapi, each team would work from a distinct hapi plugin, and the single server would then load both plugins. This would allow each piece of code to be completely isolated from each other and have very little coupling. Each plugin can register its own routes, listen for events, have its own cookie-managed state, and have its own list of other plugins as dependencies. Covering all of what plugins can do is outside the scope of this book, but the full documentation can provide better insight to working with plugins.[8]

Plugin Example

Let's expand Listing 14-1 by adding a plugin module that will display the JSON on a web page. We'll avoid using any templating languages to keep the example simple, and construct the HTML by hand, sending the response back to the client.

```
//...original code from Listing 14-1 omitted
var plug = {
  register: function (plugin, options, next) {
```

---

[8] http://hapijs.com/api#plugin-interface

```
    plugin.route({
      method: 'GET',
      path: options.prefix + '/view',
      config: {
        handler: function (request, reply) {
          request.server.inject({
            url: '/users'
          }, function (res) {
            var users = res.result.users;
            var view = '<!DOCTYPE html><html lang="en"><body><h1>
➥User Output</h1><table>';

            for (var i = 0; i < users.length; i++) {
              var user = users[i];
              view += '<tr><td>' + user.first + '</td><td>' +
➥user.last + '</td></tr>';
            }

            view += '</table></body></html>';
            reply(view);
          });
        }
      }
    });

    next();
  }
};
plug.register.attributes = {
  name: 'viewer',
  version: '1.0.0'
};


server.pack.register({
  plugin: plug,
  options: {
    prefix: '/users'
  }
}, function (err) {
  if (err) {
    console.log(err);
  } else {
```

```
    server.start();
  }
});
```

Listing 14-6. Plugin example

This looks a little overwhelming at first, but let's walk through it. We're creating a `plug` variable that has a `register` function with `attributes` attached to the `register` function. `attributes` must have a `name` and `version` key. Those few items are everything a JavaScript object needs to be considered a plugin. The `register` function is the main entry point into the object and is where the majority of the logic will be located. The `register` accepts three arguments: `plugin`, `options`, and `next`. `plugin` is the plugin interface and has many of the same methods available to the `server` object, including `route`. The `options` object is where any plugin-specific options will reside; in this case, we've supplied a `prefix` value that we used to set the `path` value for the route registration. `next` is the callback function the method must call to return control over to the application and complete the registration process.

In the `handler`, we use `server.inject`. The `inject` method simulates an HTTP request without actually making a socket connection. It's useful for testing and, in this case, requesting information from another route to obtain the list of users. After we have the list of users available, we simply create an HTML string and respond to the client with `reply`.

To register the plugin, we use `server.pack.register`. `server.pack` is too large a concept to discuss in this book. In short, every server is grouped into a pack of servers. This lets you register the same plugin and routes for multiple hapi servers at once. It also allows developers to treat packs of servers as a single object, so that they can start and stop a pack of servers in one step. For the full explanation of a pack, please check the hapi documentation.[9]

If you start a web browser and navigate to `"/users"` and `"/users/view"`, you should see the different response. This plugin lets us separate two routes and serve a view from one and JSON from the other. Ideally, the plugin would be in another file to help keep the main server logic clean. Using plugins such as this allows for far

---

[9] http://hapijs.com/api#hapipack

greater code modularity and reuse. There are several pre-built plugins for tasks such as logging, API documentation, and working with user agents.

Summary

That was a whirlwind tour of some of what hapi has to offer. It is a completely different approach to building servers compared to Express, which makes it interesting to learn. Many of the elements feature-complete web servers need are built right into hapi. If it's not built in, there are freely available plugins to fill in the majority of missing features. The routing logic in hapi is unique because order does not matter. hapi also uses events to provide extension points to expand and change the server behavior.

Whether you use hapi or Express, I trust that after these few chapters, you'll understand why most people avoid trying to build all these features using only core modules, instead investing time to learn a framework.

15

AngularJS Overview

The final MEAN technology that we're going to explore is AngularJS. Angular is a front-end framework used for creating single-page applications (SPAs). Like the other MEAN technologies, Angular is open source and can be used freely in your applications.

Angular was created in 2009 by Miško Hevery and Adam Abrons at a company named Brat Tech LLC. Angular was initially intended to be part of an online JSON storage service, but this concept was abandoned and Angular was released to the open-source world. Adam Abrons has since left the project, but Hevery continues work on the project. Hevery became employed by Google, which is now closely associated with Angular.

Single-page Applications

Single-page applications represent the latest evolution in web design. The idea behind SPAs is that all the necessary code can be retrieved in a single page load or dynamically loaded as necessary. As the user interacts with the application, data is sent to and received from the server using Ajax requests. This provides a more

fluid user experience than page reloads, and is closer to resembling a native application. Some of the common characteristics of SPAs will now be explored:

- Ajax: Ajax requests are a necessity in SPAs. By definition, SPAs should experience a single-page load. All other requests should occur via Ajax or some other
  real-time communication mechanism such as WebSockets.

- Templating: it's considered bad practice to mix HTML into the JSON data re-
  turned by the server, hence why templating languages are often used in SPAs.
  These languages, which are often implemented in JavaScript, are able to convert
  JSON data into HTML strings that can be injected into the DOM.

- Routing: client-side routing is similar to server-side routing that you learned
  about in the chapter on Express. Routing allows you to select a piece of the application to display without requiring a page load. In SPAs, it is common for
  client-side routes to be specified in the URL's **fragment identifier**, which is the
  part that follows a hash symbol. For example, in the URL `http://do-
  main.com/#/team`, the client-side router would deal with the `/team` section that
  follows the #.

As mentioned, the biggest advantages of SPAs are improved performance and a
more fluid user experience due to reduced page loads and smaller server transactions.
However, SPAs also have drawbacks, the two biggest of which are the nature of
browser history and search engine optimization (SEO). Browser history can be
problematic because the **Back** and **Forward** buttons are based on page loads. Luckily,
using URL fragment identifiers maintains the expected behavior, as long as the application can recreate the page based on the identifier.

SPAs can be tricky for search engines because they have not historically executed
JavaScript code during the crawling process. Search engines are beginning to catch
up, though; Google has begun to crawl pages with fragment identifiers by executing
JavaScript. There are other techniques that can be implemented as well. One common
example is detecting on the server side when a page is requested by a search engine,
and then using a headless browser (a browser without a GUI) to render the page and
send back a "normal" page. Care must be exercised in this situation, as it is slower,
and search engines typically incorporate page load time into their rankings.

SPA Frameworks

There are a number of popular frameworks used for creating SPAs, each with different pros and cons. And, as with many aspects of technology, users tend to be very passionate about their framework of choice. This books focuses on Angular as it is traditionally part of the MEAN stack, but that's not to say we want to detract from the alternatives. We suggest that you check out each framework to evaluate its strengths and weaknesses,[1] and see who is using it. For example, for a listing of products designed with Angular, check out builtwith.angularjs.org.[2]

Here's a selection of popular competitors to Angular:

- Backbone.js[3] is a veteran front-end framework, battle-tested and likely to be the most used SPA framework. It is simple, flexible, and provides many small building blocks with which to work. Unfortunately, Backbone's simplicity often requires its users to write a substantial amount of code to fill in the missing pieces.

- Ember.js[4] is an extremely opinionated framework. It often only supports one way of solving a problem, known as "the Ember Way." This can be seen as a strength and a weakness of the framework, depending on your point of view. The Ember home page contains an impressive list of framework users[5].

- Polymer[6] is another Google offering that focuses on Web Components,[7] an up-and-coming collection of technologies that provide web developers with the ability to create customer HTML elements. Unfortunately, these technologies are yet to be considered production-ready, leaving Polymer in the position of a polyfill. Nevertheless, there is still interesting work going on in the area of Web Component-based SPAs.[8]

---

[1] http://blog.andyet.com/2014/08/13/opinionated-rundown-of-js-frameworks
[2] https://builtwith.angularjs.org/
[3] http://backbonejs.org/
[4] http://emberjs.com/
[5] http://emberjs.com/ember-users/
[6] https://www.polymer-project.org/
[7] http://webcomponents.org/
[8] https://www.polymer-project.org/articles/spa.html

So, how does Angular stack up in comparison with these competitors? It is considered one of the simpler frameworks to learn, and has a large community and core team lead by Google. You can accomplish a lot with Angular just by writing some custom HTML. One commonly noted drawback, though, is that it does too much for you, without you having an understanding of what's really happening. Additionally, there seems to be no evidence of it being used in any of Google's flagship products, and the upcoming Angular 2.0 is expected to have no simple upgrade path, meaning that full application rewrites could be on the horizon.[9]

Model–View–Controller Architecture

Angular brings the Model-View-Controller (MVC) architecture to front-end web applications. Under the MVC approach, the model defines the application at a data layer, independent of the user interface. In Angular, models are as simple as plain JavaScript objects. The view is a visual representation of the model data. Angular allows you to use HTML, in conjunction with extensions known as *directives*, as a templating language for view creation. The controller component is responsible for manipulating the model's data. In Angular applications, controllers are JavaScript functions that are registered with the application using the `controller()` method. Figure 15.1 illustrates how a generic MVC process works. Note that this image is not specific to Angular.

---

[9] http://developer.telerik.com/featured/can-angularjs-maintain-dominance/

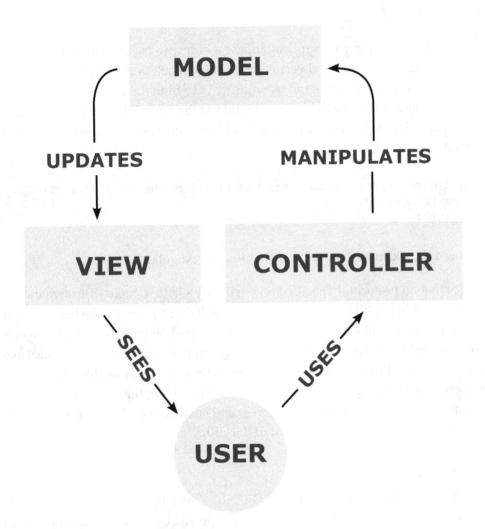

Figure 15.1. A generic MVC process[10]

One of Angular's most well-known features is its two-way data binding between models and views. This greatly simplifies the problem of keeping data synchronized between two application components. **Two-way data binding** means that when the user updates the view, the model data is automatically updated to reflect the changes. Similarly, if the controller modifies the model, the view is updated as well.

---

[10] Image courtesy of Regis Frey via Wikimedia Commons.

Getting Angular

To include Angular in your application, use a `<script>` tag as shown in Listing 15-1. This tag imports a minified version of Angular 1.2.23 from Google. You can also download a nonminified version by omitting `.min` from the URL. The minified version should always be used in production as the nonminified code is several times larger, leading to increased download times and therefore greater page load latency.

```
<script src="//ajax.googleapis.com/ajax/libs/angularjs/1.2.23/
➥angular.min.js">
</script>
```

Listing 15-1. Example `<script>` tag that imports Angular

Notice that no protocol is specified on the library's URL. Google will serve the Angular library over HTTP or HTTPS. By not specifying a protocol, the browser will load the library with whatever protocol is being used on your page. This prevents potential mixed content[11] errors and warnings from occurring when your page uses one protocol and Angular loads using another. One caveat is that this style will fail to work when running code locally without a server (over the `file://` protocol). If you are not running your code on a server and encounter a "file not found" error, try adding `http` or `https` to the front of the URL.

Building from Source

The Angular project is maintained on GitHub in the angular/angular.js repo.[12] If you are so inclined, you can contribute to the project by submitting a pull request to this repo; however, be warned that setting up an Angular development environment requires Java, Grunt (a task runner), and Bower (a client-side package manager), in addition to git and Node.

After installing all the prerequisite software,[13] you can build Angular using the series of commands shown in Listing 15-2. The first command clones the repo from GitHub. Alternatively, you may want to fork the repo first, then clone your fork and

---

[11] https://developer.mozilla.org/en-US/docs/Security/MixedContent
[12] https://github.com/angular/angular.js
[13] https://docs.angularjs.org/misc/contribute

add the official repo as a remote. The `npm install` and `bower install` commands are used to install all dependencies. The final command, `grunt package`, is used to build Angular.

```
git clone "git@github.com:angular/angular.js.git"
cd angular.js
npm install
bower install
grunt package
```

Listing 15-2. Commands for cloning and building Angular

After running `grunt package`, the build output can be found in the `build` directory. This directory should contain the following files and folders:

- `angular-<version>.zip` — the complete zip file, containing all the release build artifacts

- `angular.js` — the nonminified Angular code

- `angular.min.js` — the minified Angular code

- `angular-scenario.js` — the Angular End2End test runner

- `docs` — a directory containing all the files needed to run an Angular documentation site

- `docs/index.html` — the main documentation page

- `docs/docs-scenario.html` — the End2End test runner for the documentation application

Releases

Unlike the npm ecosystem, Angular does not adhere to semantic versioning. In Angular, breaking changes occur between minor releases. It tries to avoid breaking changes, but this is not always possible; for example, when potential security issues are discovered. For instructions on upgrading to specific versions and details on breaking changes, see the migration documentation.[14]

---

[14] https://docs.angularjs.org/guide/migration

One interesting aspect of the Angular ecosystem is its naming convention for new releases. Release code names are formed by two seemingly random words that are joined with a hyphen. Example release names are finicky-pleasure, timely-delivery, increase-gravatas, and temporal-domination, which correspond to versions 1.2.22, 1.2.0, 1.1.0, and 1.0.0 respectively.

As a front-end framework, Angular has to deal with issues such as legacy browsers. The term legacy browser essentially translates to Internet Explorer 6, 7, and 8. Currently, Angular's Travis CI server is configured to run tests against IE9, 10, and 11. Angular dropped support for IE6 and 7 as from version 1.2. Angular 1.3 and later drops support for IE8.

Angular "Hello World"

Listing 15-3 shows a simple Angular application that utilizes data binding. This page contains an `<input>` element whose `ng-model` attribute is set to `"example"`. `ng-model` is an example of an Angular directive. Angular directives, the subject of Chapter 17, are extensions to HTML syntax defined in an Angular application (or the Angular core library). This directive signifies that this input's value is bound to the model's `example` property.

Next, notice the `<div>` element whose content is `{{example}}`. In an Angular application, HTML can be used for templating. The double opening and closing curly braces are used to bind JavaScript expressions; hence, this example binds the value of the `<input>` element to the contents of the `<div>` element.

The only task left to figure out is how a page is defined as an Angular application. Notice the `ng-app` directive on the `<html>` element. This directive marks the `<html>` element and its children as an Angular app. In this case, the app is fittingly named `"app"`.

Finally, notice the two `<script>` tags near the end of the `<body>`. The first script imports the Angular codebase, while the second script defines an Angular module based on our HTML using the `angular.module()` method. The first argument to `module()` is the name of the module, and must match the value of an `ng-app` directive. The second argument to `module()` is an array of modules that the current module imports. In this case, our simple module does not have any dependencies. `module()` returns the newly created module. Note that, ideally, the JavaScript code

would be separated out into another file. For the purposes of this basic example, it
has been left in the HTML.

```html
<!DOCTYPE html>
<html lang="en" ng-app="app" class="no-js">
  <head>
    <meta charset="utf-8">
    <meta http-equiv="X-UA-Compatible" content="IE=edge">
    <title>Data Binding Example</title>
  </head>
  <body>
    <input ng-model="example" />
    <div>
      {{example}}
    </div>
    <script src="//ajax.googleapis.com/ajax/libs/angularjs/1.2.23/
➥angular.min.js">
    </script>
    <script>
      'use strict';
      var app = angular.module('app', []);
    </script>
  </body>
</html>
```

Listing 15-3. An example Angular application that utilizes data binding

An example of our application in action is shown in Figure 15.2. In this example,
the text "Wow such binding!" has been entered in the text box. At the same time,
the contents of the <div> are updated. This feature is much more impressive to
watch in real time, so we encourage you to implement this example on your own.

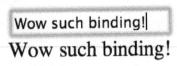

Figure 15.2. Data binding in action

Of course, this is a trivial example. It does not define any controllers, custom directives, routes, or anything else commonly used in Angular applications. These features
will be explored in more detail in the coming chapters.

Summary

This chapter has introduced the AngularJS ecosystem, as well as some of the related topics, such as MVC architectures and single-page applications. It has shown you how to add Angular to a web page, as well as build it from source. In the next few chapters, we'll continue our dive into Angular by exploring the concepts of data binding, directives, controllers, and routing in detail. After we've thoroughly explored the Angular framework, we'll add a front end to our example Human Resources application.

Chapter **16**

Data Binding

In programming, **data binding** is the automatic synchronization of data is between a program's data layer and the associated view layer. Think back to some of the database code in this book. We would execute a query in the database, collect the result in a variable, and then send the JSON to the requesting client. If we take this one more logical step, that JSON would be used by the display layer to show the database results to the user. This can be thought of as one-way data binding; the data from the database is *bound* to the view we display to the user. For our purposes, our application is going to be a web page and the view is going to be HTML.

One of the marquee features of Angular is the built-in **two-way data binding system**. This allows Angular developers to create rich, interactive web applications with very little UI code. (In fact, later on in the chapter, Listing 16-1 will provide a non-trivial interface with zero JavaScript.) In this chapter, we're going to discuss one- and two-way data binding, and walk through some Angular code examples to demonstrate leveraging this powerful feature.

One-Way Data Binding

One-way data binding is useful in specific applications. Suppose you had a web page that was an online storefront. The HTML would only require the data from the database once before displaying the page. After the initial load, the user is unable to interact or change the data in the database, only observe it through the HTML. One-way data binding is much easier to implement and requires less code complexity. Most one-way data binding can be achieved without any support from a framework; however, most applications accept input from users and the view layer needs to update based on users' interactions.

There are several limitations to one-way data binding. Once the data is loaded and the view rendered, the view is static. Even if the model changes five minutes later—via an Ajax call, for example—the view won't automatically update. The developer would have to reset the data model, clear the HTML representing the data, and recreate the changed parts of the DOM to update the view. This might sound like minimal work for a very small web application, but once there are multiple pages with different user controls and input mechanisms, managing those data changes by hand can quickly spiral into a maintenance and debugging nightmare.

So far, we have only been focusing on data moving in one direction, from the server to the view. Just as often, data needs to move from the user back to the server, and keep the view up to date during data flow. Suppose you were using a simple to-do web application. When you add a new task, you expect both the view and the database on the server to update. With one-way data binding, all of those updates are up to the developer to make happen. The workflow would go like this:

1. The user would fill out a small form to add a new task and press an **Add** button.

2. The JavaScript array in the memory would be updated to include the new object.

3. The view would need to be updated to include the new item in the array.

4. The JavaScript object would be sent to the web server to update the database.

The developer would be responsible for keeping data flowing correctly through this workflow and handling any errors that might occur. So far, we've only been focusing on adding, but what about deleting? That would be even harder because there needs to be an artificially created relationship between the view and underlying object model. Remember, HTML is just a string; it has no knowledge about the in-memory JavaScript objects to which it is bound.

To achieve this level of interactivity, developers must rely heavily on DOM events and DOM manipulation. Back to our storefront example, what if the user wanted to change the currencydisplay from USD to EUR? There would need to be an event listener for the change event on the drop-down. There also needs to be some edge-case conditional logic for the first time the page loaded. This has led to the community term "jQuery spaghetti" code. It's used when many event handlers and DOM manipulations have to be written by hand using jQuery to create a responsive user interface.

Ideally, web developers would have access to a framework that lets them operate on native JavaScript objects with the view automatically updating as the model changes. In addition, changes to the view would also make updates to the object to which it is bound. Then developers could focus on writing business logic and excellent user interfaces. Two-way data binding empowers web developers to do exactly that.

Two-Way Data Binding

Two-way data binding solves the data model and view syncing problem. It allows the developer to manipulate the bound data directly and not be concerned with keeping the DOM in sync. For example, suppose you had a sign-up form with two inputs for first and last name. With two-way data binding, as the user enters information, the underlying data model stays in sync with the view. There's no need for any `onChange` or `onKeyUp` events to keep the data layer in sync with the view.

Suppose that one of the requirements for the user screen was a "full name" display, with first name and last name concatenated together. With two-way data binding, the developer can bind the result of `firstName` + `lastName` to a `span` tag. The focus can then solely be on building that computed value without having to worry about keeping the DOM up to date if either of the name parts change.

As stated, one of the main features of Angular is two-way data binding. It provides a framework to bind simple and complex values, collections, functions, and Angular expressions. It also comes with many built-in functions that can be combined with bound values to control data display, which is useful for locale-aware formatting.

A Simple Example

The best way to demonstrate the usefulness of two-way data binding is with an example. Listing 16-1 is a simple sign-up form that hooks into the Angular data binding system.

```
<!DOCTYPE html>
<html lang="en" ng-app>
  <body>
    <input type="text" ng-model="firstName" placeholder="first name"
➡>
    <input type="text" ng-model="lastName" placeholder="last name">
    <h2>Gender {{gender}}</h2>
    <input type="radio" ng-model="gender" value="male"
➡ng-click="style={color:'yellow'}">Male
    <input type="radio" ng-model="gender" value="female"
➡ng-click="style={color:'orange'}">Female
    <br />
    <h2 ng-style=style>Welcome {{firstName + ' ' + lastName}}</h2>
    <button ng-disabled="!(firstName.length && lastName.length)"
➡ng-click="signup()">Sign Up</button>
    <script src="//ajax.googleapis.com/ajax/libs/angularjs/1.2.16/
➡angular.js"></script>
  </body>
</html>
```

Listing 16-1. Simple Angular data binding

This small amount of HTML gives us a remarkable amount of functionality, and we're yet to write any JavaScript. What you should first notice is that this is just regular HTML. Angular does not introduce a new markup language or foreign syntax to memorize—just plain HTML with attributes. Let's examine the markup line by line and explain how to use some of these HTML attributes.

The Meaning of ng

In Angular applications, you'll see attributes or tags that start with "ng". This alerts you to the attribute or tag being Angular-specific, and will let you look up the documentation on the Angular website.

Markup Explanation

The first feature you should notice is the ng-app attribute on the html tag. This attribute is particularly important, yet often overlooked. You only ever need this once for the whole Angular application. The ng-app attribute is used to instruct Angular that the html element is the root element for this application. In general, you'll see this attribute on the html or body tags. If you forget to useit, none of the Angular code will execute.

The two text box inputs have ng-model attributes attached to them. ng-model is the specific keyword that establishes the two-way data binding used throughout Angular. The ng-model attribute instructs Angular to bind to the value in the available scope named firstName and lastName.

Throughout the markup, you can see values referenced with {someValue}. This is how you display/use the data-bound values. If you interact with the view, you'll see the h2 elements dynamically update as firstName, lastName, and gender change. Notice how even though gender is bound to a radio button list, the binding still works correctly. The bound value is correctly updated when you toggle the various radio options.

Another new concept is the ng-click directive. This is one way to attach click events to DOM nodes using Angular. You'll notice, though, that the value of ng-click isn't true JavaScript; it's what is known as an Angular expression.[1] An Angular expression is a JavaScript-like code snippet with a few important differences. First, the context used in an Angular expression is a scope object, rather than the global window object. Second, developers can enjoy more defensive handling when working with values that may be null or undefined. Last of all, expressions lack any notion of control flow. Many of the Angular attributes can be set to expressions as well as values, so it's worth understanding how to use them.

When clicking on each of the radio buttons, we're setting the style value based on the selection. The style value is used with the ng-stlye directive to control how the h2 name tag is displayed. This is a simple demonstration on how setting different values can control the view layer. A second feature used in the h2 name tag displays the result of an Angular expression. Using an expression, we can show the computed

---

[1] https://docs.angularjs.org/guide/expression

result of `firstName` plus `lastName` without any additional logic to keep the display in sync when either value changes.

Finally, we use one more Angular directive on the `button` tag: `ng-disabled`. This directive toggles the enabled state of the element based on an expression. In this example, the button stays disabled until the user has entered a first and last name. We also have another `ng-click` attribute set to `signup()`. This presently does nothing, but we'll leave it in for the next example later in the chapter.

Summary

Reviewing Listing 16-1 should illustrate a few critical points about two-way data binding with Angular. We were able to achieve a high degree of front-end polish without writing any JavaScript (yet). To achieve this level of responsiveness using only jQuery or vanilla JavaScript would be a significant effort. There would need to be several event handlers created to respond to the text and radio button changes, another few lines of code to manage the color changes of the `h2` tags, and one or two functions for toggling the enabled state of the **submit** button. Two-way data binding lets us focus more on data and data interactions, instead of ensuring that the DOM is in sync with our data layer.

Technical Overview

Let's go a little deeper into exactly *how* data binding works in Angular. Fundamentally, data binding consists of functions associated with a scope object (also called an Angular context). A **scope object** is a JavaScript object created with an Angular constructor that is used as the model for HTML markup. In a complete Angular application, the scope object is instantiated via a controller and made available to the view, but in Listing 16-1 we are using the global scope that is automatically created by the framework. The rules governing scope objects work similarly to native JavaScript scope rules. For example, if a page has several nested Angular scope objects, the inner object can see and access the outer scope object that contains it.

$watch

Any time you bind data to the UI, Angular automatically creates a new `$watch` entry in what is known as the `$watch` list. Think of a `$watch` as a very small event emitter that can send and receive events when the underlying data model or UI changes.

There is one $watch entry automatically created for every property that's bound in the UI. The $watch value and $watch list are used in the next topic, the digest loop.

Digest Loop

Any time there is a browser event (click, change, key press) that should be handled by the related Angular context, the **digest loop** will run. This means that the loop will run many, many times. When a user enters a single **A** into the firstName input box, the digest loop runs. The digest loop is relatively simple in its functionality. It iterates over every item in the $watch list and goes through a few simple steps. First, it interrogates the object for the current value. Then it asks the value if it has changed since the last time the digest loop ran. If any of the $watch items report a change, another digest loop is run. The loop continues to run until none of the $watch items report a change. At this point, the DOM is updated with all of the changes to the object layer.

When talking about the digest loop, it's important to remember that JavaScript is single-threaded. So when the digest loop starts, Angular has control of the thread, which means that during the loop user input is temporarily blocked. This explanation of how two-way data binding works has been drastically simplified for the scope of this book. Most of the time, there will be no need to understand the nuts and bolts of how data binding works, only how to use it.

Simple Controllers

Listing 16-1 demonstrates some of the power of two-way data binding using Angular; however, no real application is built that way. Angular is an MVC framework at heart and Listing 16-1 only really has a view. We are going to rewrite this example and introduce some new concepts that will form some of the building blocks for the rest of the Angular chapters.

In Listing 16-1, you'll notice that no JavaScript was written. But suppose we wanted the click button to make an Ajax request to a server. Currently, there is nowhere for this code to go. That's because Angular applications are supposed to have controllers behind them.

For now, let's keep the exact HTML as Listing 16-1 and add the JavaScript code needed to make a functional controller:

```
var app = angular.module('app', []);
app.controller('main', ['$scope', function($scope) {
  $scope.firstName = $scope.lastName = undefined;
  $scope.gender = 'female';
  $scope.style = {color:'orange'};

  $scope.signup = function () {
    var person = {
      first: $scope.firstName,
      last: $scope.lastName,
      gender: $scope.gender
    }
    console.log(person);
  };
}]);
```

Listing 16-2. A simple controller

Before trying to wire this JavaScript into the HTML in Listing 16-1, you'll need to make two tiny changes to the HTML. First, change ng-app to ng-app=app on the html tag. This instructs Angular that the application we are building is named app, and it needs to instantiate a new app object. The second HTML change is to add ng-controller="main" to the body tag. This instructs Angular that all the elements inside the body tag should use the main controller as their scope context. Now you can copy the code in Listing 16-2 into the HTML file from Listing 16-1 and the application should continue to function. You'll know you have everything set up if the default value of gender is "female" and information is logged to the console when you click **Sign Up**.

Functionally, everything remains the same compared to Listing 16-1; however, by adding in a controller, we now have more control over the scope object being used inside the body tag. The data binding should still function exactly as it did in Listing 16-1. The $scope argument passed into the function is the context object for this controller. When data and functions are bound to this controller, they have a reference to this $scope object. The next chapter will focus solely on working with controllers, so don't worry if you feel a little confused. For now, just know that it creates a new Angular context instead of using the global one, and we have much more control over how it functions. The controller also provides a place to write our business logic.

Data Binding with Lists

One of the best features of working with data binding is the relative ease in working with lists. Listing 16-3 is a simple list viewer and editor:

```
<html lang="en" ng-app="app">
  <body ng-controller="main">
    <input type="text" ng-model="firstName" placeholder="first
name">
    <input type="text" ng-model="lastName" placeholder="first name">
    <button ng-disabled="!(firstName.length && lastName.length)"
ng-click="add()">Add</button>
    <table>
      <tr ng-repeat="p in presidents">
        <td>{{p.first}}</td>
        <td>{{p.last}}</td>
        <td><button ng-click="$parent.remove(p)">Remove</button>
</td>
      </tr>
    </table>
    <script src="//ajax.googleapis.com/ajax/libs/angularjs/1.2.16/
angular.js"></script>
    <script>
        var app = angular.module('app', []);
        app.controller('main', ['$scope', function($scope) {
          $scope.firstName = $scope.lastName = '';

          $scope.presidents = [{
            first: 'Abraham',
            last: 'Lincoln'
          }, {
            first: 'Andrew',
            last: 'Johnson'
          }, {
            first: 'Ulysses',
            last: 'Grant'
          }];

          $scope.add = function () {
            $scope.presidents.push({
              first: $scope.firstName,
              last: $scope.lastName
            });
```

```
            $scope.firstName = $scope.lastName = '';
        };

        $scope.remove = function(president) {
            $scope.presidents.splice($scope.presidents.indexOf
➥(president), 1);
        }
      }]);
    </script>
  </body>
</html>
```

Listing 16-3. Data binding with lists example

Just like the controller in Listing 16-2, there is a `$scope` object passed into the controller function. In this example, we once again attach `firstName` and `lastName`. We also attach a list of presidents and two functions that will be used as event handlers. Remember, the `$scope` object is used by the view to bind to the values and functions in this controller's context.

This example will display a table of presidents with buttons to delete them from the list. The first new feature used is the `ng-repeat` directive. The HTML and all the children inside of it will be repeated for every item in the `presidents` collection of the Angular context, which is an array in our controller. There are a few other tasks you can achieve with `ng-repeat` and we encourage you to read more about it in the Angular documentation[2].

Another new feature is `$parent.remove`. Remember, every DOM element inside the the Angular application has a scope associated with it. Inside a `ng-repeat` directive, the scope is the current item in the collection. In this example, it's an object with a first and last name. The `remove` function is up one scope level on the `main` controller. You'll recall that scopes are nested just like variables in standard JavaScript. `$parent` is a pointer to the immediate parent scope, which is the `main` controller object and has the `remove` function defined. We want to pass p, the current item in the collection, into the `remove` function so that the event handler knows which object to remove from the bound collection.

---

[2] https://docs.angularjs.org/api/ng/directive/ngRepeat

The `add` event handler creates a new object with `first` and `last` keys and then adds that object to the `presidents` collection. As soon as this happens, the `$digest` loop starts up, notices that the `presidents` collection has changes, and redraws the new items. This adds a single row to the DOM table. Removing items is just as easy as adding. In the markup, we indicated that we wanted to pass the current item into `remove`. Then we use some standard array methods to locate the item and then `splice` is out of the array. This triggers another `$digest` loop, and the table is redrawn to match the contents of the array. If you want to play with a few more examples, try sorting the list of presidents and see how easy it is to keep the DOM in sync with the sorting.

To duplicate this level of functionality using only JavaScript and jQuery would require many more lines of code, and would be very brittle. Adding sorting, for example, would be a nontrivial change. The developer would have to either sort the data layer and redraw the DOM by hand, or sort the DOM and update the data layer by hand. Both of these approaches would be susceptible to bugs and quickly become difficult to maintain. Using Angular's two-way data binding system, working with lists is easy and adding new features is a piece of cake. Speaking of food, think of how many lines of jQuery spaghetti code you can now replace in your own projects!

Summary

In this chapter, we scratched the surface of two-way data binding using Angular. Working with the DOM and keeping it up to date with data can be a frustrating and dull task. Using a framework that supports two-way data binding lets developers focus on what they are good at: working with and manipulating data. The DOM just comes along for the ride, so to speak. Changes to the underlying object model automatically update the bound DOM objects.

We gave a high-level overview of how data binding works in Angular by discussing how the `$digest` loop iterates over all the `$watch` objects to determine what values have changed since the last time the loop ran. Remember, because JavaScript is single-threaded, the `$digest` loop phase takes control away from the browser and blocks user input. After Angular determines what has changed in the context and after refreshing the DOM, the browser regains control.

We created a more involved example of a very common use case: list management. Our example demonstrated how to add and remove items to a list using a controller.

Writing that same application without a data-driven framework would have been a very tedious exercise. The list example, we trust, drove home the ability to operate at the data layer, and the need to just let the DOM update automatically without any developer interaction.

We also introduced the concept of an Angular controller and explained why we use them. They are the way to control the context of a specific part of the DOM, rather than by using the global Angular context. As mentioned, a future chapter is dedicated to controllers; we only gave a high-level overview of what was required to make the example work.

17

Angular Directives

This chapter continues our exploration of Angular's core principles. Specifically, this chapter focuses on directives, which are what allow Angular to extend HTML syntax. Angular ships with a number of built-in directives, but developers can also define custom directives to suit their application's needs. This chapter will explain how to use directives, as well as how you can create your own.

Overview

Let's begin by defining exactly what is a **directive**. According to the official documentation:[1]

> At a high level, directives are markers on a DOM element (such as an attribute, element name, comment or CSS class) that tell AngularJS's **HTML compiler** (`$compile`) to attach a specified behavior to that DOM element or even transform the DOM element and its children.

---

[1] https://docs.angularjs.org/guide/directive

In other words, directives are additional pieces of markup that Angular interprets to extend the default behavior of HTML. Directives can be specified as custom HTML elements, attributes, classes, or comments. For example, given a fictional directive named ngFoo, Listing 17-1 shows how it can be used as an element, attribute, class, and comment:

```
<ng-foo>Here is it used as an element</ng-foo>

<div ng-foo="Here is it used as an attribute"></div>

<div class="ng-foo">Here it is used as a class</div>

<!-- Here it is used as a comment -->
<!-- directive:ng-foo -->
```

Listing 17-1. An example directive used as an element, attribute, class, and comment.

There are a number of points to make about this example. First, our fictional directive can be used as an element, attribute, class, or comment, but in reality, not all directives can be used in each way. For example, the ngRepeat directive, which is used to loop items in a collection, can only be used as an attribute. This topic will be covered in more detail later in the chapter. It's also worth mentioning that best practice dictates that directives should be used as elements and attributes while avoiding classes and comments, which exist to support legacy applications.

The next point worth mentioning in Listing 17-1 is the way ngFoo is referenced in HTML. By convention, Angular directives are named using camelCasing; however, when used in HTML, directives are written in all lowercase letters with dashes used to separate words. When Angular processes directives embedded in HTML, it normalizes names using the following steps:

1. Strip x- and data- from the name.
2. Convert :, -, or _ delimited names to camel case.

This means that ngRepeat can be written as ng-repeat, x-ng-repeat, data-ng-repeat, ng:repeat, and ng_repeat. The simple dash-delimited form (ng-repeat) is the preferred format, but the data- prefixed version is acceptable if you're using an HTML validation tool. The other versions should be avoided, and exist primarily for legacy reasons.

You'll also notice that Angular prefixes its official directives with ng. When creating custom directives, you should prefix your names as well; however, you should avoid using ng, as it could potentially conflict with an Angular directive in the future. For example, if you were writing a directive named match for a SitePoint product, you might consider naming it spMatch.

An Example Using Common Directives

Next, we're going to look at an Angular application, shown in Listing 17-2, containing a few common directives. The first is ngApp,[2] which is attached to the html element as ng-app. ngApp is used to create a new Angular application, and should be attached to the root element of the application. ngApp can only be used once per HTML document. In this example, the Angular application is named app.

The next directive used in Listing 17-2 is ngController. As you've already learned, Angular supports the MVC approach to application design. ngController allows you to specify a controller for a specific section of an application. In Listing 17-2, a controller named ExampleCtrl is attached to the body element. The functionality of ExampleCtrl is found in the JavaScript near the bottom of the example. This particular controller only adds a variable named people to the model (referred to as $scope in the controller code).

```
<!DOCTYPE html>
<html lang="en" ng-app="app">
  <head>
    <meta charset="utf-8">
    <title>Angular Directives</title>
  </head>
  <body ng-controller="ExampleCtrl">
    <div ng-repeat="person in people">
      {{person.firstName}} {{person.lastName}}
    </div>
    <script src="//ajax.googleapis.com/ajax/libs/angularjs/1.2.25/
➥angular.js">
    </script>
    <script>
      'use strict';
      var app = angular.module('app', []);
```

---

[2] https://docs.angularjs.org/api/ng/directive/ngApp

```
app.controller('ExampleCtrl', ['$scope', function($scope) {
  $scope.people = [
    {
      firstName: 'Colin',
      lastName: 'Ihrig'
    },
    {
      firstName: 'Adam',
      lastName: 'Bretz'
    }
  ];
}]);
    </script>
  </body>
</html>
```

Listing 17-2. An example Angular application containing several directives

The final directive used in Listing 17-2 is ngRepeat. ngRepeat is used to iterate over the elements of a collection. In this case, ng-repeat="person in people" loops over all the members of the people in the model. During each iteration, the current element is available via the person loop variable. In this example, we're simply displaying the first and last name of each person. The output of running Listing 17-2 is shown in Figure 17.1. The bottom panel of the figure also shows how ngRepeat expands people.

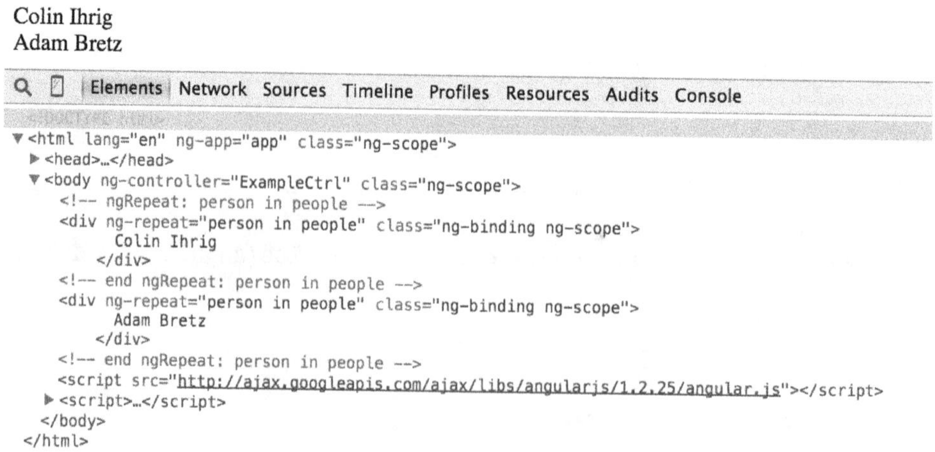

Figure 17.1. Directive example output and generated code

Creating Directives

Angular ships with a number of useful built-in directives, but you will inevitably come across a situation where you need to extend what Angular provides out of the box. Luckily, Angular provides a convenient API for creating directives.

Directives are registered to individual modules using the `directive()` method. `directive()` takes two arguments. The first argument is the normalized directive name (`myDirective` as opposed to `my-directive`). The second argument to `directive()` is a factory function that returns an object telling Angular's HTML compiler, `$compile`, how the directive should behave.

The object returned by the factory function argument is known as a **directive definition object**, and is a plain JavaScript object whose properties define the directive's behavior. The following list explains some of the properties that can be used by a directive definition object:

priority   If multiple directives are defined on a single DOM element, `priority` can be used to specify the order in which they are compiled. Directives with higher `priority` values are compiled first. The compile order of directives with the same `priority` is undefined. The default value is 0.

scope   If this is set to `true`, a new scope will be created for the directive. If `scope` is an object literal, a new isolate scope is created. **Isolate scopes** do not inherit from the parent scope. This is useful when creating reusable components that should not read or modify the parent scope. The properties of an isolate scope object define the local scope as derived from the parent scope. These values can be defined in one of three ways:

- `@` or `@attr` — Binds a local scope property to the value of a DOM attribute. The result is always a string since DOM attributes are strings. As an example, `scope: {name: '@'}` would bind the `name` property to the `name` property in the parent scope. Similarly, `scope: {name: '@otherName'}` would bind `name` to the parent's `otherName` property.

      = or =attr — Sets up bi-directional binding between a local scope property and a parent scope property.

      & or &attr — Provides a way to execute an expression in the context of the parent scope.

controller   A controller constructor function.

transclude   Compiles the content of the element and makes it available to the directive. When `true`, transclude the content of the directive's element. When `'element'`, transclude the directive's element, including any directives on the element with a lower priority.

compile   The `compile()` function is used to transform the template DOM, although it is rarely used. The function takes two arguments, `tElement` and `tAttrs`, and returns either a post-link function or an object with function properties, `pre` and `post`. `tElement` is the element where the directive has been declared. `tAttrs` is a normalized list of attributes declared on the element.

link   `link()` is a function responsible for registering DOM listeners as well as updating the DOM. `link()` is only used if the `compile()` function is not defined. This is where most directive logic resides. `link()` takes five arguments:
- `scope` — the scope to be used by the directive
- `iElement` — the element where the directive is to be used
- `iAttrs` — a normalized list of attributes declared on this element
- `controller` — a controller
- `transcludeFn` — a transclude linking function prebound to the correct transclusion scope

terminal   When `terminal` is true, no lower `priority` directives will be compiled. Directives with the same `priority` are still compiled.

template   Used to specify the HTML generated by the directive. `template` can be an HTML template string or a function that takes two arguments, `tElement` and `tAttrs`, and returns a HTML string. If the function version is used, `tElement` is the element where the directive has been declared. tAttrs is a normalized list of attributes declared on the element.

templateUrl   Similar to the string version of template; however, the string is loaded asynchronously from a file.

restrict   A string containing a subset of the string EACM. If E is present, the directive can be used as an element. If A is included, the directive can be used as an attribute. Similarly, the presence of C or M allow the directive to be used as a class or comment respectively.

An Example Custom Directive

Listing 17-3 revisits the code from Listing 17-2; however, in this example, a custom authorNames directive has been created instead of using the built-in ngRepeat. The first point to notice about the custom directive is that restrict: 'E' is used, meaning that authorNames can only be used as an element. Next, the controller is defined using the controller property (notice that the ngController has been removed from the DOM). Finally, a link() function is used to create a template string, compile it, and replace the new author-names element with the freshly compiled DOM.

```
<!DOCTYPE html>
<html lang="en" ng-app="app">
  <head>
    <meta charset="utf-8">
    <title>Angular Directives</title>
  </head>
  <body>
    <author-names></author-names>
    <script src="//ajax.googleapis.com/ajax/libs/angularjs/1.2.25/
➥angular.js">
    </script>
    <script>
      'use strict';
      var app = angular.module('app', []);

      app.directive('authorNames', function($compile) {
        return {
          restrict: 'E',
          controller: function($scope) {
            $scope.people = [
```

```
              {
                firstName: 'Colin',
                lastName: 'Ihrig'
              },
              {
                firstName: 'Adam',
                lastName: 'Bretz'
              }
            ];
          },
          link: function(scope, element, attrs,
                    controller, transclude) {
            var template = scope.people.map(function(person) {
            var str = '<div>' + person.firstName +
                      ' ' + person.lastName + '</div>';

              return str;
            }).join('');
            var newElement = $compile(template)(scope);

            element.replaceWith(newElement);
          }
        };
      });
    </script>
  </body>
</html>
```

Listing 17-3. An example Angular application containing a custom directive

Summary

This chapter has explained how Angular's built-in directives work, as well as how you can create your own directives. We haven't covered all of Angular's built-in directives, nor have we covered all the possible options that can be set on a directive definition object. What we have done is cover the major points of directive development and, we hope, armed you with enough information to read through the Angular docs and develop some awesome directives of your own.

Controllers

Controllers create a framework to promote code reusability and testability. They are the basic building blocks of an Angular application. In previous chapters, we covered data binding and directives. We briefly touched on Angular controllers at the end of Chapter 16. In this chapter, we're going to cover controllers in greater detail. We'll discuss what they are and what purpose they serve; we will then cover some syntax issues, best practices, and examples.

Like everything related to Angular, it is important to remember that controllers are just JavaScript functions. These functions are used to create a new Angular (or scope) context and are bound to sections of HTML markup. A controller provides a place to put application and view logic that is specific to a particular set of HTML tags. Keep in mind that a single view can use multiple controllers: the view to controller relationship is not one-to-one. It is also possible to reuse controllers in different views.

Syntax

We've already seen some controllers defined, but let's go over the specific syntax used to define an Angular controller:

```
var app = angular.module('app', []);
app.controller('main', ['$scope', '$http', function($scope, $http) {
  //...
}]);
```

Listing 18-1. A controller stub

The first line creates an Angular module. A module represents a logical unit within an application. It has one or more controllers, services, filters, and directives packaged inside of it. In this example, we are creating a new module called app with angular.module. Here, think of app as the entire Angular application where we'll place all of our controllers. The function signature is the module name, followed by a string array of dependencies.

A dependency is a reference to another module that the current module needs to function correctly. Angular will ensure that every module listed in the dependency list is loaded before creating the app module. In a future chapter on client-side routing, we'll need a few modules loaded before our application module; however, for this simple example we don't need anything beyond the Angular boilerplate, so we pass an empty array.

app.controller lets us add a controller object to app. Similar to the module function, the first argument is the controller name and the second argument is another list of dependencies with a function as the last element in the array. The function is where the logic for the main controller will reside. The first two items in the dependencies list are ones that this controller needs: $scope and $http. $scope is the local scope context that every controller has and $http is an Angular HTTP module used to make HTTP requests for remote resources.

The function signature suggests that inside the controller function, we'll have access to both a $scope and $http variable. Any time a main controller is created, Angular will execute this function with a new $scope object and the $http object because they are listed as dependencies to this controller function. While you can rename the function arguments (for example, s and h), it is generally preferred to keep the function argument and dependency name the same for readability.

There are other ways to declare controllers and specify dependencieswith Angular, but the approach in Listing 18-1 is preferred, as the code will continue to function after minification. In Listing 18-1, we have explicitly alerted Angular to what dependencies this controller needs by calling them out by name. Angular can infer dependencies by name, but that will fail to work after the code is minified. After minification, most variables are reduced to a single character and dependency lookup by name no longer functions.

Dependencies

$scope is a child scope object whose parent is the global application scope. Generally, these are automatically created by Angular when a controller is specified with ng-controller in the HTML. There are way too many properties and functions associated with $scope to cover in this book, so check out the full documentation on the Angular website.[1] $scope has methods attached to it for interacting with the $digest loop, and for creating additional $watch values and mechanisms for sending and receiving events from other Angular objects.

$http[2] is the promise-based module for making HTTP requests. The main function takes a configuration object where you specify the route, method, and payload, as well as many other attributes of an HTTP request. The $http() function returns a promise object that has .then(),.success(), and .error() methods available. We're going to use it in our example to make a request to our Express server to retrieve a list of employees.

Angular has a built-in dependency injection system. If you're unfamiliar with **dependency injection**, it's an easy enough concept. It's a design pattern where dependencies are *injected* into a dependent object (the main controller in this case) when it's created and become part of the client object's state. This separates the client and dependency logic and further decouples the client from the dependency. If you're looking for a more in-depth look at dependency injection, check out the official Angular documentation.[3]

By injecting the $http module into the controller, the controller is not responsible for finding and creating the $http module; instead, $http is passed in as a parameter. We want to make tests as small as possible and test only developer code. Using dependency injection, we can pass a mock $http module that just returns static

---

[1] https://docs.angularjs.org/api/ng/type/$rootScope.Scope
[2] https://docs.angularjs.org/api/ng/service/$http
[3] https://docs.angularjs.org/guide/di

values to the controller. This allows us to just test the controller logic in isolation, taking a server and the Angular $http module completely out of the test.

Expanding on Our Example

Let's fully flesh out Listing 18-1. We want to retrieve a list of employees from our server and display them. We should also be able to add and delete employees from the list with the proper HTTP calls. This example will only focus on the client-side code.

Express Integration

If you've been following along with the code and examples, you should have a functional Express server at this point that we started building in Chapter 13. Place Listing 18-2 in an HTML file in the **public/html** directory and point a browser to that file. This will bring up the example and enable you to interact with it.

When the controller first loads, it makes a GET request using $http back to the Express server to get a list of employees. The /employees route we built in Chapter 13 communicates with the MongoDB instance and returns a list of employees from the database.

The other two routes, POST to /employees and DELETE to /employees/:id gives you a chance to expand on the functionality of the Express server on your own. You'll need to use router.post and router.delete to set up the routes in the Express server. Inside the handler functions, utilize the Employee model to communicate with the Employee collection in the database. Employee.remove is used for deleting and Employee.save for creating new employees. After successfully deleting an employee, respond to the client with the updated employee document collection. Finally, after creating a new employee in the database, respond to the client with the newly created employee document. Looking back at Chapter 8 should provide some helpful hints and examples on how to make these two new routes functional.

```
<html lang="en" ng-app="app">
  <body>
    <div ng-controller="main">
      <input type="text" ng-model="firstName" placeholder="first
➥name">
      <input type="text" ng-model="lastName" placeholder="first
```

```
➥name">
      <button ng-disabled="!(firstName.length && lastName.length)"
➥ng-click="add()">Add</button>
      <table>
        <tr ng-repeat="p in employees">
          <td>{{p.id}}</td>
          <td><span>{{p.first}} {{p.last}}</span></td>
          <td><button ng-click="$parent.remove(p)">Remove</button>
➥</td>
        </tr>
      </table>
    </div>
    <div ng-controller="logger">
      <pre>
        <p ng-repeat="e in events track by $index">{{$index}} -
➥{{e}}</p>
      </pre>
    </div>
    <script src="//ajax.googleapis.com/ajax/libs/angularjs/1.2.16/
➥angular.js"></script>
    <script>
        var app = angular.module('app', []);

        app.controller('main', ['$scope', '$http', '$rootScope',
➥function($scope, $http, $rootScope) {
          $scope.employees = [];
          $scope.firstName = $scope.lastName = '';

          $http.get('/employees').success(function(data) {
            $scope.employees = data;
            $rootScope.$emit('log', 'GET /employees success');
          });

          $scope.add = function () {
            $http.post('/employees', {
              first: $scope.firstName,
              last: $scope.lastName
            }).success(function(data) {
              $scope.employees.push(data);
              $scope.firstName = $scope.lastName = '';
              $rootScope.$emit('log', 'POST /employees success');
            });
          };

          $scope.remove = function(employee) {
```

```
                    $http.delete('/employees/' + employee.id).
➥success(function(data) {
                        $scope.employees = data;
                        $rootScope.$emit('log', 'DELETE /employees success');
                    });
                }
            }]);
            app.controller('logger', ['$scope', '$rootScope',
➥function ($scope, $rootScope) {
                $scope.events = [];

                $rootScope.$on('log', function (event, data) {
                    $scope.events.push(data.trim());
                });
            }]);
        </script>
    </body>
</html>
```

Listing 18-2. A complete controller example

That is a lot of code, so we'll break it down into two parts: JavaScript and HTML.

JavaScript

We start by creating a new Angular module that will house all of our controllers and name it app. You can name the module anything you like, but most examples will use app for the module and variable names. Then we declare the main controller. Basically every controller needs the $scope object, so that is added to the list of dependencies. We are going to make requests to our server, so we'll need the $http module as well. Finally, to facilitate communication between multiple controllers, we include $rootScope. The $rootScope object gives us a direct reference to the global scope object for the entire Angular application.

The controller's first few lines set its initial state. We are going to use employees as the data store for the list of employees. Just like the Express router, $http has convenience methods exposed that map to the most common HTTP verbs. The first task is to retrieve the list of employees from our server and load $scope.employees with that data. To accomplish this, we make a GET request to /employees. In success we set employees equal to the response from the web server, which is an array of employee objects.

Because `employees` is data bound to the view, as soon as its value changes, a new `$digest` loop is triggered, automatically updating the view. Notice that no additional code was required to update the view. Angular's two-way data binding took care of everything, even though we retrieved data from the server asynchronously.

Then we make use of `$rootScope` to emit a custom event. The first argument is the event name and the second argument is the event payload that we want to pass to any clients that may be listening. We want to use the `$rootScope` object because the two controllers we'll be working with are siblings and not nested inside each other.

Next we create the two event handlers for adding and removing items, similar to what was done in Listing 16-3. The big difference is that these methods are mapped back to a web server with a real data store. The `add` method uses `firstName` and `lastName` to create a new object literal that we POST to the web server. On the server we create a new object and insert it into the database. In this example, the server responds with the created object represented by `data`. After a successful creation, we push `data` into the `employees` array. Because of data binding, a new row is automatically added into the HTML table that represents the new employee.

Finally we add `remove` to the `$scope` object. This function makes a DELETE request to the web server and passes an employee ID via a route parameter. The response is the updated list from the database, so we can reset `$scope.employees` to the returned result and let the view layer update.

The second controller, `logger`, is simple by comparison. We are going to use it as an event logger. When a `log` event occurs, we want to add that event into the internal `events` array.

We attach `events` to `$scope` and initialize it as an empty array. `$rootScope.$on` is used to set up a listener for any `log` events that occur on `$rootScope`. The callback function takes two arguments, the first being the Angular event object. It contains information about how the event originated, the source and target scope, and functions to manage event bubbling through different Angular scopes. The second argument is any payload data that is passed in from the emitting function. We are going to push `data`, which will be a simple string, into the `events` array.

We will be able to leverage the `logger` controller throughout the application. The advantage of making a new controller for event logging is that it can be reused on many pages without knowing about any of the other controllers used in the same view.

HTML

The HTML in Listing 18-2 should look familiar by this point, so we are only going to highlight a few of the key changes. First, we introduced a new div to wrap the DOM elements that are related to the `main` controller and set `ng-controller="main"`. This instantiates a new `main` controller and binds the DOM elements to the new instance of `main`. We've also added a second div with `ng-controller="logger"` set. It's important to note that these controllers do *not* have a parent/child relationship. They are direct siblings, which keeps their contexts from being nested.

Note also that we are using the `full-name` directive inside `ng-repeat`. We want to pass the current item in the loop into the directive by setting `person=p`. This creates an isolate scope inside the directive with a reference to the correct p object.

One new thing being used in the HTML is `track by $index` in the logger section of the DOM. The optional `track by` argument to `ng-repeat` tells Angular how to associate collection items to corresponding DOM elements. By default, Angular uses JavaScript identity to make this association, which is generally fine for collections of objects; however, in the `logger` controller we are maintaining a list of strings, and duplicates are unavoidable. Angular dislikes having duplicated DOM elements that would occur using regular JavaScript identity on strings. Tracking the elements with `$index` lets us specify that each unique index in the array should be treated as a unique item.

Listing 18-2 is looking good now. It is a feature-complete user listing web application that provides a nice user experience with code that's easy to read and maintain. We could also add sorting, highlighting, and validation quite effortlessly. But there is still some room for improvement. What if we wanted to retrieve the list of employees in a different controller? Additionally, because we wrote our server to be RESTful, should there be a less code-heavy way to communicate with it?

Simple Service

We are going to refactor our HTTP requests to an Angular service that uses another of Angular's built-in modules: $resource.[4] $resource is a factory object that was specifically designed to interact with RESTful web services. The factory pattern is a well-established design that's meant to solve the issues of working with class constructors. Using a factory, a single function can return different types of objects. We will use $resource to create a simple Employee service that will replace all of our HTTP calls. It will also be able to be used by any other controller that needs access to employee CRUD functions. ngResource is located in a separate script file, so you'll need to update your HTML to include it after Angular. We loaded this script via the Angular CDN at //code.angularjs.org/1.2.16/angular-re-source.js.

One of the benefits of using services is that they are created as singletons, once per ng-app block, and are shared among any controller nested inside it. This means that when we have our service defined, it can be injected like any other dependency and used by any controller in our application. It can also be tested in isolation outside of any controller, providing another level of testability as well. For a complete discussion on the different types of factory objects, please refer to the Angular documentation.[5]

```
var app = angular.module('app', ['ngResource']);
app.factory('EmployeeService', ['$resource', function($resource) {
  return $resource('/employees/:employeeId', {}, {
    get: {
      isArray: true
    },
    delete: {
      isArray: true,
      method: 'DELETE'
    },
    post: {
      method: 'POST',
```

---

[4] https://docs.angularjs.org/api/ngResource/service/$resource
[5] https://docs.angularjs.org/guide/providers

```
    }
  });
}]);
```

Listing 18-3. Creating the `Employee` service

In Listing 18-3, we are creating the `app` module and specifying that `ngResource` is now a dependency for this module. `ngResource` makes the `$resource` dependency available to any dependency list inside `app`. `$resource` is the object needed to create our employee service. The second line is the exact same syntax as creating a controller. The `$resource` dependency is referring to the `ngResource` module installed into the global `app` module.

You'll notice that the majority of the `Employee` service is just a configuration object. The full particulars of everything you can configure with this object is outside the scope of the book, but the Angular site has all the documentation.[6] Effectively, we've created a RESTful connector to our server using the `/employee/:employeeId` resource. We've configured the `get` action to return an array, and `delete` has also been configured to return an array and use the DELETE HTTP method. Finally, we've included a `post` action that issues a POST request to the server.

These settings are specifically designed to work with the routes outlined in the Express integration section. If your implementation deviates from our suggested course, you'll need to update the settings for your `EmployeeService` to match your implementation of the Express routes.

Using EmployeeService

Finally, in Listing 18-4, we will replace `$http` with our new `EmployeeService`:

```
app.controller('main', ['$scope', 'EmployeeService', '$rootScope',
➥function($scope, EmployeeService, $rootScope) {
  EmployeeService.get(function (data) {
    $scope.employees = data;
  });

  $scope.add = function () {
    EmployeeService.post({
```

---

[6] https://docs.angularjs.org/api/ngResource/service/$resource

```
      first: $scope.firstName,
      last: $scope.lastName
    }, function (data) {
      $scope.employees.push(data);
    });
  };

  $scope.remove = function(employee) {
    EmployeeService.delete({
      employeeId: employee.id
    }, function (data) {
      $scope.employees = data;
    });
  }
}]);
```

Listing 18-4. Using `EmployeeService`

We have removed some code from the original `main` controller to focus solely on integrating `EmployeeService`. `EmployeeService` can now be `required` into the `main` controller exactly like any of the built-in Angular modules. We have replaced `$http` in the dependencies list, as well as in the controller function signature.

These code changes should not impact the application functionality. They just clean up the server interactions by removing all the `$http` boilerplate code. They also encapsulate the employee server operations in a single module, which can be used in many places and tested in isolation outside of a controller.

Summary

In this chapter, we've discussed Angular controllers, which are responsible for communicating back and forth with the view. A controller creates a new context that is a child of the parent scope. We discussed the preferred way to declare a controller and how to specify different dependencies the controller needs. We talked about one of the built-in Angular modules, `$http`, and demonstrated how to use it to make requests to our existing Express server.

Next, we wrote a complete example in Listing 18-2 that employed all the Angular topics covered so far. This includes directives, controllers, the `$http` module, event handling, and controller-to-controller communication.

Finally, we did some refactoring of Listing 18-2 by writing our first service. This enabled us to remove all of the `$http` boilerplate and replace it with a configuration-centric `$resource` module. We also talked about injecting this module into our controllers.

Client-side Routing

In Chapter 18, we demonstrated how to make Ajax requests to our Express server and load the results into `$scope` to display the results. That's great for a single-page website, but most applications span more than a single page. In Listing 18-2, what if we wanted to add a new screen that could be used to edit an employee? The application needs to change pages and display a new view, but we want to use the benefits of an Ajax request and not lose all of our JavaScript state and static files in the browser's memory. We also want that page to be bookmarkable, so the page has to be stateless.

This is where client-side routing really shines. Client-side routing allows developers to create standard anchor tags throughout the HTML that will be handled by the Angular router. The Angular router intercepts these links before they are sent to the web server and runs them through a client-side routing table, responding with a new page of content. The new page can have its own Angular controller and completely new block of HTML. To the user, it appears exactly the same as traditional navigation, except the change is almost instant.

In this chapter, we are going to expand Listing 18-3 and move it one step closer to our complete human resources application. We are going to use the list view from

Listing 18-3 and add an edit view as well. Each view will be stored in a discrete HTML file. We'll also use a "layout" style HTML page, which will act as the static part of the site and provide a "window" area where the client-side routing changes will occur.

Getting Started with `ngRoute`

Routing in Angular has changed a few times during the development cycle. The module needed used to come packaged in the Angular runtime; however, the Angular team have since broken `ngRoute` out into a standalone file. The primary reason for this was to reduce the download size of Angular web applications if there's no requirement for the routing module. Installing the `ngRoute` module exposes both `$routeProvider` and `$routeParams` dependencies to controllers and configuration blocks. We'll cover both of these dependencies in more detail in the code example part of this chapter. Just like `ngResource`, we recommend using the Angular CDN for this example. The version we'll be using can be found at `//code.angularjs.org/1.2.16/angular-route.js`.

Application Overview

In this section, we're going upgrade our existing application with client-side routing. We want to display a list of users and some information about each of them. Then we want to provide an edit button that takes the user to a new page and displays an edit UI with which the user can interact. For simplicity's sake, we'll skip implementing the save functionality.

First, we'll need three HTML files: **index.html**, **edit.html**, and **view.html**. Remember, `app.use(express.static(__dirname + '/public'));` creates a static file server that looks in the **/public** directory for files. Create these files under **public** so that the Express static middleware will serve them directly from the hard drive. After creating the files, verify that the web server can properly send them to the browser.

Second, we want to create a place for our JavaScript code. For this example, we're going to use an external JavaScript file instead of inline `<script>` tags as in some of our other examples. Create **webapp.js** under **/public/scripts** to keep the script files separate from the views. **webapp.js** is where all the JavaScript code for this example will be housed.

Code

First, let's look at **index.html** to see how we're going to structure the rest of the application:

```html
<html lang="en" ng-app="app">
  <body>
    <h1>Your Human Resource Application</h1>
    <ng-view></ng-view>
  </body>
  <script src="//ajax.googleapis.com/ajax/libs/angularjs/1.2.16/
➥angular.js"></script>
  <script src="//code.angularjs.org/1.2.16/angular-route.js">
➥</script>
  <script src="//code.angularjs.org/1.2.16/angular-resource.js">
➥</script>
  <script src="scripts/webapp.js"></script>
</html>
```

Listing 19-1. The **index.html** file

Listing 19-1 will serve as the static portion of the application. We have script tags to load Angular, the Angular router (`ngRoute`), and Angular resource (`ngResource`). Finally, we add a reference to our own **webapp.js** script file. You should be familiar with `ng-app` at this point; however, the `ng-view` is a new element in our toolbox of Angular directives.

ng-view is a new element that's exposed by `ngRoute` because they are used together. It's a placeholder for where the contents of a rendered HTML file will reside inside the markup. Every time the current route changes, the content inside `ng-view` changes according to the configuration of the route. This will make some sense when we talk more about the routing.

 Why Are All the Scripts in index.html?

All the scripts we need are located in **index.html**. This is so they stay loaded throughout the life cycle of the application. If we put them inside either **view.html** or **edit.html**, they would need to be downloaded every time the route changed. If we had some CSS, we'd also want to include that in **index.html** as well.

Router

These are the first few lines of **webapp.js**. We'll continue to append code to this example for the rest of this chapter:

```
var app = angular.module('app', ['ngRoute', 'ngResource']);

app.config(['$routeProvider', function($routeProvider) {

  $routeProvider
    .when('/view', {
      templateUrl: 'view.html',
      controller: 'view'
    })
    .when('/edit/:employeeId', {
      templateUrl: 'edit.html',
      controller: 'edit'
    })
    .otherwise({
      redirectTo: '/'
    });
}]);
```

Listing 19-2. The Angular Router

The first line creates our `app` module and installs `ngRoute` and `ngResource`. We used `ngResource` in Listing 18-3, so that should be familiar to you. As previously noted, `ngRoute` gives us access to the `$routeProvider` dependency. `$routeProvider` is the object we'll use to set up client-side routing.

First, a word about `app.config`. Angular modules, such as `app`, can have many configuration blocks via `.config` and `.run`. At a high level, both these methods are used to run configuration code during different phases of application bootstrapping. The Angular documentation sums up the different block types as follows:[1]

1. Configuration blocks (`.config`) — get executed during the provider registrations and configuration phase. Only providers and constants can be injected into configuration blocks. This is to prevent accidental instantiation of services before they have been fully configured.

---

[1] https://docs.angularjs.org/guide/module

2. Run blocks (`.run`) — get executed after the injector is created and are used to kickstart the application. Only instances and constants can be injected into run blocks. This is to prevent further system configuration during application run time.

In Listing 19-2, we're using `.config` because we want to fully configure `$routeProvider` before the application starts. This makes sense because without the client-side routing being completely set up before the application starts, navigation would be broken, rendering the entire site useless. By tapping into the Angular bootstrap process, we can be sure that our configuration code blocks (`app.config`) will run before we receive any user input. This makes `.config` blocks the perfect place to store code that runs once before the application starts.

The `$routeProvider` code should be fairly easy to read. Each `.when` call represents a different URL in the browser. The second argument contains the options for the router to use: `templateUrl` and `controller`. `templateUrl` instructs the router of the location from which the template for the associated URL can be loaded. Note the existence of `":employeeId"` in the first parameter to `.when`. The Angular router uses the same notation for route parameters as Express.

Programmatically setting the controller for a view can be helpful if you want to use the same view but different controllers for two routes. You can keep `ng-controller` in each of the views if you wish, but we feel it's better to declare `controller` here and make the views more controller-agnostic.

Routing Life Cycle Example

To really appreciate how powerful client-side routing is, let's walk through an example from request to response. If you were to enter `index.html#/view` into a browser, the Angular router would examine the incoming request and try to match a route defined in the routing table. If it finds one, it will make an Ajax request to `templateUrl` and instantiate a new controller based on the `controller` option, rendering that into the `ng-view` directive. If there are multiple matches for a route, the last match is the one whose code is executed. If the route starts with `index.html#` but there's no match for any configured route, the `.otherwise` block will execute and send the request back to `/`. By default, the Angular router will try to intercept routes that have `#` in them. Routes without `#` will be normal requests and go through the web server router.

Service and Controllers

Most of this code should be familiar if you've read Chapter 18:

```
app.factory('EmployeeService', ['$resource', function($resource) {
  return $resource('/employees/:employeeId', {}, {
    list: {
      isArray: true
    },
    get: {
      isArray: false
    }
  });
}]);

app.controller('view', ['$scope', 'EmployeeService',
➥function($scope, EmployeeService) {
  $scope.employees = [];
  $scope.firstName = $scope.lastName = '';

  EmployeeService.list(function (data) {
    $scope.employees = data;
  });
}]);

app.controller('edit', ['$scope', 'EmployeeService','$routeParams',
➥ function($scope, EmployeeService, $routeParams) {
  $scope.employee = {};

  EmployeeService.get({
    employeeId: $routeParams.employeeId
  }, function (data) {
    $scope.employee = data;
  });
}]);
```

Listing 19-3. Service and Controllers

We have slightly tweaked EmployeeService in Listing 19-3 from its appearance in Listing 18-3. If you recall the discussion about $resource from Chapter 18, most of the code in Listing 19-3 should be recognizable. The first argument to $resource is the route for this resource object, complete with route parameter :employeeId. The second argument isn't used in this example and is an empty object. We are using the third argument to declare what methods will be defined in the resultant `$resource` we're building.

We've added a `list` action that makes a GET request to `/employees/:employeeId`. However, when we use the `list` method, we're going to omit the `employeeId` because we are treating `list` as the full list of employees. If a route parameter is omitted, it is treated as an empty string. While this may be a little confusing, it's how you can use a single object, `EmployeeService`, and interact with all the Express server resources. `isArray` indicates that the result for this request should be an array. The `get` has been changed to no longer be an array because we're going to use that action to retrieve a single employee from the database. When we use the `get` function, we're going to pass an `employeeId` into the function, which will be used when the `EmployeeService` object builds the URI to request from the Express server. So `list` doesn't need an `employeeId` because it's expected to return all the employees, and `get` needs an `employeeId` to return a specific employee.

The `view` and `edit` controllers are very simple. Only a few items are attached to their respective `$scope` values, and just a single call is requiredto retrieve data with `EmployeeService`. The `edit` controller introduces the `$routeParams` dependency. `$routeParams` gives developers a convenient way to extract route parameters from client-side routes, similar to `req.params` on the Express side. This module essentially parses the current browser URL and tries to extract the route parameters for the current route, attaching the values to `$routeParams`. This concept is the same as route parameters in Express, just using slightly different syntax. In this example, it provides an easy way to get the `employeeId` from the browser URL. Without `$routeParams`, you'd need to use a regular expression to get data from the URL.

Views

Finally, to complete this example, we'll build views that work with the Angular router.

view.html

```html
<table>
  <tr ng-repeat="p in employees">
    <td>{{p.id}}</td>
    <td>{{p.first}}</td>
    <td>{{p.last}}</td>
```

```
    <td><a href="#/edit/{{p.id}}">Edit >>> </a></td>
  </tr>
</table>
```

```
                                                                 edit.html
<fieldset>
  <legend>{{employee.first}} {{employee.last}}</legend>
  <input type="text" name="first" ng-model="employee.first">
➥<label for="first">First Name</label>
  <input type="text" name="last" ng-model="employee.last">
➥<label for="last">Last Name</label>
</fieldset>
<a href='#/view'>Back <<< </a>
```

Listing 19-4, Router views

Both of these views should feel familiar. The main details to note are the a tags: notice that href includes the # sign. This alerts the Angular router to intercept this URL and try routing it client side instead of forwarding it to the server. By using the Angular router, we can navigate to different pages in the application simply by decorating URLs with #.

Putting It Together

Once you've made all the changes outlined, start your server and point a browser to index.html#/view to engage the Angular router. It will match on /view, make an Ajax request to view.html, create a view controller, and send the result to the browser. You should see a table of employees with clickable **EDIT** links. Clicking on one of these links starts the routing process all over again. You should see the edit view, and the browser should be pointed to a URL similar to /index.html#/edit/69c3974488bc9fe6. If you refresh the browser, the same employee and view should be displayed. This is what is meant by *bookmarkable*: the display state of the page is transmitted entirely through the URL. If you change the URL to /index.html#/unknown, you'll see the default landing page. The .otherwise option in the router was engaged and sent the request back to the route URL. If you're looking for more of a challenge, update the edit view and EmployeeService to make updating employees functional. Everything you need to make that work has been covered in the last few chapters, so use this as a chance to test your understanding of the topics discussed through to this point.

Summary

In this chapter, we've demonstrated how to set up client-side routing with Angular. It requires the ngRoute module, which gives us access to the dependencies `$routeProvider` and `$routeParams`. `$routeProvider` is used to build the routing table in an application configure block using `.when`, and `.otherwise`. `templateUrl` tells the router to issue a GET request for the named file or resource when there's a matching client-side route. The `controller` option gives us a way to create the correct controller for the related view. This gives developers more flexibility to mix and match controllers instead of using the `ng-controller` directive.

`$routeParams` provides an easy way to extract information out of the URL without having to resort to regular expressions. `ngRoute` also exposed the `ng-view` Angular directive that acts as a target when new views are rendered. It is the part of the site that changes when client-side routes are rendered. Everything outside of that element stays intact when navigating to different client-side routes.

We discussed how the # symbol acts as an indicator for Angular to try to route the current request client side. In our views, we were able to create traditional a tags and set the `href` property to other client-side links without any special configuration. These anchor tags were used to move from page to page without any additional coding. This reduces the amount of maintenance and potential bugs that a custom routing solution could introduce.

Chapter 20

Angular in Our App

Throughout Chapters 6, 9, and 13, we've created a reasonably straightfoward human resources application API using Node, MongoDB, and Express respectively. In this chapter, we're going to create the front end of our application using Angular. The result will be a full-blown MEAN application. This chapter contains a considerable amount of code as it ties the rest of the application together, but we'll do our best to explain it clearly.

All the work done in this chapter will take place in the project's `public` directory. This directory is used to serve static resources such as HTML, CSS, JavaScript, and image files. This is set up in `index.js` by the line in Listing 20-1. For the purposes of this chapter, you should delete the existing contents of the `public` directory. Our final `public` directory structure is shown in Figure 20.1.

```
app.use(express.static(path.join(__dirname, 'public')));
```

Listing 20-1. Configuration of `static` middleware

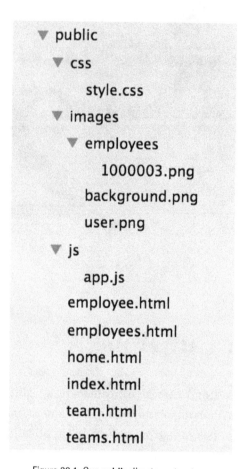

Figure 20.1. Our **public** directory structure

The Home Page

A defining feature of a single-page application is that it has a single HTML page. The contents of our project's home page are shown in Listing 20-2. There are a few points to note in this code. First, the html tag defines an Angular application named app. Second, our application utilizes Bootstrap to simplify the styling process,[1] as well as Font Awesome to provide useful icons.[2]

Inside the body tag, an unordered list is used to provide a menu at the top of the screen, while a div tag is used to display the Angular views. The Angular core lib-

---

[1] http://getbootstrap.com/
[2] http://fortawesome.github.io/Font-Awesome/

rary, as well as the $route and $resource services, are imported using three script tags. Our own CSS file, **style.css** is also imported.

```
<!DOCTYPE html>
<html lang="en" ng-app="app" class="no-js">
  <head>
    <meta charset="utf-8">
    <meta http-equiv="X-UA-Compatible" content="IE=edge">
    <title>HR App</title>
    <meta name="viewport" content="width=device-width,
➥initial-scale=1">
    <link rel="stylesheet" type="text/css" href="//netdna.bootstrap
➥cdn.com/bootswatch/3.1.1/flatly/bootstrap.min.css"/>
    <link rel="stylesheet" type="text/css" href="//netdna.bootstrap
➥cdn.com/font-awesome/4.0.3/css/font-awesome.min.css">
  </head>
  <body class="container">
    <ul class="nav nav-pills">
      <li class="active"><a href="#">Home</a></li>
      <li><a href="#/employees">Employees</a></li>
      <li><a href="#/teams">Teams</a></li>
    </ul>
    <div ng-view></div>
    <script src="//ajax.googleapis.com/ajax/libs/angularjs/1.2.25/
➥angular.js"></script>
    <script src="//code.angularjs.org/1.2.25/angular-route.js">
➥</script>
    <script src="//code.angularjs.org/1.2.25/angular-resource.js">
➥</script>
    <script src="js/app.js"></script>
    <link rel="stylesheet" type="text/css" href="/css/style.css">
  </body>
</html>
```

Listing 20-2. The single, standalone HTML page in the application

CSS and Image Files

We'll only be covering CSS and image files in limited detail, but it's worth pointing out that they exist. The contents of our custom stylesheet, **css/style.css**, are shown in Listing 20-3.

```css
body {
  background: url('/images/background.png');
  background-repeat: repeat;
  min-width: 320px;
}

ul.nav.nav-pills {
  margin: 10px 0;
  background-color: #fff;
}

.employee-list-item .panel-body {
  display: -webkit-box;
  display: -moz-box;
  display: -webkit-flex;
  display: -ms-flexbox;
  display: box;
  display: flex;
}

.employee-list-item .panel-body > * {
  -webkit-align-self: center;
  align-self: center;
  -ms-flex-item-align: center;
}

.employee-list-item .panel-body .btn {
  margin-left: auto;
}

.employee-avatar {
  height: 200px;
  width: 200px;
  border-radius: 6px;
}

span.icon-container {
  display: inline-block;
  text-align: center;
  width: 48px;
  height: 48px;
  border: 1px solid #3498db;
  margin-right: 15px;
  border-radius: 4px;
}
```

```
div.button-bar {
  text-align: left;
  margin-bottom: 10px;
}

div.form-offset {
  padding-top: 15px;
}

.margin-top-reset {
  margin-top: 0;
}

ul.address-lines {
  list-style: none;
  margin: 0;
  padding: 0;
}

ul.address-lines div.address-edit, .margin-bottom-space {
  margin-bottom: 5px;
}

ul.address-lines .in-line-input {
  margin-bottom: 5px;
}
```

Listing 20-3. Custom CSS code found in `style.css`

The **images** directory contains a background image (**background.png**), a default profile picture (**user.png**), and an **employees** directory that contains profile pictures. Currently, only one user has a profile picture in the system. All other users will use the default image.

app.js

The most interesting file in this chapter is **js/app.js**, which contains all our Angular code. This code is shown in Listing 20-4. We begin by declaring our module, named app, which depends on `ngRoute` and `ngResource`. A constant is defined to list abbreviations for each US state. This is going to be used in an employee directive that updates employee information.

The `config()` call is used to inject `$routeProvider` in order to create a client-side router. In this example, the router supports five routes and an `otherwise` case that sends the user back to the home page. The routes related to employees and teams each have a controller that's defined later in the code.

Next, two calls to `factory()` are used to create the `EmployeeService` and `TeamService`. The `factory()` calls depend on `$resource`, which makes interacting with RESTful APIs (such as our Express API) extremely easy.

We then define two custom directives using the `directive()` method. The first directive, `imageFallback`, is used to set a fallback image for an `img` element. This sets a default profile picture for employees without one. The second directive, `editInLine`, is used to edit employee information without going through a different route.

Finally, four controllers are created to use with our team and employee routes. With the exception of `EmployeeCtrl`, these controllers are trivial. The `EmployeeCtrl` controller is used to work with the individual employee view page. This controller needs to perform a number of actions, and relies on the `q` promises library. For example, this controller's `save()` function is used to persist any changes to the MongoDB database. If users begin to edit information but then change their mind, the `cancel()` method is called. This method calls `$route.reload()`, which causes the `$route` service to reload the current route even though the location hasn't changed. This wipes out any changes that had been made.

```
'use strict';
var app = angular.module('app', ['ngRoute', 'ngResource'])
  .constant('config', {
    states: ['AL','AK','AZ','AR','CA','CO','CT','DE','FL','GA','HI',
➡ 'ID','IL','IN','IA','KS','KY','LA','ME','MD','MA','MI','MN','MS',
➡ 'MO','MT','NE','NV','NH','NJ','NM','NY','NC','ND','OH','OK','OR',
➡ 'PA','RI','SC','SD','TN','TX','UT','VT','VA','WA','WV','WI','WY']
  });

app.config(['$routeProvider', function($routeProvider) {
  $routeProvider
    .when('/', {
      templateUrl: 'home.html'
    })
    .when('/employees', {
      templateUrl: 'employees.html',
```

```
      controller: 'EmployeesCtrl'
    })
    .when('/employees/:employeeId', {
      templateUrl: 'employee.html',
      controller: 'EmployeeCtrl'
    })
    .when('/teams', {
      templateUrl: 'teams.html',
      controller: 'TeamsCtrl'
    })
    .when('/teams/:teamId', {
      templateUrl: 'team.html',
      controller: 'TeamCtrl'
    })
    .otherwise({
      redirectTo: '/'
    });
}]);

app.factory('EmployeeService', ['$resource', function($resource) {
  return $resource('/employees/:employeeId', {}, {
    update: {
      method: 'PUT'
    }
  });
}]);

app.factory('TeamService', ['$resource', function($resource) {
  return $resource('/teams/:teamId');
}]);

app.directive('imageFallback', function() {
  return {
    link: function(scope, elem, attrs) {
      elem.bind('error', function() {
        angular.element(this).attr('src', attrs.imageFallback);
      });
    }
  };
}).directive('editInLine', function ($compile) {
  var exports = {};

  function link (scope, element, attrs) {
    var template = '<div class="in-line-container">';
    var newElement;
```

```
    var displayValue;
    var options;

    switch (attrs.editType) {
    case 'select':
      displayValue = attrs.displayValue ? 'displayValue' : 'value';
      options = attrs.editOption;
      options = options.replace(attrs.editList, 'editList');

      template += '<div class="in-line-value" ng-hide="editing">
➤{{' + displayValue + '}}</div>';
      template += '<select class="in-line-input form-control"
➤ng-show="editing" ng-model="value" ng-options="'+ options +'">
➤</select>';

      break;
    case 'number':
      template += '<div class="in-line-value" ng-hide="editing">
➤{{value}}</div>';
      template += '<input class="in-line-input form-control"
➤ng-show="editing" type="number" ng-model="value" step="any"
➤min="0" max="99999" />'

      break;
    default:
      template += '<div class="in-line-value" ng-hide="editing">
➤{{value}}</div>';
      template += '<input class="in-line-input form-control"
➤ng-show="editing" type="text" ng-model="value" />';
    }

    // Close the outer div
    template += '</div>';
    newElement = $compile(template)(scope);
    element.replaceWith(newElement);

    scope.$on('$destroy', function () {
      newElement = undefined;
      element = undefined;
    });
  }

  exports.scope = {
    value: '=',
    editing: '=',
```

```
    editList: '=',
    displayValue: '='
  };
  exports.restrict = 'E';
  exports.link = link;

  return exports;
});

app.controller('EmployeesCtrl', ['$scope', 'EmployeeService',
➡function($scope, service) {
  service.query(function(data, headers) {
    $scope.employees = data;
  }, _handleError);
}]);

app.controller('EmployeeCtrl', ['$scope', '$routeParams',
➡'EmployeeService', 'TeamService', '$q', 'config', '$route',
  function($scope, $routeParams, employee, team, $q, config,
➡$route) {

    $scope.address = {};

    function getTeam (teams, teamId) {
      for (var i = 0, l = teams.length; i < l; ++i) {
        var t = teams[i];
        if (t._id === teamId) {
          return t;
        }
      }
    }

  $q.all([
    employee.get({
      employeeId: $routeParams.employeeId
    }).$promise,
    team.query().$promise
  ]).then(function(values) {
    $scope.teams = values[1];
    $scope.employee = values[0];
    $scope.employee.team = getTeam($scope.teams,
➡$scope.employee.team._id);
  }).catch(_handleError);

  $scope.editing = false;
```

```
  // To prevent multiple references to the same array, give us a new
➥copy of it.
  $scope.states = config.states.slice(0);

  $scope.edit = function() {
    $scope.editing = !$scope.editing;
  };

  $scope.save = function() {
    // To prevent empty lines in the database and keep the UI clean
    // remove any blank lines
    var lines = $scope.employee.address.lines;

    if (lines.length) {
      lines = lines.filter(function (value) {
        return value;
      });
    }

    $scope.employee.address.lines = lines;

    employee.update({
      employeeId: $routeParams.employeeId
    }, $scope.employee, function() {
      $scope.editing = !$scope.editing;
    });
  };

  $scope.cancel = function () {
    $route.reload();
  }

  $scope.address.addLine = function (index) {
    var lines = $scope.employee.address.lines;

    lines.splice(index + 1, 0, '');
  }

  $scope.address.removeLine = function (index) {
    var lines = $scope.employee.address.lines;

    lines.splice(index, 1);
  }
}]);
```

```
app.controller('TeamsCtrl', ['$scope', 'TeamService',
➥function($scope, service) {
  service.query(function (data) {
    $scope.teams = data;
  }, _handleError);
}]);

app.controller('TeamCtrl', ['$scope', '$routeParams', 'TeamService',
➥function($scope, $routeParams, service) {
  service.get({
    teamId: $routeParams.teamId
  }, function(data, headers) {
    $scope.team = data;
  }, _handleError);
}]);

function _handleError(response) {
  // TODO: Do something here. Probably just redirect to error page
  console.log('%c ' + response, 'color:red');
}
```

Listing 20-4. Contents of **app.js**

Template Files

Our application has five template files: **home.html**, **employees.html**, **teams.html**, **employee.html**, and **team.html**. The simplest of these is **home.html**, which is used on a minimal home page. The contents of **home.html** are shown in Listing 20-5, while the resulting page is shown in Figure 20.2.

```
<div class="jumbotron hero-spacer">
  <h1>Human Resources</h1>
  <p>This page is your destination for all HR related tasks.</p>
</div>
```

Listing 20-5. Home page template

Figure 20.2. Home page view

Team and Employee Listing Views

The template code for the team and employee listing pages is shown in Listing 20-6 and 20-7 respectively. Both templates use the ng-repeat directive to loop over the members of the collection. Each member generates a link to the individual team or employee page. An example of the employee list page is shown in Figure 20.3.

```
<div class="col-xs-12 col-sm-6 col-lg-4" ng-repeat="team in teams">
  <div class="panel panel-default employee-list-item">
    <div class="panel-body">
      <span class="icon-container"><i class="fa fa-3x fa-group"></i>
➥</span>
      <span class="h4">{{team.name}}</span>
      <a href="#teams/{{team._id}}" class="btn btn-sm btn-info">
        <i class="fa fa-eye"></i> View
      </a>
    </div>
  </div>
</div>
```

Listing 20-6. Team listing template

```
<div class="col-xs-12 col-sm-6 col-lg-4" ng-repeat="employee in
➥employees">
  <div class="panel panel-default employee-list-item">
    <div class="panel-body">
      <span class="icon-container"><i class="fa fa-3x fa-user"></i>
➥</span>
      <span class="h4">{{employee.name.last}}, {{employee.name.
➥first}}</span>
      <a href="#employees/{{employee.id}}" class="btn btn-sm
➥btn-info">
```

```
          <i class="fa fa-eye"></i> View
      </a>
  </div>
</div>
```

Listing 20-7. Employee listing template

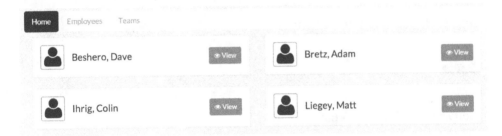

Figure 20.3. Employee listing page view

Individual Team View

The individual team page displays a list of all employees on the team, making it similar to the employee list page. The template file, `team.html`, is shown in Listing 20-8. The template is fairly basic, displaying a few fields from the model and using `ng-repeat` to loop over all the members of the team. An example of the rendered template is shown in Figure 20.4.

```
<ul class="breadcrumb">
  <li><a href="#teams">Teams</a></li>
  <li class="active">{{team.name}}</li>
</ul>
<div>
  <h3>{{team.name}}</h3>
</div>
<div>
  <h4>Team Members</h4>
</div>
<div class="col-xs-12 col-sm-6 col-lg-4" ng-repeat="employee in
➥team.members">
  <div class="panel panel-default employee-list-item">
    <div class="panel-body">
      <span class="icon-container"><i class="fa fa-3x fa-user"></i>
➥</span>
      <span class="h4">{{employee.name.last}}, {{employee.name.
```

```
➥first}}</span>
      <a href="#employees/{{employee.id}}" class="btn btn-sm
➥btn-info">
        <i class="fa fa-eye"></i> View
      </a>
  </div>
</div>
```

Listing 20-8. Individual team template

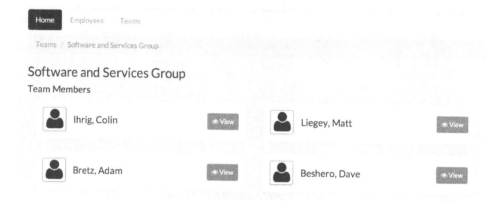

Figure 20.4. Individual team page view

Individual Employee View

The final and most complex template belongs to the individual employee view page. This page not only displays employee information, but also allows information to be updated using our customer `edit-in-line` directive. The code for the template is shown in Listing 20-9, while the rendered page is shown in Figure 20.5. Note that there is currently no way to modify the user's profile picture.

```
<ul class="breadcrumb">
  <li><a href="#employees">Employees</a></li>
  <li class="active">{{employee.name.last}}, {{employee.name.first}}
➥</li>
</ul>
<div class="panel panel-default clearfix">
  <div class="panel-body">
    <div class="button-bar">
      <button class="btn btn-warning" ng-click="edit()"
➥ng-hide="editing">Edit</button>
```

```
      <button class="btn btn-success" ng-click="save()"
➥ng-show="editing">Save</button>
      <button class="btn btn-danger" ng-click="cancel()"
➥ng-show="editing">Cancel</button>
    </div>
    <div class="col-xs-12 col-md-4 text-center">
      <h3 class="margin-top-reset">{{employee.name.first}}
➥{{employee.name.last}}</h3>
      <img ng-src="{{employee.image}}" image-fallback=
➥"images/user.png" class="employee-avatar">
    </div>
    <div class="col-xs-12 col-sm-6 col-md-4 form-offset">
      <div class="form-group">
        <label class="control-label">Employee ID</label>
        <div>#{{employee.id}}</div>
      </div>
      <div class="form-group">
        <label class="control-label">First Name:</label>
        <edit-in-line value="employee.name.first"
➥editing="editing" />
      </div>
      <div class="form-group">
        <label>Last Name:</label>
        <edit-in-line value="employee.name.last"
➥editing="editing" />
      </div>
      <div class="form-group">
        <label>Team:</label>
        <edit-in-line value="employee.team" editing="editing"
➥edit-list="teams" edit-option="t.name for t in teams"
➥edit-type="select" display-value="employee.team.name" />
      </div>
    </div>
    <div class="col-xs-12 col-sm-6 col-md-4 form-offset">
      <div class="form-group">
        <label class="control-label">Address</label>
        <ul class="address-lines">
          <li ng-repeat="line in employee.address.lines track
➥by $index">
            <span ng-hide="editing">{{line}}</span>
            <div ng-show="editing" class="input-group address-edit">
              <input type="text" class="form-control"
➥ng-model="employee.address.lines[$index]" />
              <span class="input-group-btn">
                <button ng-click="address.addLine($index)"
```

```
➥class="btn btn-success">
                <i class="fa fa-plus"></i>
              </button>
              <button ng-click="address.removeLine($index)"
➥ng-disabled="employee.address.lines.length === 1" class="btn
➥btn-danger">
                <i class="fa fa-trash-o"></i>
              </button>
            </span>
          </div>
        </li>
        <li>
          <edit-in-line value="employee.address.city"
➥editing="editing" />
        </li>
        <li>
          <span ng-hide="editing">{{employee.address.state}},
➥{{employee.address.zip}}</span>
        </li>
        <li ng-show="editing">
          <edit-in-line ng-show="editing" edit-type="select"
➥value="employee.address.state" editing="editing" edit-list="states"
➥ edit-option='s for s in states' />
        </li>
        <li ng-show="editing">
          <edit-in-line value="employee.address.zip"
➥editing="editing" edit-type="number" />
        </li>
      </ul>
    </div>
  </div>
</div>
```

Listing 20-9. Individual employee template

Figure 20.5. Individual employee page view

Summary

Readers are encouraged to experiment with and extend the existing HR demo application. You could start small by adding new data points, such as employee salary. If you want to add more advanced features, you could implement the functionality for updating employee profile pictures or add a new view for dragging employees between teams.

This chapter concludes our look at the MEAN stack. These twenty chapters should provide you a solid foundation in the MEAN technologies, as well as some of their alternatives. The remainder of this book will teach you about other JavaScript tools surrounding the MEAN stack. These tools include task runners, debuggers, and testing frameworks.

Chapter 21

Task Runners

In the examples we've shown in many of the Angular chapters, all the JavaScript code lies in a single file. There are several benefits of working with a single file. The browser only needs to download one file containing all of our JavaScript, and can reuse a cached version everywhere on the site. It also reduces download order issues because everything is contained in a single file with the code in the proper, logical order. The entire block of code can be wrapped in a function expression that keeps the contents out of the global namespace. Finally, minification can reduce the browser download size, sometimes as much as 80%. The downside of working with a single file is the maintenance, especially when working within a team. Each developer would be editing the same file, leading to conflicts in the source control; furthermore, locating specific code to change or fix for bugs can be very difficult in a ten-thousand-line file.

Breaking client-side JavaScript into multiple files makes it much easier to maintain. A developer can work on a specific feature or bug that only exists in one file, drastically cutting down on change-management conflicts. It also allows your web application to be more easily understood because each file represents a discrete section or feature of a whole application. The downside is that each JavaScript file needs to be downloaded individually from the browser. If one file requires features from another file, the ordering of the script tags becomes very important. Resource sharding can also be difficult because you lose control of the entire download order.

What we really want is the ability to write files in any way we want and have a process turn them into best-practice static resource files. This is where **task runners** are used. They are a series of tasks that run either automatically or on demand that help manage our client-side resources. Task runners can do much more than manage multiple JavaScript files, though; they can be used to compile CoffeeScript, make CSS sprite files, compress and resize images, run CSS precompilers such as Stylus or LESS, run JavaScript linters, and handle many other asset management tasks.

Introducing Gulp

Gulp is an uncomplicated asynchronous task runner written in JavaScript for Node. It is fairly new, but has already gained tremendous community adoption because of its core architecture design pattern, leveraging pipes and streams. If you skipped that part of this book, we urge you to go back and read it now.

We're going to proceed assuming that you have a fundamental understand of those two core concepts. A second Gulp architecture decision also fits in with the Node design philosophy as a whole: code specialization through modules and plugins.

Overall, Gulp provides low-level functionality. It has a few built-in methods and properties, such as task management and file watching, but the majority of the functionality comes from Gulp plugins. This should sound similar to the Node architecture. To date, there are over 600 Gulp plugins.[1] One of the core design principles governing Gulp plugins states:[2]

> Your plugin should only do one thing, and do it well.

All of the Gulp plugins perform one specialized task. Knowing this will help us later in the chapter when we want to design our Gulp workflow. Each task you want to happen will be achieved by a single Gulp plugin. A stream (usually a file stream) is piped into a series of transform streams that modify the incoming stream in a

---

[1] http://gulpjs.com/plugins/http://gulpjs.com/plugins/

[2] https://github.com/gulpjs/gulp/blob/master/docs/writing-a-plugin/guidelines.mdhttps://github.com/gulpjs/gulp/blob/master/docs/writing-a-plugin/guidelines.md

specific way, and pipe that result into the next stream. Each of these actions is handled by a unique Gulp plugin.

Setting Up Gulp

First, install `gulp` globally on your development machine with `npm install gulp -g`. This will add the `gulp` CLI tool to your environment. You'll also want to install `gulp` locally so that it can be referenced from script files. Second, create an empty script file named **gulpfile.js** in your project. Finally, we're going to create some Stylus and JavaScript files to work with. Create two new folders: **./assets/style** and **./assets/javascript** right at the root of the project. Inside **./assets/style**, create **one.styl** and **two.styl**. If you're unfamiliar with Stylus,[3] it's the Node-specific CSS precompiler. And if you're feeling ambitions, you can write your own styles in these two files; otherwise, you can copy these styles.

```
                                                                    one.styl

html
  font-size: 62.5%

body
  background-color: #000
  width: 90%
  max-width: 900px
```

```
                                                                    two.styl

.container
  background-color: #CAD
  color: #EEE

h2
    font-size: 1.4rem
    font-weight: bold
```

Listing 21-1. Two sample Stylus files

For the JavaScript, we're going to refer back to the client-side routing example in Chapter 19 and split the code across three distinct files under **./assets/javascript**.

---

[3] http://learnboost.github.io/stylus/

Looking at the sample files that follow, you should be able to see a potential problem if we were not to control the file ordering. An error would occur if the contents of **view_controller.js** appeared before the contents of **mainapp.js**, because app would be undefined. To prevent this, we will make sure to order the files properly in the build script without relying on any sorting method.

mainapp.js

```javascript
var app = angular.module('app', ['ngRoute', 'ngResource']);

app.config(['$routeProvider', function($routeProvider) {
  // See Listing 19-2 for complete code
}]);

app.factory('EmployeeService', ['$resource', function($resource) {
  // See Listing 19-3 for complete code
}]);
```

view_controller.js

```javascript
app.controller('view', ['$scope', 'EmployeeService',
➥function($scope, EmployeeService) {
  // See Listing 19-3 for complete code
}]);
```

edit_controller.js

```javascript
app.controller('edit', ['$scope', 'EmployeeService','$routeParams',
➥ function($scope, EmployeeService, $routeParams) {
  // See Listing 19-3 for complete code
}]);
```

With these files in place, we are ready to start building our Gulp file.

Designing a Gulp File

In this section, we're going to write a Gulp file that has two tasks: css and javascript. Each task will be responsible for manipulating the files under ./**assets** to create optimized browser-compatible files. Before we start coding, let's write up a list of responsibilities that each of our tasks will need to perform. This will come in handy once we start coding.

Stylesheet files

1. Compile all the Stylus files into plain CSS

2. Minify the CSS to reduce the file size

3. Combine all the CSS files into a single file

4. Write the minified version to **./public/css/main.min.css**

JavaScript files

1. Combine all the JavaScript files into a single file in the correct order

2. Wrap the code in a function to keep the data out of the global namespace

3. Run a linter (JSHint)[4] and report any code issues

4. Write the nonminified version to **./public/javascript/main.js**

5. Minify the code to reduce the file size

6. Write a minified version to **./public/javascript/main.min.js**

css Task

Every Gulp file should have at least one default task: `default`. The syntax to declare a task is easy: `gulp.task('default', function() {})`. `default` is the task that the `gulp` command will try to run when you execute `gulp` from the command line. Inside the callback is where you start any of the other defined tasks. Let's start by declaring our `default` and `css` tasks:

```
var gulp = require('gulp');

gulp.task('css', function() {
    // Transform contents of one.styl and two.styl to CSS
});
```

---

[4] http://www.jshint.com/about/

```
gulp.task('default', function() {
  gulp.start('css');
});
```

Listing 21-2. Gulp file stub

In Listing 21-2, we've created the `default` task and the stub of the `css` task. Inside the default task, we execute `gulp.start('css')`, which will start the `css` task.

If you look back at the list of responsibilities this task needs to complete, the first one is "Compile all the Stylus sheets into plain CSS." `gulp-stylus`[5] wraps the existing Stylus compiler in the Gulp interface, and compresses the result via function options. Install `gulp-stylus` locally and ensure that you update the **package.json** file when you do.

```
var stylus = require('gulp-stylus');

gulp.task('css', function() {
  gulp.src('./assets/style/*.styl')
    .pipe(stylus({
      compress: true
    }))
    .pipe(gulp.dest('./public/css'));
});
```

Listing 21-3. Compiling and writing Stylus files

The first line instructs Gulp to create a file stream for anything inside **./assets/style/** that has a **.styl** extension. We want to pipe that into the `stylus` plugin, which will compile the files into compressed CSS. Finally, we want to pipe that result to `gulp.dest`, which will write the results to **./public/css**. If you run `gulp` from the command line, you'll see some logging information and, finally, a line indicating that `default` is finished.

If you open **./public/css**, you'll see **one.css** and **two.css**. They will be standard, compressed CSS files. All that's left to do is combine them into a single file. There are ways to do this using only Stylus, but that requires writing the files differently; for brevity, we'll just concatenate them as strings into a single output file.

---

[5] https://github.com/stevelacy/gulp-stylus

```
var concat = require('gulp-concat');

gulp.task('css', function() {
  gulp.src('./assets/style/*.styl')
    .pipe(stylus({
      compress: true
    }))
    .pipe(concat('main.min.css', {
      newLine: ''
    }))
    .pipe(gulp.dest('./public/css'));
});
```

Listing 21-4. Concatenating CSS files

In Listing 21-4, we've loaded `gulp-concat`, which concatenates files together. We piped in the result of `stylus` into `concat`, named the file **main.css**, and passed an option to specify the `newLine` to be an empty string. If you rerun `gulp`, you should now see a single **main.css** file in **./public/css**.

That should be everything we need for our `css` task. If you look back at the steps under *Stylesheet Files*, each step lines up closely with the code in Listing 21-4. All the Stylus files are compiled, minified, and combined into a single file that our web server can send to clients.

`javascript` Task

Let's apply what we've learned from the `css` task to the `javascript` task. We want to perform some of the same responsibilities in this task as well (pipe files in a specific folder, combine them into one, compress them, and then write them to a different location). Since we've covered much of the basics in Listing 21-4, we can use that as a starting point for Listing 21-5.

```
var jsSource = './assets/javascript/';
gulp.task('javascript', function() {
  return gulp.src([jsSource + 'mainapp.js',
  jsSource + 'edit_controller.js',
  jsSource + 'view_controller.js'])
    .pipe(concat('main.js'))
    .pipe(gulp.dest('./public/javascript'))
});
```

```
gulp.task('default', function() {
  gulp.start('javascript');
  gulp.start('css');
});
```

Listing 21-5. Combining JavaScript files

Here we are just setting up the basics: declaring the javascript task, combining all the .js files in that directory into main.js, and writing the result to ./public/javascript. We also should add a start command for the javascript task, as well inside the default task. If you run the Gulp file now, you'll see the **main.js** file inside ./**public/javascript**.

Remember, the order that the JavaScript files are combined in is important. To control the order during processing, we pass an array of filepaths to **gulp.src** instead of a wildcard. The order of the arguments is the order Gulp will process the files. In this way, we have control over the order and can prevent any file order-related bugs being introduced when the files are combined.

Let's expand on our example to create a compressed copy inside ./**public/javascript**.

```
var rename = require('gulp-rename');
var uglify = require('gulp-uglify');
var jsSource = './assets/javascript/';

gulp.task('javascript', function() {
  gulp.src([jsSource + 'mainapp.js',
  jsSource + 'edit_controller.js',
  jsSource + 'view_controller.js'])
    .pipe(concat('main.js'))
    .pipe(gulp.dest('./public/javascript'))
    .pipe(rename({
      suffix: '.min'
    }))
    .pipe(uglify())
    .pipe(gulp.dest('./public/javascript'))
});
```

Listing 21-6. Compressing JavaScript files

In Listing 21-6, we've added two new Gulp plugins, `rename` and `uglify`. After writing the combined file, **main.js**, we want to make a copy of the file and rename it to **main.min.js** and pipe that result into `uglify`. `uglify` is the Gulp plugin wrapper for UglifyJS2[6] that minifies (or compresses) the resulting string of JavaScript. That result is then piped into `gulp.dest`, and **main.min.js** is written into our public JavaScript folder.

If you rerun `gulp` now, you should see both the compressed and normal **main** file inside the JavaScript directory. The only job left to do is to wrap all the code in an immediately invoked function expression and run the result through a linter, JSHint in this case. If you are unfamiliar with linters, they warn developers about common JavaScript mistakes and enforce style rules as well.

```
var wrap = require('gulp-wrap');
var jshint = require('gulp-jshint');
var jsSource = './assets/javascript/';

gulp.task('javascript', function() {
  gulp.src([jsSource + 'mainapp.js',
  jsSource + 'edit_controller.js',
  jsSource + 'view_controller.js'])
    .pipe(concat('main.js'))
    .pipe(wrap('(function(a, window){<%= contents %>}(angular,
➥ window));'))
    .pipe(jshint({
      predef: ['window', 'angular']
    }))
    .pipe(jshint.reporter('default'))
    .pipe(gulp.dest('./public/javascript'))
    .pipe(rename({
      suffix: '.min'
    }))
    .pipe(uglify())
    .pipe(gulp.dest('./public/javascript'))
});
```

Listing 21-7. Our final JavaScript task

---

[6] https://github.com/mishoo/UglifyJS2

Finally, we've added `wrap` and `jshint` into our Gulp task. `wrap` implements the Gulp interface to wrap stream contents with a lo-dash template.[7] This allows us to wrap the output of the concatenation, `contents`, in a function expression.

That result is then piped into the `jshint` Gulp plugin. This plugin wraps the core JSHint[8] functionality up in a Gulp wrapper. There are several configuration options you can supply to JSHint either directly through the plugin, or through a configuration file. For our example, we just want to alert `jshint` about the global variables `window` and `angular`, since they are provided from external sources. The result of JSHint are piped into the `reporter`, which will log the results out to the console.

Lastly, you need to update all your `script` tags to reference **/javascript/main.js** or **/javascript/main.min.js**, depending on your deployment environment.

watch Task

Let's add one more basic task, just for convenience. If you've been following along, you should notice that you have to keep running `gulp` every time there are changes to the JavaScript and Stylus source files in assets. It would be nice if Gulp would run any time a source file changed. Let's create one more task that watches our assets folders, running the appropriate task any time there is a file change.

```
gulp.task('watch', function() {
  gulp.watch('./assets/javascript/*.js', ['javascript']);
  gulp.watch('./assets/style/*.styl', ['css']);
});
```

Listing 21-8. Creating a `watch` task

This task uses `gulp.watch`, which watches the matching files for changes. When there are changes, it will `gulp.start` each task listed in the second argument. Now you can open a new terminal session, run `gulp watch`, and Gulp will continue to run and watch for changes to the files under assets, running the appropriate task when necessary.

---

[7] http://lodash.com/docs#template
[8] https://github.com/jshint/jshint/

Summary

In this chapter we covered task runners, which can also be referred to as build scripts. Task runners take client-side resources and transform them into more optimized, browser-friendly formats. This enables developers to leverage better code organization and higher-order languages such as Stylus or CoffeeScript.

Then we covered the task runner Gulp. Gulp is a stream and pipe system, making it very fast and easy to use. Every action in Gulp generally boils down to stream manipulation that is handled by a Gulp plugin. The results of a single plugin are piped into the next one, creating a Gulp task.

Finally, we wrote a functional **gulpfile.js** that had a task for handling Stylus files and one for managing JavaScript files. The `css` task compiled the Stylus down into standard CSS, combined the two files, and minified the result into **main.min.css**. The `javascript` task was much more involved; it combined multiple files, created a minified and a nonminified copy, ran the result through JSHint to check for code quality, and wrapped everything in a function expression.

We finished our Gulp discussion by creating a `watch` task that watches specific files for changes and runs tasks when a change occurs. This makes using a build step almost completely transparent.

Gulp is a very easy and powerful task runner. It embraces many of the same core philosophies as the Node core. If you understand pipes and streams, you can pick up Gulp very quickly. We hopes this demonstrates the utility and flexibility of using a task runner for your own site.

Chapter 22

Debugging

Unfortunately, bugs are a part of life when writing software, no matter what language you're working with. **Debugging**, as the name suggests, is the process of tracking down bugs and fixing them. The process of debugging can be as simple as adding `console.log()` calls to your code to verify that certain variables hold expected values. But for more involved bugs, you'll want to use a debugger. Debuggers are extremely successful at tracking down bugs, as they allow you to step through an application line by line, inspecting (and modifying) variable values.

This chapter will teach you how to debug JavaScript applications using Google Chrome's DevTools. All modern browsers have similar debugging facilities, but we've chosen to focus on Chrome for two reasons. First, at the time of writing, Chrome is the most popular browser in both the desktop and mobile markets.[1] Second, Node has a fantastic debugger called node-inspector that works with DevTools.[2]

---

[1] http://www.sitepoint.com/browser-trends-september-2014-chrome-top-mobile-browser/
[2] https://github.com/node-inspector/node-inspector

The debugger Statement

All major JavaScript environments (browsers, Node.js, and so on) come with a built-in debugger; however, the debugger is not typically enabled by default. The process of running an application with the debugger enabled is known as "attaching the debugger", and it varies slightly from each debugger. JavaScript's debugger statement is used to invoke a debugger on an application, if one is attached. If an application has no debugger associated with it, the debugger statement has no effect.

To illustrate how the debugger statement works, let's look at the example in Listing 22-1. The JavaScript on this page displays a greeting if the variables i and j are equal. So, for our program to function correctly, we want these two values to be equal. In looking at the code, clearly they are unequal, but for the sake of this example, we want to see why the code inside the if statement fails to execute.

```html
<!DOCTYPE html>
<html lang="en">
<head>
  <meta charset="utf-8">
  <title>Debugging Intro</title>
</head>
<body>
  <span></span>
  <script>
    var span = document.querySelector('span');
    var i = 0;
    var j = 1;

    if (i === j) {
      span.innerText = 'Hello!';
    }
  </script>
</body>
</html>
```

Listing 22-1. An HTML page that behaves unexpectedly

The same code is shown again in Listing 22-2, but in this example a debugger statement has been added just before the if statement. Now open this page in Chrome and notice that nothing happens—no greeting, no debugger magic, nothing.

We haven't enabled the debugging tools, so the `debugger` statement doesn't do anything. Let's change that.

```
<!DOCTYPE html>
<html lang="en">
<head>
  <meta charset="utf-8">
  <title>Debugging Intro</title>
</head>
<body>
  <span></span>
  <script>
    var span = document.querySelector('span');
    var i = 0;
    var j = 1;

    // Set a breakpoint before the conditional
    debugger;

    if (i === j) {
      span.innerText = 'Hello!';
    }
  </script>
</body>
</html>
```

Listing 22-2. The same page from Listing 22-1 with a `debugger` statement added

Running Chrome's Debugger

Open Chrome's developer tools by right-clicking on the page and clicking **Inspect Element**. Next, refresh the page. Doing this with the developer tools enabled allows the debugger to be attached. This time, you should invoke the debugger as shown in Figure 22.1, which reveals the file and line where execution was paused on the `debugger` statement. This predefined pause in execution is known as a **breakpoint**. On the right-hand side of the image, notice the two panels, **Scope Variables** and **Global**. These panels can be expanded to view the variables and values in the local and global scope respectively. Our code is currently executing in the global scope, so nothing is listed in the **Scope Variables** panel. Expand the **Global** panel and scroll down until you find i and j (you'll probably have to scroll down quite a long way, as there are a lot of items defined in the global scope, such as browser API objects). You'll see that i is zero, and j is one.

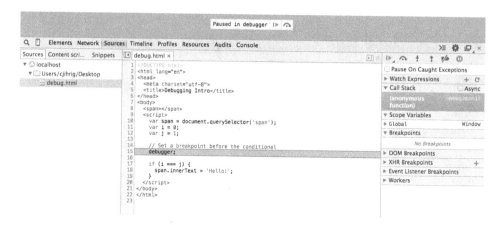

Figure 22.1. Chrome's debugging tools

Controlling the Debugger

Now that we can see the values of the variables, let's step through the `if` statement
to see if it is executed (though, we do know it hasn't). Figure 22.2 shows the debugger
with the control buttons highlighted. These six buttons, from left to right, allow you
to resume execution, step over a function, step into a function, step out of a function,
deactivate breakpoints, and break on exceptions.

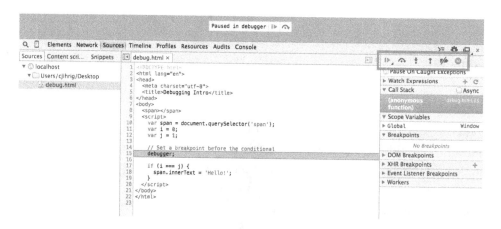

Figure 22.2. Debugger controls

The **resume** button will cause the application to begin executing as normal until
another breakpoint is encountered or the program ends. The **step over** and **step in**
buttons are used to execute the next line of code. If the line is a function, step over
will treat it as a single line of code, while step in will allow you to debug the function

line by line. The step out button will cause the debugger to execute the rest of the current function normally, and then continue debugging.

 Paused Execution Disables Refresh

> If execution is paused in the debugger, you may not be able to refresh the page. You can solve this by exiting out of DevTools or pressing the resume button. However, pressing the resume button may cause execution to pause if another breakpoint is encountered.

The deactivate breakpoints button causes breakpoints encountered in the future to be ignored. If this is enabled and you refresh the page, the `debugger` statement will fail to pause execution. The pause on exceptions button causes uncaught exceptions to be treated as breakpoints. When this is enabled, you are shown a checkbox that allows you to also pause on caught exceptions.

Now that we've gone over the basic debugger controls, refresh the page so that you are paused on the `debugger` statement. Press the step over or step in button to advance to the `if` statement. Press the button again, and notice that the code inside the `if` statement has not executed. Next, we'll look at how you can modify the values of variables inside the debugger to test out different scenarios.

Modifying Variables

There are a few ways to modify variables while the debugger is running. The simplest way is to find the variable in the `Scope Variables` or `Global` panels, double-click on the variable name, and then edit the variable's value. Note that any changes made to these values will persist even outside the debugger.

As an example, refresh the page, find the variable j in the `Global` panel, and set its value to zero. If you step through the `if` statement, you'll notice that the conditional now evaluates to `true`. Similarly, if you set the value of j and simply resume execution, the page will display the expected greeting.

A second way to inspect and modify values is by switching to the `Console` tab. This offers you a fully featured REPL environment. In our example, you might switch to the **Console** tab, inspect and set some values, and then switch back to the `Sources` tab where the debugger controls live. An example that uses the `Console` tab is shown in Figure 22.3. After running these commands in the **Console** tab, switch back to the debugger controls and either step through or just resume execution, and the greeting should be displayed.

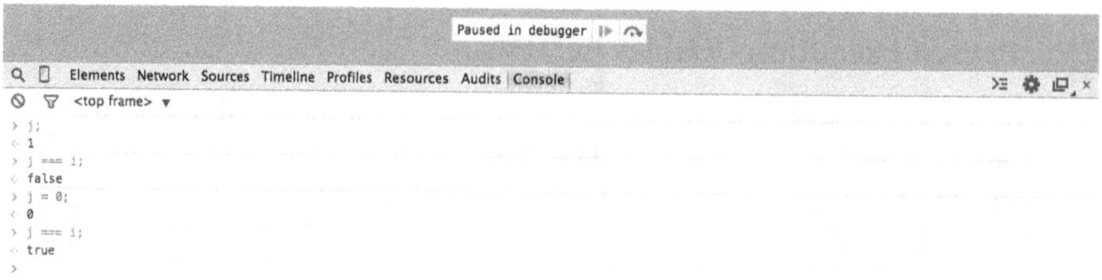

Figure 22.3. Using the debugger console

We trust that with your newfound debugging skills, you can identify the line that causes our simple page's greeting to not display. Now we'll look at the same problem in Node.js.

Node's Debugger

Node ships with a built-in debugger. Be warned, it is not too user-friendly, hence why we'll be covering node-inspector later. To attach the debugger to your application, run **node** with the **debug** flag as shown in Listing 22-3. The contents of **app.js** are shown in Listing 22-4.

```
node debug app.js
```

Listing 22-3. Running a Node application in interactive debug mode

```
var i = 0;
var j = 1;

// Set a breakpoint before the conditional
debugger;

if (i === j) {
  console.log('Hello!');
}
```

Listing 22-4. Contents of **app.js** from Listing 22-3

Running with the `debug` flag launches an interactive debugger session, which sets a breakpoint on the first line of the application, shown in Listing 22-5. Notice that the line numbers are printed next to the code, with the > character indicating the current line.

```
< Debugger listening on port 5858
connecting to port 5858... ok
break in app.js:1
> 1 var i = 0;
  2 var j = 1;
  3
debug>
```

Listing 22-5. Output from starting `app.js` in the interactive debug model

> ### -debug and --debug-brk
>
> The `debug` argument launches an interactive debugger session; however, you can also use the arguments `--debug` or `--debug-brk`, which causes the debugger to listen for connections on port 5858. The difference between `--debug` and `--debug-brk` is that `--debug-brk` also sets a breakpoint on the first line of the application. You can also change the debug port using the `--debug-port` argument. For example, `node --debug-port=4000 --debug-brk app.js` would set a breakpoint on the first line of **app.js** and listen for debugger connections on port 4000.

You can control the debugger by entering commands at the `debug>` prompt. Table 22-1 provides a basic listing of debugger commands, which are self-explanatory. Notice the parallel between the `cont`, `next`, `step`, and `out` commands and the DevTools debugger controls. Also note that you can exit the debugger using **Control-C** or **Control-D**.

Table 22.1. Useful debugger commands

Command	Description
cont or c	Resumes execution
next or n	Steps to the next instruction
step or s	Steps into a function call
kill	Kills the executing script
restart	Restarts the script
pause	Pauses running code
scripts	Lists all loaded scripts
list(n)	Displays source code, showing n lines before and n lines after the current line

Inspecting and modifying variables in Node's debugger is a bit tricky. You cannot access the variables directly from the debugger. Instead, you must issue the repl command. This will launch a REPL in the debugger, where you can issue JavaScript commands. Once you're finished, you must exit the REPL using **Control-C** to return to the debugger. Any changes to variables made in the REPL will persist.

Listing 22-6 shows a full run of **app.js** that sets j to zero so that the greeting is displayed. Note that Node 0.11 is required for this example to run properly. Running this in Node 0.10 results in the variable failing to update properly. Anyway, if this seems like an arduous process just to change a value from one to zero and execute an if statement, you would be correct. That's why node-inspector was created.

```
< Debugger listening on port 5858
connecting to port 5858... ok
break in app.js:1
> 1 var i = 0;
  2 var j = 1;
  3
debug> c
break in app.js:5
  3
  4 // Set a breakpoint before the conditional
> 5 debugger;
  6
  7 if (i === j) {
```

```
debug> repl
Press Ctrl + C to leave debug repl
> j
1
> j = 0;
0
debug> n
break in app.js:7
  5 debugger;
  6
> 7 if (i === j) {
  8    console.log('Hello!');
  9 }
debug> n
break in app.js:8
  6
  7 if (i === j) {
> 8    console.log('Hello!');
  9 }
 10 });
debug> n
< Hello!
break in app.js:10
  8    console.log('Hello!');
  9 }
>10 });
debug>
```

Listing 22-6. Modifying a variable via the Node debugger

```
debug> repl
Press Ctrl + C to leave debug repl
> j
1
> j=0;
```

```
0
> j
1
```

node-inspector

node-inspector is a third-party module that creates an interface between Node's built-in debugger and Chrome's DevTools interface. The first step is to install node-inspector using the command shown in Listing 22-7.

```
npm install node-inspector -g
```

Listing 22-7. Globally installing node-inspector

Next, run your application with either the --debug or --debug-brk flag. This choice will depend on the nature of your application. If it's a server that waits for connections, then --debug will work; however, if your application will run to completion when you start it, you're going to want to use --debug-brk to create a breakpoint. For a basic application such as the one in Listing 22-4, we're going to use --debug-brk, as shown in Listing 22-8.

```
node --debug-brk app.js
```

Listing 22-8. Launching an application with the --debug-brk flag

Next, launch node-inspector in a separate terminal window. It will connect to the debugger running in your application. Listing 22-9 shows the command being issued and the resulting output.

```
node-inspector
Node Inspector v0.7.4
Visit http://127.0.0.1:8080/debug?port=5858 to start debugging.
```

Listing 22-9. Connecting to your application's debugger using node-inspector

Note the URL http://127.0.0.1:8080/debug?port=5858. If you visit this URL in Chrome, you'll be greeted with the DevTools interface. You might notice that the code is unfamiliar. This is because the breakpoint has been set just before your application runs. Press the resume button and you'll be taken into your application code as shown in Figure 22.4. From here you can access all the familiar DevTools features covered earlier in this chapter. Take a look at the values in the expanded `Scope Variables` panel. You'll see your application variables, `i` and `j`, as well as familiar Node variables such as `__dirname`, `__filename`, and `exports`.

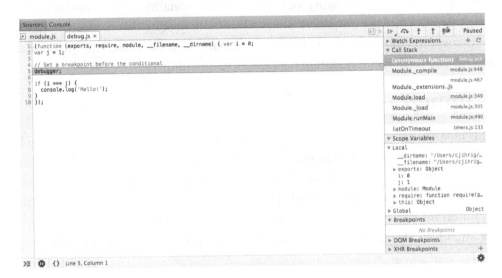

Figure 22.4. Debugging a Node application using node-inspector

node-debug

node-inspector is leaps and bounds ahead of the built-in Node debugger in terms of usability. Yet running your application and node-inspector, as well as opening a browser window, are all repetitive tasks that could be automated. The node-debug[3] module makes debugging with node-inspector extremely straightforward. Start by installing node-debug as shown in Listing 22-10.

```
npm install node-debug -g
```

Listing 22-10. Globally installing node-debug

Now, anytime you want to use node-inspector, simply launch your application with `node-debug` instead of `node`, as shown in Listing 22-11. This will automatically open DevTools with a connection to your Node application.

---

[3] https://github.com/jfirebaugh/node-debug

```
node-debug app.js
```

Listing 22-11. Running node-inspector via node-debug

The maintainers of node-inspector found this functionality to be so useful that they've added it to the newest versions, essentially making this module obsolete. node-inspector have been kind enough to maintain the `node-debug app.js` interface to avoid confusion and maintain backwards compatibility.

Summary

This chapter has introduced you to JavaScript application debugging. It started by teaching you the basics of Chrome's DevTools debugger, but, as usual, there is still a lot more to learn about DevTools. We encourage you to learn more via the DevTools documentation.[4] From there, the chapter moved on to Node's built-in debugger that is, unfortunately, far from user-friendly. Finally, we looked at node-inspector, a tool that uses DevTools as a more adaptable interface on top of Node's debugger.

---

[4] https://developer.chrome.com/devtools

Chapter 23

Testing

No one would debate that writing tests for software is valuable. There are arguments about which testing methodology might be better or more comprehensive, but there's one fact that all developers can agree on: any production code should have comprehensive tests. In well-tested software, the amount of test code written often exceeds the amount of functional code. Tests provide a safety net to optimize, refactor, and upgrade the code without fear of introducing unexpected bugs. Good tests can also help developers discover issues before the code is deployed into production. In modern web applications that combine multiple frameworks and libraries, proper testing is the most reliable way to ensure everything continues to run smoothly.

JavaScript is no exception. It could be argued that JavaScript requires an even *greater* amount of testing because of the loosely typed nature of the language. The differences in the JavaScript implementation from browser to browser also increase the need to thoroughly test client-side JavaScript. Even when working within well-tested frameworks such as Express and Angular, you should have unit tests that cover your application code.

In this chapter, we're going to touch on testing both the Express server and the Angular application using testing frameworks. We recommend always using a testing framework, rather than a long list of `if` and `else` statements.

A framework provides a uniform way to structure tests, offers different reporting options, and makes maintaining test code easier. The frameworks presented in this chapter are far from being the only testing frameworks available, but they are the ones we chose to showcase.

Testing Node

There are a number of modules and frameworks designed to test Node applications. For the purposes of this book, we're going to focus on a framework named Mocha.[1] We chose to focus on Mocha because it's extremely popular and works in both Node and the browser. Mocha can be installed via `npm` using the command shown in Listing 23-1.

```
npm install -g mocha
```

Listing 23-1. Installing Mocha via `npm`

Once Mocha is installed, you can invoke it by issuing the `mocha` command. This will attempt to execute any JavaScript files in the current directory's `test` directory. If this directory does not exist, `mocha` will try to run a JavaScript file named **test.js**. Alternatively, you can pass the name of the file you want to execute as an argument to `mocha`.

Defining Tests

When Mocha executes a file, it expects tests to be defined using the `it()` function. `it()` takes two arguments. The first is a string that describes what the test does, while the second is a function representing the test. A file can contain any number of tests. A test is considered to have passed if it runs to completion, and failed if it throws an exception.

Tests can also be grouped together hierarchically into **suites**, which can also be nested in a hierarchy. A suite is defined using the `describe()` function. `describe()`

---

[1] http://visionmedia.github.io/mocha/

also takes two arguments. The first is a string describing the test suite. The second argument is a function containing zero (although an empty suite would be fairly useless) or more tests.

Listing 23-2 shows an example file that can be understood by Mocha. This file consists of a top-level test suite, a nested test suite, and four tests. Tests 1 and 2 belong to the nested suite, while Test 3 belongs to the top-level suite, and Test 4 belong to no suite. Technically, Mocha defines a nameless top-level suite that contains everything else, including Test 4. Save this code in a file named **test.js** and then run the command `mocha`. You should see output similar to Listing 23-3. Notice that Test 2 fails because it throws an exception. Your output will likely contain an additional stack trace for the error, which has been omitted here.

```
describe('Top Level Tested Suite', function() {
  describe('Nested Test Suite', function() {
    it('Test 1', function() {
    });

    it('Test 2', function() {
      throw new Error('problem');
    });
  });

  it('Test 3', function() {
  });
});

it('Test 4', function() {
});
```

Listing 23-2. A sample Mocha input file containing suites and tests

 ## Mocha's Testing Interfaces

Mocha provides several testing interfaces.[2] The two most popular are behavior-driven development (BDD) and test-driven development (TDD). The same functions are available in each interface, but with different names. For example, `describe()` and `it()` are BDD functions. The equivalent functionality is available via the

[2] http://mochajs.org/#interfaces

`suite()` and `test()` functions as part of the TDD interface. This book uses the BDD functions.

```
✓ Test 4
Top Level Tested Suite
  ✓ Test 3
  Nested Test Suite
    ✓ Test 1
    1) Test 2



  3 passing (8ms)
  1 failing

  1) Top Level Tested Suite Nested Test Suite Test 2:
     Error: problem
```

Listing 23-3. Example output from running the code in Listing 23-2

Asynchronous Tests

Node is typically associated with asynchronous code. For Mocha to work well with Node, it needs to support asynchronous tests. Marking a test as passing is inadequate with asynchronous code, as the function could very easily complete while some long-running asynchronous operation is still happening.

Mocha supports asynchronous tests by allowing you to pass a callback function to `it()`. This callback is typically named `done` by convention. Calling `done()` indicates that the test was successful, while a failure is still marked by a thrown exception. Listing 23-4 shows an example of an asynchronous test. In this example, `fs.read-File()` is invoked on a file named `some_file.txt`. If an error is passed to the `readFile()` callback, it's thrown as an exception, causing the test to fail. If there is no error, `done()` is called and the test passes.

```
var fs = require('fs');

it('Asynchronous Test', function(done) {
  fs.readFile('some_file.txt', function(error, data) {
    if (error) {
      throw error;
    }
```

```
    done();
  });
});
```

Listing 23-4. An asynchronous test that reads a file

`skip()` and `only()`

Mocha allows you to selectively run a certain subset of your tests or suites. The methods `skip()` and `only()` are used to denote whether a test should be skipped or run respectively. `skip()` is useful if a test needs to be temporarily disabled for whatever reason. `only()` is useful for marking a few tests to be run without the need to comment out large blocks of code. An example that uses `skip()` is shown in Listing 23-5. If you run this code through Mocha, only Test 2 will execute. If you were to replace `skip()` with `only()`, then only Test 1 would execute. Note also that this example applies `skip()` to a test. The same task can be accomplished for an entire test suite (`describe.skip()`).

```
it.skip('Test 1', function() {
});

it('Test 2', function() {
});
```

Listing 23-5. An example use of `skip()`

Test Hooks

Mocha provides optional hooks that can be used to execute code before and after test runs. This is useful for setting up data before a test, and cleaning up after a test. Specifically, there are four hooks that can be associated with a test suite:

- `before()` — runs once before the test suite is executed
- `beforeEach()` — runs before each test in the suite is executed
- `after()` — runs once after the test suite executes
- `afterEach()` — runs after each test in the suite executes

All four of these functions take a function as their only argument. If you need to execute asynchronous code in one of these hooks, pass done() to the function argument.

Listing 23-6 shows an example test suite containing two tests and all four hook functions. The output from running this code is shown in Listing 23-7. Notice that the run starts with begin() and ends with after(). Additionally, beforeEach() runs prior to each individual test, and afterEach() follows each test.

```
describe('Suite', function() {
  before(function() {
    console.log('before()');
  });

  beforeEach(function() {
    console.log('beforeEach()');
  });

  afterEach(function() {
    console.log('afterEach()');
  });

  after(function() {
    console.log('after()');
  });

  it('Test 1', function() {
    console.log('Test 1');
  });

  it('Test 2', function() {
    console.log('Test 2');
  });
});
```

Listing 23-6. A test suite with hooks

```
  Suite
before()
beforeEach()
Test 1
    ✓ Test 1
afterEach()
```

```
beforeEach()
Test 2
    ✓ Test 2
afterEach()
after()
```

Listing 23-7. Partial output from Listing 23-6

Assertions

Up to this point, the simple tests that we created explictly threw errors. This is a valid way to write tests, but not the most elegant. A preferred method involves writing assertions. **Assertions** are pieces of logic that test that certain expected conditions of the test are being met. For example, an assertion might state that a variable holds a specific value, or that a certain function is expected to throw an exception based on its inputs.

For very basic tests, you might be interested in using Node's core `assert` module.[3] For the purposes of this book, we'll use the more powerful Chai assertion library.[4] Like Mocha, Chai can be used in both Node and the browser. Chai also makes the claim on its home page that it "can be delightfully paired with any JavaScript testing framework". It can be installed using the command shown in Listing 23-8.

```
npm install chai
```

Listing 23-8. Command to install `chai`

Chai also supports several assertion interfaces: `should`,[5] `expect`,[6] and `assert`.[7] This book is going to use the `expect` style, which is designed for BDD style testing. The `expect` style allows you to write your tests in in a fashion that reads very much like natural language. For example, the Mocha test in Listing 23-9 asserts that the variable `foo` is equal to 4 using Chai's `expect` style.

---

[3] http://nodejs.org/api/assert.html

[4] http://chaijs.com/

[5] http://chaijs.com/guide/styles/#should

[6] http://chaijs.com/guide/styles/#expect

[7] http://chaijs.com/guide/styles/#assert

```
var expect = require('chai').expect;

it('Addition Test', function() {
  var foo = 2 + 2;

  expect(foo).to.equal(4);
});
```

Listing 23-9. A simple test that uses a Chai expect style assertion

Notice how simply the assertion in Listing 23-9 reads. Listing 23-10 includes several other common examples of `expect` style assertions.

```
var expect = require('chai').expect;

it('expect style assertions', function() {
  expect(2).to.be.greaterThan(1);
  expect(null).to.not.exist;
  expect(false).to.be.false;
  expect('foo').to.be.a('string');
  expect(function(){
    throw new Error('foo');
  }).to.throw;
  expect([1, 2, 3]).to.have.length(3);
  expect({foo: 'bar'}).to.have.property('foo').and.equal('bar');
});
```

Listing 23-10. Common `expect` style assertions

Testing Angular

One of the reasons many developers choose Angular over other client-side offerings is *testability*. Angular was built to be tested. This is evident by the dependency injection pattern used throughout the Angular core. Recall that the second argument to most Angular constructs is a list of dependencies. This allows the dependency objects to be created outside the constructor and passed in as arguments, which can drastically increase a code's testability because tests can focus solely on developer code instead of framework code. Let's start by first writing a basic Angular controller, and then we'll set up our project to test it.

Listing 23-11 is the controller we want to test. Create **main.js**file under
/public/javascript. EmployeeService is the $resource from previous examples in the
Angular chapters.

```js
                                                                    main.js
var app = angular.module('app', ['ngResource']);
app.factory('EmployeeService', ['$resource', function($resource) {
  return $resource('/employees/:employeeId', {}, {
    get: {
      isArray: true
    },
    post: {
      method: 'POST',
      isArray: false
    }
  });
}]);

app.controller('main', ['$scope', 'EmployeeService', function($scope,
➥ EmployeeService) {
  $scope.employees = [];
  $scope.firstName = $scope.lastName = '';

  EmployeeService.get(function (data) {
    $scope.employees = data;
  });

  $scope.addDisabled = function () {
    return !($scope.firstName.trim().length && $scope.lastName.
➥trim().length);
  }

  $scope.add = function () {
    EmployeeService.post({
      first: $scope.firstName,
      last: $scope.lastName
    }, function (data) {
      $scope.employees.push(data);
      $scope.firstName = $scope.lastName = '';
    });
  };
}]);
```

Listing 23-11 Our testing controller

Looking at the controller, here's what we want to test:

▨ `employees` is properly set with the results of `EmployeeService.get`

▨ `addDisabled` should return `true` until a valid first and last name both have values

▨ `add` will call `EmployeeService.post` and the newly created employee will be added to `employees`

▨ after adding a new employee, `addDisabled` should return `true`

In a complete example, we'd want to test `EmployeeService` in isolation before testing the main controller in Listing 23-1; however, `EmployeeService` is not indicative of the majority of testing code needed to test Angular applications. The majority of developer logic is in the controllers, so that's what we'll focus on testing in this chapter.

Set Up

First, we'll install the Karma test running local to the current project with `npm install karma --save`. Second, we'll install the Karma CLI module globally via `npm install -g karma-cli`. Karma is a *test runner*,[8] not a testing library, that the Angular development team uses during development. It's a tool to launch an HTTP server, serve static files, watch files for changes, create an HTML test report, and load a proper test framework into the browser.

Once both the Karma modules have been installed, run `karma init` in your project. This will walk you through creating a **karma.conf.js** file in the current directory. Accept the default value for the prompts. You'll need to make two small changes for everything to be functional. After the generator has finished, open **karma.conf.js** and make these changes:

```
frameworks: ['mocha', 'chai'],
files: [
    'http://ajax.googleapis.com/ajax/libs/angularjs/1.2.16/angular.js',
    'http://cdnjs.cloudflare.com/ajax/libs/angular.js/1.2.16/angular-
➥mocks.js',
    'http://code.angularjs.org/1.2.16/angular-resource.js',
```

---

[8] http://karma-runner.github.io/0.12/index.html

```
  'public/javascript/*.js',
  'public/javascript/test/*.js'
],
```

Listing 23-12 Karma configuration changes

The `files` setting configures Karma to load all the listed files into the browser. It also sets up logic to watch the local folders for changes and rerun the test suite when there are file changes. In Listing 23-2, we are instructing Karma to load several Angular libraries first and then load our JavaScript last. All the files listed should be familiar except for **angular-mocks. angular-mocks** gives us access to `$httpBackend`,[9] which lets us mock HTTP requests without involving the web server. We will cover `$httpBackend` in more detail shortly. **angular-mocks** overrides a few core Angular functions as well to aid in testing.

`frameworks` instructs Karma to load `mocha` and `chai` into the browser. Our tests will use `mocha` as a testing library and `chai` as an assertion framework.

Next, create a file in **public/javascript/test** called **main_test.js**. This is where we are going to write our Mocha tests. Everything you learned about Mocha while testing the Express server applies to testing client code as well. Now we need to install a few more modules so that we can use both Chai and Mocha with Karma. Run the following command in a terminal window: `npm install mocha karma-mocha karma-chai --save-dev`.

You should be familiar with `mocha` at this point. The other two packages are just adapters that let Karma communicate with both `chai` and `mocha` through the Karma framework. Although you won't be interacting with either of them directly, you will need them installed for testing to work properly.

Test Code Setup

Finally, let's flesh out **main_test.js** with some basic tests. First, we'll show and discuss the test code setup in Listing 23-13, and then we'll cover the actual tests in Listing 23-14.

---

[9] https://docs.angularjs.org/api/ngMock/service/$httpBackend

```
describe('main controller', function() {
  beforeEach(module('app'));
  var _scope;
  var _httpBackend;

  beforeEach(inject(function($controller, $rootScope,
➥EmployeeService, $httpBackend) {
    _scope = $rootScope.$new();
    _httpBackend = $httpBackend;

    $httpBackend.when('GET', '/employees').respond([{
      first: 'Abraham',
      last: 'Lincoln'
    }, {
      first: 'Andrew',
      last: 'Johnson'
    }]);

    $httpBackend.when('POST', '/employees').respond({
      first: 'Grover',
      last: 'Cleveland',
    });

    $controller('main', {
      $scope: _scope,
      EmployeeService: EmployeeService
    });
  }));
  // Tests go here
  // {...}
});
```

Listing 23-13 Test code setup

Remember, we are using Mocha to test our client-side code. The functions and conventions used to test server-side code are the same here. In the first `beforeEach` function, we call `module` and pass `app`. This instructs Mocha to load the `app` module and its dependencies before each test in this spec. `module`, in Listing 23-12, is one of the Angular features that has been overwritten by `angular-mocks`. `app` has the `main` controller attached to it, which is the controller we're trying to test.

The second `beforeEach` is where the meat of the test setup is located. At a high level, this `beforeEach` creates a new `main` controller before each test—the one defined in Listing 23-11. We want a new controller for each test. because we want to avoid any changes to the controller in one test from having unpredictable downstream impacts on a future test. Creating a new controller for each test ensures that each one starts with a controller in a known state.

During testing, the developer has to act like Angular and create a controller object that manages all the dependencies by hand. `inject` might look a little odd at first, but it is merely another of the mock functions provided by `angular-mocks`. It creates a new instance of `$injector`, which is used to resolve dependency references. This is the same function that's used behind the scenes for all of Angular's dependency injection logic. In our test, we want to tap into this directly to control some of the dependencies `main` will use.

To create a functional `main` controller, we'll need `$controller`, `$rootScope`, `Employ-eeService`, and `$httpBackend`. `$controller` is the internal function Angular uses to create controllers, which we'll use to manually create a controller object. Remember, `$rootScope` is the global Angular scope object that has functions for creating children scope. The `EmployeeService` is the data access service built using `$re-source` that communicates to the RESTful web server. Finally, `$httpBackend` is another Angular mock dependency that we'll use to intercept and mock HTTP requests.

First, we create a new child scope object with `$rootScope.$new()` and store it in `_scope`. If you notice the scope of `_scope`, it is available to every function nested inside the `describe` block. This is intentional, otherwise, there would be no way to observe changes internally to the `$scope` object inside the `main` controller. Because objects are passed by reference, any changes in the controller to `$scope` will also be reflected in `_scope`. We use `_scope` to observe changes that happen inside the controller to the `$scope` value.

Next, we want to mock HTTP requests that will be going through `EmployeeService`. The first argument to `$httpBackend.when` is the HTTP verb and the second is the URI. The returned object has a `respond` method that accepts a response object. The response object will be the payload of the mocked response when the associated route is called via the `$http` module. The two routes we have set up with `$http-Backend` are the same two routes available inside `EmployeeService`. So in `main` when `EmployeeService.get` is run, normally the low-level `$http` module would make a GET request to the correct route on the web server. By using `$httpBackend`, we are intercepting this request, returning a mocked response, and taking the web server out of the testing loop. Similar to the `_scope` variable, we've created a `_http-Backend` variable that can be accessed from any function inside `describe`.

Finally, we instantiate a new `main` controller with `$controller`. The first argument is the controller name and the second is a hash object, where the key is the dependency name and the value is the dependency object. We pass in `_scope` as the child scope and pass `EmployeeService` through unmodified.

Controller Tests

Now that all the setup code is prepared, we are finally ready to write our controller tests.

```
                                                          main_test.js
//Test one
it('should not allow add initially', function () {
  expect(_scope.addDisabled()).to.equal(true);
});
//Test two
it('should allow add when firstName and lastName have been set',
➥function() {
  _scope.firstName = 'Grover' ;
  _scope.lastName = 'Cleveland';
  expect(_scope.addDisabled()).to.equal(false);
});
//Test three
it('should have a list of employees after the "get" call is
➥complete', function () {
  _httpBackend.flush();
  expect(_scope.employees.length).to.equal(2);
});
//Test four
it('should return the new item after adding and disable the add
➥button', function () {
  _httpBackend.flush();

  _scope.firstName = 'Grover' ;
  _scope.lastName = 'Cleveland';
  _scope.add();
```

```
  _httpBackend.flush();
  expect(_scope.employees.length).to.equal(3);

  var result = _scope.employees[2];
  expect(result.first).to.equal('Grover');
  expect(result.last).to.equal('Cleveland');

  expect(_scope.addDisabled()).to.equal(true);
});
```

Listing 23-14 main controller tests

Test one checks to make sure that addDisabled is true, initially because both first
and last names are blank. In test two, we set _scope.firstName and _scope.lastName
to strings. Now when we interrogate addDisabled, we expect the value to be false.
The business rule inside addDisabled should return false because the first and
last names have values. By having test code to demonstrate, it should be clear why
we created the _scope variable and how we can use it.

Tests three and four demonstrate how we use _httpBacked. In test three, the first
step is to invoke _httpBackend.flush. flush allows unit tests to control when
_httpBackend sends (flushes) responses. Every call to flush will send out any
pending responses currently held inside the state object inside _httpBackend. By
using flush, we can keep our code asynchronous while avoid writing asynchronous
tests.

When main initially loads, one of its first actions is to request a list of employees
with EmployeeService.get. $httpBackend intercepted that request and holds it in
an internal list of pending mock requests. flush empties out this internal list of requests and sends out the mocked responses. In test three, after we flush the stored
requests, the callback in main will execute and set $scope.employees to the result
of the mocked GET request. After that happens, the length of _scope.employees
should be 2.

In test four, we flush the GET request to ensure the list of employees is populated.
Then we set the first and last names of _scope and invoke add. This calls Employ-
eeService.post and passes in the name values. Just like the GET request, the POST
request is stopped inside $httpBackend, so the callback function has yet to be fired
and the list of employees should be unchanged. We call _httpBackend.flush a

second time to return the mocked POST request. This will cause the callback function to fire, and will add the newly created employee into the list of employees attached to _scope. The last few expect calls in test four validate that this has happened as expected.

Running the Tests

Now that everything is set up, lets run these tests to see how our main controller holds up to automated testing. In an open terminal, run karma start. A web browser should open and display a connection message, and in the terminal where you ran the start command, the test results should print out. If you've been following along closely, all four tests should pass. At this point, if you make any changes to the controller or test JavaScript files, the tests should rerun. This lets you refactor and clean up with constant feedback.

Currently, the browser is displaying nothing useful. It is simply acting as a place-holder for the tests and all the client-side libraries needed to run the tests. Our configuration is only using the default reporters that log information directly to the console. If you want well-formatted HTML in the browser or other reporting options, check out the list of reporters on npm.[10]

Next Steps

We've only tested a controller here. If we wanted to thoroughly test our applica-tion—and we should—we'd need tests for our custom directives and services as well. We could also expand our testing efforts to include coverage measurements too. Additionally, we could restructure our tests to be more modular. This was just a short introduction to the tools and set up required to continue writing tests for your Angular applications.

Summary

This chapter has discussed several methods for testing the various parts of a JavaScript application. We began by looking at the Mocha framework for Node.js testing. From there, we moved on to Angular testing with Karma. Conveniently, Karma allows us to reuse a lot of our knowledge about Mocha.

---

[10] https://www.npmjs.org/browse/keyword/karma-reporter

This concludes this chapter, and, indeed, this book. We sincerely thank you for reading, and hope that you've learned a thing or two. We certainly learned a lot by writing it.

CPSIA information can be obtained
at www.ICGtesting.com
Printed in the USA
JSHW041243050123
35764JS00004B/95